LIFE IN
IRELAND

For Katie

LIFE IN IRELAND

A Short History
of a Long Time

CONOR W. O'BRIEN

MERRION
PRESS

First published in 2021 by
Merrion Press
10 George's Street
Newbridge
Co. Kildare
Ireland
www.merrionpress.ie

© Conor W. O'Brien, 2021

9781785373848 (Paper)
9781785373855 (Kindle)
9781785373862 (Epub)

A CIP catalogue record for this book is
available from the British Library.

Typeset in Sabon LT Std 11/15 pt

Cover design by Claire Prouvost.

Text images: p. 14, Alamy; pp. 16, 28, 78, 83, 89, 100, 109, 115,
118, 124, 134, 137, 145, 157, 165, 170, 179, 191, 208, 222, 229,
233, 248, Adobe Stock; p. 52, Wikimedia Commons; p. 76, iStock;
pp. 149, 193, 195, 213, 250, courtesy of the Royal Society for the
Protection of Birds/Mike Langman; pp. 90, 182, 204, 239, 244,
courtesy of the author.

Plate images: 1, 5, 6, 10, 11, 12, 14, 26, 28, 30, Adobe Stock; 2, 3,
7, 8, 9, 13, 15, 16, 18, 19, 20, 21, 22, 23, 24, 25, 27, 29, courtesy
of the author; 3, courtesy of Brendan Arrigan; 5, Wikimedia
Commons; 17, Pixabay.

Merrion Press is a member of Publishing Ireland.

Contents

PART III
Life in the Human Age

Epilogue

Acknowledgements

T
his book would not have been possible without the input of so many people, and the amazing research they have conducted into the prehistoric past.

Special thanks go to Patrick Wyse Jackson, Associate Professor and Curator of the Geological Museum of Trinity College Dublin for reviewing Parts I and II, as well as Aodhán Ó Gogain, PhD candidate at Trinity College, for the invaluable information he provided on Ireland's Devonian and Carboniferous wildlife.

My sincere thanks to Nigel Monaghan, Curator of the Natural History Museum in Dublin, and Dr Mike Simms, Curator of Paleontology at the Ulster Museum in Belfast, for all their help as well.

Thanks also to Brendan Arrigan (discoverer of the *Phanerotinus* specimen in Tuam), Sean Forde (Conservation Ranger at Killarney National Park), Ruth Carden (of University College Dublin), Matt Riley (of the Sedgewick Museum in Cambridge), Jonathan Jeffery (of the University of Bristol), Hallie Street (of the University of Alberta), Dr Anthea Lacchia (of University College Dublin), the late Matthew Parkes (of the Natural History Museum in Dublin),

Jesmond Harding (of Butterfly Conservation Ireland), Dr Eamon Doyle (Geologist for the Burren and Cliffs of Moher UNESCO Global Geopark), Gerd Geyer (of the University of Würzburg), Steve Brusatte (of the University of Edinburgh), David Dunne (of the Wild Deer Association of Ireland), Olf Elicki (of Freiburg University), David Peterman (of Wright State University), Nichola Salmon (of Castlecomer Discovery Park), Heather Sparks and Ryan Phelan (of Revive & Restore) and Ted Daeschler (of Drexel University) for their input.

To all those making an effort – however big or small – to save Ireland's wildlife in the here and now, I salute you.

Introduction

Clinging onto a rocky promontory, the ruins of the Black Castle have stood guard over Wicklow Town, on Ireland's east coast, for over 300 years. The skeletal remains of the outer walls are but a shadow of the castle at the height of its splendour, built by the Anglo-Normans in the wake of their conquest in the late 1100s.

Holding, as it does, an imposing command over the Wicklow coastline, the castle affords you sweeping views of the rocky outcrops and piers that puncture the Irish Sea on either side, growing into the Wicklow Mountains in the distance. It makes for a picturesque setting today. The builders of the castle, though, had more life-and-death concerns: how to spot and repulse the impending attacks of the native Gaelic Irish. These would prove frequent. The castle was razed several times before being finally abandoned to the elements in the 1600s.

Walking around the husk of the castle, I like to think about those who stood at this exact spot centuries before: all those lords and ladies, warriors, bards and brigands. Theirs was quite a different world to the one we live in now – and not just for its people. Back then, a different cast of wild characters also made its home in Ireland. When the Black Castle was at its most impressive, the grey wolf still haunted the hills of Wicklow. The pine forests still played host to the leks of mating capercaillie. And the great auk – a bird now lost not just to Ireland, but to the world – still swam the waters around our coasts, perhaps swirling within sight of the Black Castle itself.

Even now, centuries after human habitation, the castle is not lifeless. Lichens still form a patina across its crumbling walls, lending them a rich orange hue. These ancient organisms – a cocktail of fungi and algae – were colouring rocks for at least 150 million years before the dinosaurs came along. They have survived long after them too, weathering every extinction event nature could throw at them. Meadow pipits dip in and out of the structure, searching for insects that cleave to creases in the stone. And hooded crows, omnipresent with man in Ireland, still use the topmost portion of free-standing wall as a lookout point; it offers a commanding view from which to survey the area or project their hoarse croaks onto the surrounding seascape.

Seeing this is a reminder of the sheer resilience of life. In the far-off future will this be the fate of all man-made structures – to be shelter and calling posts for wild things long after the last humans have, like millions of species before us in the tapestry of life, become extinct? Just as our civilisation is built on bedrock formed from plants and animals that came before us, what creatures will make bedrock of the remains we leave behind? In tens of thousands of years' time, will our most imposing concrete edifices be nothing more than eyries for eagles, their plumbing tunnels for rats and their ceilings festooned with wasps' nests and roosting bats?

The Black Castle is just one of the thousands of timestamps that history has left strewn across the Irish countryside.

They're windows into a world far removed from our own. But in their potency and charisma, they can distract us from a much, much deeper history that lies below our very feet.

As you stand at the castle, the rock beneath you seems to flow, like the ebb of waves incised in stone. It's a legacy of the volcanic activity that helped mould Wicklow's dramatic coastline – not hundreds, but hundreds of millions of years ago.

The Wicklow Mountains that define the skyline to the north are yet more offspring of this process, forged in the tectonic fires that ravaged and sundered Ireland through the eons. Since then, the Ice Age has left its own imprint on the mountains. The uplands of Wicklow, where snow pooled and hardened into ice, would prove a breeding ground for great glaciers. Crawling through the mountains, these helped to carve out the dramatic landscape we enjoy today.

Neither the Normans nor Gaels were here to witness these titanic changes to Ireland's landscape. But what creatures were? What were they like? And what clues did they leave behind?

These are the very clues I spent a childhood searching for. As a boy, I excavated every garden I could (parents', grandparents', cousins') in my hunt for fossils. The rocks that emerged from the soil would then be set upon with chisels and toothbrushes. With these, I hoped to tease a tooth or eye socket out of the rock, and gaze at the form of an extinct creature. Every now and then I'd find a rock which was unusual in shape. I'd convince myself it was the delicate skull of a long-dead dinosaur. Sadly, more often than not it would turn out to be nothing more than a product of the Earth's convulsions millions of years ago.

It wasn't until a family trip to The Burren in County Clare that my luck would turn. Here, amid the jagged karst that criss-crossed the landscape, I could see the limestone riddled with the scintilla of the distant, living past. These were not bleached tumours of rock masquerading as bones. Clear in the stone you could make out the creases and grooves of corals and shellfish that lived and died millions of years before the first dinosaur drew breath. In death they became the essence of limestone, the compacted detritus of the sea built up and set like concrete.

Fortunately, others have had far better luck uncovering traces of Ireland's deep past over the years. Even today, on an island as small and thoroughly explored as Ireland, fascinating finds are still occasionally made. From the remains of great marine reptiles on the coast of Antrim to the amazing Ice Age caves of Cork and Waterford, a litany of clues about an Ireland long gone have been found – and are still being found today. Our rocks have yielded some of the first primitive plants, some of the oldest flying insects in Europe, and some of the first vertebrates (that great dynasty of backboned animals to which we humans belong) ever to crawl onto terra firma – all of them pioneers that would change the course of life on Earth forever. Over the eons, the land that would become Ireland played host to armoured dinosaurs, mighty mammoths and giant deer. Our oceans, meanwhile, were once the province of shelled monstrosities the size of a man, and terrifying marine lizards that tracked their prey with forked tongues through the water.

With advances in dating techniques and an ever-growing knowledge of the world as it once was, we can glean more from these discoveries than ever before. Even where the fossil record in Ireland is patchy – the evidence for dinosaurs in Ireland could fit into your pocket – we can augment it with the growing mountain of evidence unearthed around the world to help fill in the gaps and build up a record of Ireland as it once was, and of the weird and fascinating creatures that once lived here. The present has never been a better time to delve into the past.

These creatures lived in an Ireland that changed drastically throughout the history of life on Earth, from a pristine tropical ocean to a frozen waste to the fertile, temperate island we now know today. Hundreds of millions of years was not only enough time for our wildlife to change drastically, it also saw us crawl across the face of the Earth, from below the equator to our present position ensconced at one end of the Old World.

An island the size of Ireland, while very geologically diverse, will inevitably have a lot more of some rocks than of others. Dinosaur fossils are scarce in Ireland because rocks from the Mesozoic era, the age of the dinosaurs, are rare here, except in the northeast. The bulk of Ireland's rocks are actually much older. These more ancient rocks may not harbour dinosaurs – but the clues contained within them are no less significant for the history of life on Earth. This is where our journey into Ireland's deepest past will begin. Part One of this book will begin by considering some of the first inklings of life on Earth and take us right up to the age of the reptiles, when the land, ocean and sky were dominated by things with scales and feathers. It envelopes a huge chunk of Earth's history, including that landmark moment when a vertebrate crawled out of the water for the very first time. In so doing, this creature set in motion a chain of events that would give rise to reptiles, birds,

"Over the eons, the land that would become Ireland played host to armoured dinosaurs, mighty mammoths and giant deer."

[5]

mammals and culminate today in the evolution of modern humans.

In the pantheon of prehistoric life, dinosaurs are the superstars. But there were many charismatic denizens that came before them – and yet more that came after. The demise of the dinosaurs and the other great reptiles created a vacuum that would be filled by our relatives: the mammals, small furry creatures that, until then, had clung to safety in tree holes or underground burrows while dinosaurs, pterosaurs (in the air) and marine reptiles achieved their supremacy.

With the cataclysmic end of the Mesozoic era 66 million years ago, reptiles would never again dominate life on Earth. Instead, the time of the mammals had come. Over the tens of millions of years that followed, they exploded into a myriad of forms. Cetaceans took to the sea, bats to the sky. Ungulates grazed the plains and prairies as carnivorans (cats, dogs, bears, hyenas) evolved to hunt them. Primates started to spread out across what is now the Old World, eventually giving rise to our own lineage. Through it all, the mammals survived the crashing of continents and climactic upheavals big and small. But one of their most severe tests came around 2.6 million years ago, as the Earth started to chill and the snows outlived the winter. The Ice Age had begun.

This is where Part Two of our prehistoric safari takes us. In it, we'll meet the remarkable mammals of Ice Age Ireland – among them some of the most impressive beasts ever to make their home here. Much of Ireland's fauna of that time outlived the Ice Age, but would look perversely out of place in the Ireland of today. Using the fossil clues left behind, we'll build up a picture of the fauna and flora of Ireland as it was thousands of years ago, when the plains were home to mammoths and giant deer, harassed by wolves and hyenas.

The Ice Age may have been a stern test for life in prehistoric Ireland, but the greatest challenge – and for some, the greatest opportunity – would come with the arrival of a new creature on Irish soil – that most remarkable of mammals: *Homo sapiens.*

Modern humans would go on to shape the landscape and wildlife of Ireland like no creature before them. Part Three of this book will explore Ireland since the arrival of man – and the immense impact this has had upon our natural world, as the fauna and flora of twenty-first century Ireland started to take shape. In the story of life in Ireland, the time since the arrival of man makes up one of the shortest chapters. And yet, for us, it is probably the most compelling. It encompasses Ireland's natural history as we can still see, hear and smell it from the streets of our towns and cities to our forests, bogs and farms today. It is a period when human history and natural history collide. And while there's not much we can do to resurrect ecosystems that have been gone for millions of years, the wild Ireland that has coexisted with man since the last Ice Age is still here – if in a degraded state – and can still be saved if we choose to save it.

Much as successive waves of colonists – Celts, Vikings, Normans – left their mark on our towns, cities and surnames, they also played a role in shaping the fauna we still enjoy to this day. Ireland was left with a meagre legacy of land animals after the Ice Age. Many of the creatures specialised for cold climates (mammoths, reindeer, muskox) became extinct here. The filling in of the Irish sea severed the land bridge between Ireland and Britain, preventing further colonisation by foot.

As a result, many of the animals that made their home in Ireland in the millennia after the last glaciation did so with human help. The red deer – that most charismatic symbol of our wild, native woodlands – was probably among them. The sika and fallow deer were introduced for hunting and decoration, before escaping their masters and finding the wild woods and uplands of Ireland to their liking. Even the rabbit was likely brought here by the Normans in the Middle Ages, presumably for easy meat; not as imposing an heirloom as the mighty suite of castles, perhaps, but a living legacy that now forms a resolute part of our natural heritage.

What would ensue over the centuries that followed, right up to the present day, was an escalating trend towards urbanisation, coupled with the concession of more and more countryside to farming. As we shall see, for some creatures this was a boon. Towns and cities are rarely short of the detritus of human existence – rich pickings for wildlife willing to take to the suburbs. As for farms, open spaces, clear of constricting trees, were a perfect habitat for species that might not otherwise have found Ireland – a forested island, if left to nature – to their liking. With farms come crops, seeds, fruit ... food for herbivores great and small. And in turn, the pests that proliferate on farms made ready food for some predators, completing a farmland eco-system which still exists in Ireland today.

While humans and the habitats they constructed offered new routes to colonisation for a host of species, they would prove the undoing of some of Ireland's most spectacular wildlife. Some of these creatures have lingered on in myth and literature long after their physical forms walked or flew across our countryside. It's a tragedy that Ireland's wildlife – particularly on land – is, for the most part, on a much smaller scale than it used to be. Once, our ancestors had to be wary of straying into an unknown cave or risk the wrath of a hibernating bear. It's hard to conceive of something so large and dangerous in Ireland today.

Compared to times gone by, the beasts that populate our countryside today are relative midgets. This, sadly, is the case across not just Ireland but much of Europe, where the big beasts – the ones that compete with people for space, or even (in the case of wolves) for food – increasingly find themselves squeezed out. These days, even many of our largest birds are gone; our seas are no longer home to great auks, or our bogs to stately cranes. Our rivers and estuaries once played host to spawning sturgeon, primeval giants that could grow up to three metres long. No more.

This is something that doesn't truly ring home, I think, until you go somewhere where there are still large animals to be seen stalking the countryside. Ireland was once home to a cast of creatures on a par with the African savannah of today, albeit built for a much colder world. Many of these were lost at the end of the Ice Age – and many of those that replaced them eventually fell at the hands of man.

We cannot, though, arrest the past. Recognising what has been lost should encourage us to treasure the wild things we still have with us, no matter how great or small.

With man's mastery of nature, a redoubled resolve to preserve it has grown. This book will finish not with a simple compendium of the sins of our forebears against Irish wildlife, it will also commend the stellar conservation efforts being made to preserve nature on our changing island.

We will reflect on what the future has in store for life in Ireland – and discover how exciting (if controversial) new technology could be used to bring back what we thought was gone forever.

PART I

From the Dawn to the Dinosaurs

1

The First Life
in Ireland

Surmounted by its iconic cross, Bray Head towers nearly 250 metres over the town of the same name. The headland ascends in three humps like the coils of a great, green sea serpent, overshadowing the long expanse of Bray seafront with its arcades, bars and fish and chip shops. The path to the summit winds its way past raucous fulmars' nests in summer and sea-battered cliffs in winter. It concludes with a striking vista. Bray lies sprawled out below you, like flotsam washed up by the Irish Sea, before disintegrating into the carbuncled expanse of north Wicklow, chequered with fields and homesteads between the hills.

But one of Bray Head's greatest claims to fame lay embedded in its rock. The bulk of the Wicklow Mountains are comprised of granite with varying amounts of quartzite on top. Bray Head stands out – both physically and geologically. True, there's quartzite here too, but this is one of the few places in the whole of Ireland where sedimentary shales, formed from the mud of an ancient ocean, can be found. They date back to the Cambrian period, more than 500 million years ago. It was a dramatic time for life on Earth. And this is where the story of life in Ireland begins.

Earth would have looked like an alien world during the Cambrian, 541–485 million years ago. Observing the planet from space, you would have beheld a smattering of continents totally different in shape to those we know today. Ireland at this time was cleaved in two, and largely submerged beneath the sea. The northwest of the country lay with the landmass of Laurentia, at the centre of this strange world. The southeast, meanwhile, was held by the microcontinent of Avalonia, along with portions of Britain, North America and Western Europe.

A walk through a Cambrian landscape would have been a lonely experience. There were no reptiles, no mammals, no birds, no amphibians. Land plants had yet to evolve. Insects had not yet appeared either. There weren't even worms to tunnel through the soil. In their absence, the land would have looked like a vast, empty theatre of sand and rock, as lifeless on first glance as the surface of Mars is today. Even the very air you breathed during the Cambrian would have been different; carbon dioxide levels were up to fifteen times higher than they are now.

The land might have been largely desolate during Cambrian times. In the sea, though, it was a different story. All life on Earth ultimately traces back to the sea. The oldest fossils on the planet date back over three billion years, way before the start of the Cambrian. For billions of years, life on Earth had been confined to a film of microbes carpeting the sea bed, a vast submerged layer of stagnant life. All that was to change during the Cambrian. This period saw one of the most incredible events in Earth's history take place: the Cambrian Explosion. Oxygen, the fuel that drives animal life, became far more common in the oceans. A motley crew of tiny creatures – the first plankton – began to float in the open sea. These would lay the foundation for a whole new ecosystem, providing food for larger animals to follow. The first predators arose at this time. Suddenly, animals had to formulate methods of attack and defence, ambush and evasion. Creatures that had until then been soft evolved the first shells; others developed jaws and early eyes. This spurred an evolutionary arms race that led to a massive explosion of animal life. Suddenly the seas of the world were populated by a whole host of new animals, the ancestors of every living creature we see around us today.

Some of these strange creatures were the ones that left their fossils etched in the Cambrian rocks at Bray Head. These faint impressions show two distinct patterns in the stone, furrows in either a radiating pattern or diverging from a central stem, like the veins of a leaf. But this fossil is no plant; leaves were still many millions of years away. In fact, these are not the physical remains of a lifeform at all. The creature that left them is unknown to science as it left no hard parts behind it; its soft, worm-like body was far too delicate for that. Instead, all we have to go on are what are known as trace fossils, impressions left by long-dead beings. These fossils, called *Oldhamia*, are the remains of the burrows these creatures left behind them, much as earthworms still do today. They were – and still are – of huge significance to our understanding of

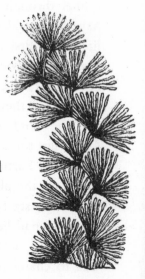

the history of life on Earth; at the time of their discovery in 1840, they were the oldest fossils known anywhere in the world.

In life, the maker of these burrows would have tunnelled away beneath the vast mat of bacteria that carpeted the Cambrian ocean. The microbes gained all the sustenance they needed either from sunlight or chemical compounds that they broke down. The decomposing material, the detritus that built up beneath the microbial mats, was probably what this animal was after. It fed on the excrement of this alien Earth, half a billion years removed from our own.

Even without physical remains to go by, the tunnels it left behind on Bray Head tell us something of its behaviour. From the initial tunnel drilled into the mud, the animal would subsequently dig in a radiating pattern, one branch at a time, in its quest for food. The result of this labour is the patterned, almost plant-like imprints left behind on the rocks of Bray Head.

Even the tiniest living things can exert an enormous influence on the world around them. It is likely that creatures like this, tunnelling and respiring at the bottom of the sea, consumed what oxygen there was in the oceans of the time. Concomitantly, they released enough carbon dioxide that some scientists even think they set in motion a chain of environmental ructions that would spur mass extinctions, the dying-off of multiple animal species that took place throughout the Cambrian. Ultimately, it was these catastrophes that would separate the Cambrian from the Ordovician period that followed it.

If Cambrian fossils are rare in Ireland, it is from Ordovician rocks that we start to build a more rounded picture of our ocean ecosystems for the first time. This was a period of enormous change. Marine biodiversity tripled during the Ordovician; new groups of animals arose, while others that had their origins in the Cambrian evolved into new forms. Many of them had their remains immortalised in Ireland's Ordovician stone. Here, instead of trace fossils, we have solid remains to go on. Among them are some of the most iconic creatures ever to live on the planet: the trilobites.

In a world before fish came to prominence, trilobites were some of the most dominant creatures in the sea. They were among the very first members of that great group of animals known as arthropods, whose living members include lobsters, crabs, spiders, millipedes and insects. Trilobites, though, had a greater resemblance to woodlice, with overlapping segments of armour shielding the legs on which the animal crawled across the sea floor. (Like woodlice, at least some trilobites could curl up in a ball for protection.) They evolved into a huge range of shapes and sizes; over 15,000 trilobite species are known to science, more than any other extinct animal group. They ranged in size from the infinitesimal to alarming giants nearly half a metre long. Some were active predators. Others scavenged detritus on the seabed. Others still probably fed on the plankton they filtered from the water. This allowed a menagerie of trilobite species to coexist in the same space, making the most of every resource in the primordial seas.

The trilobites were some of the first creatures on Earth to develop eyes – made up of thousands of lenses, much like the compound eyes of insects. They would have been invaluable in helping the animal detect prey or predators, including other

"Their adaptability made the trilobites one of the most successful families of animals ever."

trilobites. In some species, enormous eyes (to detect incomers from all angles) and a flatter, more flexible body suggest they got their food by swimming through the seas. Others had their eyes mounted on storks, implying that they buried themselves in the sand. Some trilobites were completely blind, relying on other senses to steer them to food – or perhaps waiting for food to come to them.
Many, such as the ones unearthed in Counties Waterford and Cavan, crawled along the seabed. Their adaptability made the trilobites one of the most successful families of animals ever. Although they enjoyed their heyday in the Cambrian and Ordovician, the group would patrol the prehistoric oceans for over 250 million years.

Other weird creatures plied our Ordovician seas as well. Perhaps the strangest emerged from County Tyrone: a nautiloid. These animals were distant relatives of squid and octopus. Unlike them, they possessed an external shell, with a distinctive conical shape tapering to a fine point at one end and projecting eyes and tentacles at the other. With propulsion from a tube called the hyponome, the nautiloid would have been able to power itself through the water.

In life, this animal might have been brightly coloured, with stripes along its shell helping to camouflage it, adding a dash of beauty to its deadly form. The shell would also have given the nautiloid protection from its own predators. Another key to its success lay inside; nautiloids possessed one of the first circulatory systems, allowing oxygenated blood to travel through their bodies far more efficiently than the other creatures they shared the Ordovician oceans with.

Thanks to these advantages, nautiloids were among the top predators in this strange sea. They exploded in numbers during the Ordovician, evolving into a range of sizes – including giants, the largest creatures alive at the time. Equipped with the strong tentacles and formidable beaks that their living cousins still possess, they would have been more than able to tackle the trilobites and other prey fighting for survival in the Ordovician oceans.

More benign shelled animals also made their home here. Among the most prominent were the brachiopods, a group of animals that were once common but have only a handful of members living today, mainly in deep water. With two shells of unequal size, encasing the soft flesh within, they looked a lot like the bivalve molluscs (clams, cockles, oysters) that still pebble our beaches. Brachiopods like *Sowerbyella* spent their lives fastened to the seabed, straining their food from the water. They shared the sea with the tiny bryozoans, which first appeared during the Ordovician. They spent their lives on the sea floor, clinging to stones or dead shells. Unlike brachiopods, these minute animals eschewed the safety of shells for strength in numbers, forming colonies within calcite skeletons that branched up out of the seabed. Within this, each individual creature – called a zooid – had its role. Most used a fan of tentacles to capture food; others kept the colony clean of sediment.

Colonial living was the same strategy used by corals, that ancient lineage that still forms reefs in our modern oceans. Each cell in the honeycomb corals found in Ordovician Ireland once housed its own tentacle-tipped creature, a polyp, its arms reaching out to snag food from the current. These thrived in the warm, shallow seas of the time. Then, as now, they probably lent a dash of colour to the seabed, maybe lighting it up in fuzzy balls of pink or orange.

Not everything clung to the seabed, though. Among the Ordovician fossils found in Counties Cavan and Wexford were graptolites. These too were colonial; up to 5,000 minuscule individuals lived together, sharing a skeleton made of collagen, the same protein found in your skin and fingernails. From the safety of tunnels within the structure, they probably projected feather-like arms into the water to catch microscopic food. At first, graptolites cleaved to the sea floor just like corals and bryozoans, fastened to stones or rooted in the mud. During the Ordovician, however, they started to float. In so doing, a whole new glut of food was made available to them in the upper tiers of the ocean. They were amongst the first creatures to colonise the open sea.

They shared the waters with primitive swimming creatures, known as conodonts. These are among the most numerous fossils on Earth, yet, for a long time, the true form of conodonts was a mystery to science; all they left behind were sharp, fang-like structures up to five millimetres long. However, more complete specimens were discovered in the 1980s and these helped scientists build a picture of what they actually looked like: thin, eel-like creatures with bulbous eyes at one end and a flattened tail fin at the other. Between the head and the tail ran a stiff rod of tissue, the notochord – the precursor to the backbone we possess today. The teeth-like elements, for which they were known for so long, adorned their lips, throat and tongue; conodonts had no jaws to speak of. They swam the Ordovician seas, looking for tiny prey or probably filtering plankton from the water. Conodonts diversified during this time, colonising coastal waters as well as the open ocean. Their fossils have been found in Ordovician limestones in Dublin and Mayo.

The Ordovician came crashing to a close around 444 million years ago with one of the largest mass extinction events ever; 86 per cent of all species in the oceans died out. The climate chaos that brought the Ordovician to its end gave birth to a new period, known as the Silurian. During this time, the vast Iapetus Ocean, that had divided the two halves of Ireland, began to close. The world started to warm up after the glaciation that finished off the Ordovician, and sea levels were rising. New estuarine and fresh water habitats were opening up, and new species were evolving to exploit them. Some of them, as we shall see, would go on to jettison the water entirely – and change the course of life on Earth forever.

In the warm, tropical seas of this time, huge coral reefs, on par with the Great Barrier Reef of today, began to flourish. Small wonder then that corals were among the many fossils to leave their remains entombed in Ireland's Silurian rocks.

The other creatures that emerged were, for the most part, of the same groups that had lived in Ireland's seas during the Ordovician. In between the corals, the seafloor was still festooned with brachiopods and other molluscs, while gastropods (the family to which snails and slugs belong) crawled arduously along the sand. Brittle stars – cousins of the starfish with five flimsy tentacles stemming from a circular centre – were present too, writhing across the seafloor much as they still do today, 435 million years later. Above them, graptolites hung in the current, snaring microscopic food with their tentacles. Larger tentacled killers, the nautiloids, were still among the fiercest predators in this ecosystem, picking out prey amid the corals with their enormous eyes before swooping in.

However, the Silurian also saw the first appearance of fish in the Irish fossil record. Fish had a genesis reaching all the way back to the Cambrian. They evolved from primitive, free-swimming creatures that had made a major innovation: a stiffened, internal chord that ran the length of the body. In fish this would become the spine, the backbone from which the rest of the skeleton stems. The spine itself was made up of a chain of interlocking bones, the vertebrae. As such, fish and all the other backboned animals that would later arise from them – amphibians, reptiles, birds, mammals, humans – are known as vertebrates.

Ireland's Silurian fish were small. The primitive fish that left their remains in the Silurian rocks of Louisburgh, County Mayo would all have been less than twenty centimetres long. They had no jaws. Without a bony structure to support them, what teeth they had were probably embedded in rings of muscle instead. They also lacked the pectoral fins that modern fish use for stability while swimming. As such, these oval-shaped creatures would have been altogether less graceful than their living counterparts. They probably would have swirled in the shallows, hoovering up the remains of dead plants and animals that built up on the sea floor or on river beds, much like mullet do today. Even if they did take live prey, with no jaws to help them they could only have eaten creatures much smaller than themselves. Whether they spent their entire lives in these shallow, tropical waters (Louisburgh may have been south of the equator at this time) or migrated upstream to breed like some living fish, remains unknown.

However, for all the fossils to have emerged from the ancient Silurian seas, one of the most groundbreaking moves in the history of life on Earth was taking place on dry land. Plants and animals were advancing out of the water. Terra firma, a whole new frontier, was opening up.

Ireland's Silurian rocks bear witness to this. Among our most precious fossils from this time were found on the Devil's Bit Mountain in North Tipperary. These 430-million-year-old remains were not those of an animal but a plant. The species they belonged to was called *Cooksonia*. It was one of the first plants to colonise dry land. Its remains have been found around the world. But when they were first described in 1980, none were older than the *Cooksonia* unearthed in Tipperary. These were the oldest land plants then known to science.

Plants, like animals, evolved in the water. They made their first forays onto dry land back in Ordovician times. The first plants on land were flimsy and simple, like the mosses and liverworts of today. *Cooksonia* was different. In life, it wasn't much to look at. It didn't have leaves, much less flowers. Above ground, the entire structure consisted of a minuscule, Y-shaped stem terminating in little green ovals from which it secreted its spores (seeds had yet to evolve). The *Cooksonia* fossils found in Tipperary were so small that they had to be saturated in alcohol to make them visible. Although capable of living on land, this plant was still tied to wet, coastal habitats, where it formed dense mats on the mud.

Although it couldn't grow much taller than a pin, *Cooksonia* was still a game-changer. It was among the very first plants to possess vascular tissue, the conduit for food and water possessed by almost all the plants you see around you, from the smallest buttercup to the tallest oak. Its stem had water-conducting cells thick enough to prevent themselves collapsing as water passed through them to nourish every part of the plant. What's more, the *Cooksonia* discovered on the Devil's Bit extended the history of vascular plants – and their colonisation of dry land – by millions of years.

Cooksonia might have been a minnow, but it would give birth to giants. The evolution of vascular tissue allowed plants to grow bigger, gradually moving away from the water's edge to paint the surface of the Earth green. That legacy is still writ large everywhere we look today, from temperate and tropical rainforests to the grasslands of the steppe and savannah. The largest plants now dwarf the largest animals; the tallest trees in the world tower over 100 metres above the ground, and tip the scales at more than 5,500 tonnes. That's more than twenty-seven times bigger than the largest animal, the blue whale. And these immense dimensions would not be possible without the gift of vascular tissue, bequeathed to them by their tiny ancestors, more than 400 million years ago in the Silurian. Without the likes of *Cooksonia*, there would be no trees today – nor the myriad of animals, big and small, that depend upon them. The vibrantly resplendent flora to be enjoyed all around us owes a debt of gratitude to the tiny, primitive plants like this that came before them.

Plants like *Cooksonia* transformed the world. They played a pivotal role in terraforming dry land for the wave of animal colonists to follow. It was these plants that tempted the first plant-eating arthropods, like millipedes, out of the water. Naturally, predators such as scorpions soon followed. For the first time, a self-sustaining community of plants and animals living, reproducing and dying outside the water began to take shape.

Invertebrates, like millipedes and scorpions, were among the first animals to crawl onto dry land. But they would not have it to themselves for long. As the Silurian gave way to the Devonian period, vertebrates would get in on the act too. Our own ancestors were about to leave the water for the first time. A bombshell moment in the history of life was set to take place. And once again, Ireland's ancient rocks provide the evidence.

2

Footsteps in Stone: The Valentia Island Trackway

Tethered to County Kerry by a concrete bridge from the village of Portmagee, Valentia Island juts out into the wild tempest of the North Atlantic. The island is, in many ways, Ireland's west coast at its most picturesque. Roads that rise and fall, following the contours of the slopes, are fringed by walls of rock and purple heather, partitioning fields that slope down towards the Atlantic. Some are carpeted with ferns, clamouring over each other in a great, tangled mat, adding a brown tinge which contrasts with the green of more verdant fields. Here, lazy cattle chew the cud much as they have for centuries, oblivious to the stunning views that surround them as the mountains and islands of Kerry close in beneath brooding clouds.

Valentia is a place oozing with history. This is where Europe and North America were conjoined by the first ever transatlantic cable, allowing communication between continents to a degree never before possible. Local history abounds here too. The island, as with many in this part of the world, is strewn with ogham stones, cairns and other relics dating back to antiquity. But Valentia is home to yet another

"These footprints offer us an incredibly rare and valuable glimpse into prehistoric life."

landmark, of significance not just to the island, to Ireland or even to mankind – but to the history of life itself.

While the island's many man-made structures command attention, this natural landmark is a bit more furtive. If you didn't know where you were going, and had no signposts to guide you, you might miss it entirely. It was mere happenstance that found it in the first place; for all its thousands of years of habitation, Valentia Island did not reveal this secret to science until 1993. This was when a Swiss undergraduate student happened upon a discovery, charting back to a milestone moment in the story of life on Earth.

On the northeast corner of the island, a pathway flanked by fields leads you down to a rocky overlook of mottled grey and sandy stone stained with lurid green seaweed, overshadowed by the bulk of Valentia towering above it. As with almost everywhere else on Valentia, the first temptation is to take in the sweeping views of the Iveragh Peninsula that surround you, and the vast sky above. But as the tide retreats, casting a glance at the ground will reveal a curious trail of oval pockmarks, around 200 in total, debossed in the rippling stone. Two rows of these imprints collect the tide as it retreats, forming lines of little pools much as they have done for over 300 million years.

These footprints, forming the world-famous Valentia Island trackway, offer us an incredibly rare and valuable glimpse into prehistoric life. They date back more than 380 million years. We tend to think of prehistory in terms of the dinosaurs, but these footprints are around 140 million years older than even the most primitive dinosaur. They were made at least 378 million years before the first hominin descended from the trees and strode on two legs across the African savannah.

As precious as prehistoric bones and shells are, the odds of footprints surviving as long as these without being obliterated – by flood, by erosion, by the smashing and sundering of continents – are minuscule. What's more, while bones are the interred remains of an animal in death, locked up in stone, footprints were made by a living, breathing creature. They offer us a glimpse, however brief, into the real-life movements of an animal extinct for hundreds of millions of years.

Even within the illustrious pantheon of prehistoric footprints, the Valentia Island tracks are an amazing find. This trackway is one of the very oldest examples of a vertebrate – that great family of backboned creatures that includes all fish, amphibians, reptiles, mammals and birds – leaving the water and crawling onto land. Our deepest ancestors had finally left the water behind. Terra firma was just waiting to be conquered. Life on Earth was about to change forever.

Three hundred and eighty-five million years before the present day, we are at a time in Earth's history called the Devonian. The world would be completely unrecognisable.

By the time the Valentia trackway was laid, the two separate parts of Ireland – once divided by a vast expanse of ocean – had fused together. The scar of this collision, called the Iapetus Suture, stretches from the Shannon Estuary in the west to Clogherhead, County Louth in the east. Even today, the mountains in Counties Mayo, Donegal and Wicklow have long axes that parallel the line along which Ireland's prodigal halves were joined.

Ireland at this time was mostly land, but it lay in the tropics, perched south of the equator. All of the Earth's land was gathered together in a brace of supercontinents, Euramerica (which included Ireland) and Gondwana. These, though, were quite a lot smaller than you might expect. There were probably no ice caps during the Devonian. As such, around 85 per cent of the Earth's surface was covered in water, a vast ocean on which the sun never set, compared to 71 per cent today. The dry land was often desert. The sands of these vast deserts, washed away and deposited by enormous rivers, would one day go on to form the Old Red Sandstone, that vein of beige stone on which so much of Munster is built today.

The animals of this strange time would look equally alien to us. There were no reptiles during the Devonian. Birds and mammals had yet to evolve too; things with fur or feathers were still hundreds of millions of years away. But the vast ocean that enveloped much of the world was perfect for fish. Indeed, the Devonian is nicknamed the 'Age of the Fish' such is the dominance they held in marine ecosystems at this time. In the preceding Silurian period, primitive fish still had to contend with vicious invertebrate predators, such as the sea scorpions, giant arthropods that tore their prey asunder with their pincers and spines. But these ancient, clawed killers were in decline in the Devonian, and so the fish went from strength to strength, diversifying into new families, growing to great sizes and seizing control of ocean ecosystems to a degree they never had before.

Devonian fish, though, were altogether different from those we still have swimming in our coastal waters today.

Among the dominant families of fish at this time were the placoderms, the armoured fish. Modern fish might be relatively soft bodied. But in the placoderms, the head and upper body were covered in solid, bony plates, forming a tough armoured shell to defend them against any predators – including, as was often the case, other placoderms.

Among the most successful of all these armoured fish was *Bothriolepis*, an animal whose remains have been found on Kerry's Iveragh Peninsula. This fish was widespread during the Devonian, leaving its remains on every continent.

Measuring up to a metre long, *Bothriolepis* was a strange looking animal indeed. In true placoderm style, its head and upper body were encased in two separate armoured plates, before conceding to scale-less flesh that tapered to a long, narrow tail fin. Small beady eyes were perched comically, almost conjoined, on the very top of its head, indicating a bottom-dwelling lifestyle. A mouth on the underside of its head further suggests that, whatever this animal ate, was indeed mostly found at the bottom of the rivers or shallow

seas it lived in. The pectoral fins on either side of its armoured upper body were themselves encased in solid bony tubes, transforming them into stiff, makeshift arms. With these, it's thought that *Bothriolepis* might have dug for food, be it crunchy invertebrates hiding in the sand or the soft sludge that carpets the seafloor. These bladed paddles could have helped the animal bury itself if needed, or throw up a cloud of sand in which it could lose itself from a predator. Or, they might have served an even more remarkable purpose: helping this freakish fish zigzag over land between different water bodies. Around the world, *Bothriolepis* remains have been found in both salt and freshwater. Because of this, some scientists think they might have migrated upstream to spawn, like salmon still do in rivers around Ireland today.

Whereas placoderms like *Bothriolepis* had their shields, another group of Devonian fish, the acanthodians, had their spines. Acanthodian spines have emerged from Devonian rocks in County Kerry, showing that this unique family of prehistoric fish – nicknamed the 'spiny sharks' – also lived in Ireland during this time. Much as for the placoderms, the Devonian was also a golden age for the acanthodians. These were truly ancient creatures. Among other claims to fame, they may have been some of the very first vertebrates with jaws, a landmark development in the Earth's history. These 'spiny sharks' were so called because of their stream-lined, shark-like bodies. Most, though, did not reach the terrifying proportions we associate with sharks today; the largest acanthodian was around two metres long, and many were much smaller. These fish had mostly rounded heads and big eyes that helped them pick out the smaller fish and crustaceans they preyed on. At least some acanthodians had heavy, bony armour over their shoulders. However, their main line of defence was their characteristic spines on their back and belly, which could be up to half the length of the creature itself. These would have made them difficult to swallow.

The Devonian also saw some major developments for life on land. Land plants first evolved during the earlier Ordovician period, and vascular plants in the Silurian. But it was during the Devonian that the first forests arrived, and more complicated communities of terrestrial plants took shape. Stunning examples of this have emerged from Devonian river sediments in Kiltorcan, County Kilkenny. These plants, known as *Archaeopteris*, were yet another landmark in the history of life on Earth: the very first trees had arrived. *Archaeopteris* were massive, up to a metre wide in the trunk and capable of towering more than twenty metres into the air. These plants would have looked a bit like giant Christmas trees, with drooping fronds that became narrower towards the top. Beneath them lay a woody stem, similar to modern conifers.

Archaeopteris could grow so big because it had solved the problems of size like no other plants had before it. Swellings at the bases of its branches offered more support, while layers of wood added further reinforcement on the inside. These innovations – still employed by trees today – meant *Archaeopteris* could tower over its contemporaries. With this competitive advantage, it quickly came to dominate the forests of the Devonian.

These new giants soon began to change the world around them. Among *Archaeopteris*' other unique features was an extensive root system; it was probably the first plant whose roots delved more than a metre into the soil. This had a massive impact on soil chemistry, and all manner of plants and animals that depended on it. Just like trees today, *Archaeopteris* provided food and shelter for a whole host of creatures to exploit. The first complex land ecosystems evolved during the Devonian. The decomposing remains of these enormous ferns would also help fertilise the streams and rivers of the Devonian, abetting the explosion of freshwater fish species that occurred at this time. Without the first trees, perhaps this gilded age of fish might not have shone so bright.

So, Ireland's Devonian wildlife consisted of weird fishes in the sea and strange plants forming the first forests on land. But at the interface between the two lived the most extraordinary animal of all. This was the maker of the world-renowned trackway at Valentia Island.

We don't know the specific species that these footprints belonged too. We do know, though, that they were made by a four-footed, amphibious creature called a tetrapod.

You are a tetrapod. So is your dog, your cat, and the sheep and cattle that graze the fields of Valentia today. The gulls whose cries echo out above the trackway are also tetrapods. A tetrapod is simply any creature with four limbs – or any that evolved from a four-limbed ancestor. All living amphibians, reptiles, birds and mammals (including humans) are classed as tetrapods. Even members of those families without legs, such as snakes, are considered tetrapods as they derived from a four-legged ancestor. Tetrapods also include animals that would return to the water millions of years later, such as the whales and marine reptiles.

With only footprints to go on, what can we tell about how our Devonian tetrapod looked in life? Fortunately, we have fossil evidence from other parts of the world to supplement the Valentia footprints, and build up a picture of this strange beast that has been dead for 385 million years. Its closest living analogues are the giant salamanders that still cling on, on the verge of extinction, in Japan and China today. It would have been about a metre long, with a third

"These footprints represent an extraordinary turning point in the history of life on Earth."

or more of that made up of a flattened, paddle-like tail, like a tadpole's swollen to a great size. A long, low-lying body was supported by four short, stumpy legs. At the end of each leg was a foot with up to eight digits, which were probably webbed together to form a paddle (later tetrapods, more concerned with walking than swimming, would prune this down to the more familiar five we still have today). The hind limbs might have stuck out to the back and side rather than directly underneath the animal, again diagnostic of a creature more adept at swimming than walking. Its head was flat and rounded, with the eyes protruding from the top. Hidden within the jaws were two semi-circuits of short, sharp teeth. This animal was almost certainly a predator. Like its fishy forebears, it had a lateral line on its skull, with which it could detect the movements of its prey in the water. A weird halfway house between aquatic and terrestrial life, it would probably have come equipped with the internal gills needed to breathe in water like a fish, as well as the lungs it used in the open air – lungs that would one day be inherited by you and me.

This creature would still have been awkward and inelegant out of the water. The Valentia Island tracks confirm this. Though distorted by the nearly 400 million years of geological activity which have elapsed since their creation, we can still tell how this creature walked by looking closely at them. It had an awkward, sprawling gait, twisting its body from side to side with each step, much like a crocodile. Flanked by the footprints is a faint impression made by the tetrapod's body, suggesting that it couldn't even lift its belly clear of the ground as it moved. The long, tadpole-like tail dragged behind it, carving out a faint trench in the mud that would be entombed in stone along with the footprints. This suggests that the animal was out of the water when the trackway was laid, carrying its own weight on its four legs.

These footprints represent an extraordinary turning point in the history of life on Earth. The Devonian is when vertebrates – backboned animals like our tetrapod – left the water for the first time and started to adapt to life on land. To use a dated cliché, our tetrapod is a missing link, a transitional form between the fully aquatic fish that came before it and the dynasties of land animals (amphibians, reptiles, birds, mammals) that would follow.

Footprints of early tetrapods are extremely rare in the fossil record. Where they exist, few are as comprehensive as the trackway on Valentia Island. Brazil's Devonian rocks have yielded just a single tetrapod track. Scotland's Devonian trackways are nowhere near as well preserved; Australia's are much shorter. Crucially, all of these are younger than the footprints left on Valentia Island. Indeed, the Valentia Island trackway was the oldest tetrapod trackway in the whole world until an older set of prints was confirmed in Poland in 2009. Still, its discovery back in 1993, and its age of 385 million years, implied that tetrapods were crawling onto land for longer than the actual fossil bone evidence around the world suggested.

The transition to living on land presented the early tetrapods with a range of problems. Water affords animals a degree of support they no longer enjoy on dry land (this is why whales, for instance, can attain a size in water that they could never support on land). Locomotion on land, therefore, is completely different than in water; those ancestral fins that served our tetrapod's fish predecessors so well in the water would not have been much good for walking on solid ground. Even more important were the issues of breathing and reproducing on land. Fish, the forebears of tetrapods, breathed through gills much as they still do today. But gills are useless when it comes to drawing oxygen from the air. Fish eggs are also permeable; they would shrivel and die if laid outside water. Like all of its descendants, our tetrapod's body would have been mostly made up of water. How did it prevent this from simply evaporating in the dry air? Then there were the fluctuating hot and cold conditions on land; how would our pioneering tetrapod maintain its temperature?

To understand how tetrapods solved these issues, we need to look into their origins. As well as the armoured placoderms and spiny acanthodians, there were other groups that made up this golden age of the fish in the Devonian. The lobe-finned fishes were among them. Lobe-finned fishes still survive today, although they're much rarer than they once were. Living members include the eel-like, air-breathing lungfish that haunt tropical swamps around the world, as well as the eerie coelacanths, whose luminous eyes light up the offshore crannies in which they lurk. Incredibly, fish like this share more blood with you than they do with sharks, salmon or most other living fish.

Lobe-fins, as their name suggests, have fins mounted on muscular lobes, reinforced by bone. As well as making powerful paddles, these were also much better for wriggling about on land than the fins of other fishes, and were the precursors to the arms and legs you have now. Crucially, lobe-fins had a major advantage over other fish groups in being able to breathe air through primitive lungs – air bladders affixed to the back of the throat. With these attributes, land – while by no means comfortable – was not the death sentence for lobe-fins that it was for other fishes. Oxygen levels were lower in the Devonian than they are today, and the deficit was particularly acute in the water. This might have given the ancestors of our tetrapod an incentive to supplement the oxygen they got in the water with gulps of air – and spend more and more time on land. Tides might also have played a part. During the early Devonian, days would only have lasted twenty-one hours as the Earth spun faster on its access than it does now, while the moon – which orbited closer than today – would have loomed much larger in the night sky. These factors may have led to larger tides which, when they retreated, would have left fish stranded behind in pools. Running out of oxygen and maybe food, these marooned fish would have needed lungs to breath air – and weight-bearing limbs to escape the pools in which they were trapped.

These lobe-finned fishes were the progenitors of the first tetrapods. As they adapted to living in shallower and shallower water, their skulls flattened, and their eyes migrated to the tops of their heads to help them spot food above the water. To further help in this regard, the spine elongated into a neck on top of which the head could be moved around independently of the body (fish have no necks; the head rests directly on the shoulders). Their fins slowly flowered into limbs, with elbows, wrists and digits – far better for crawling about on land when the animal needed to leave the water. Meanwhile, within the body, interlocking pegs helped keep the spine straight without water to support it. The offspring of all these changes over a thirty-million-year transitionary period were creatures like the one that left its tracks on Valentia Island. The first tetrapods had arrived. The land beckoned.

This was still a primitive animal, and had yet to arrive at all the solutions needed to live permanently on dry land. Our tetrapod likely spent much of its time in the water, even though it was better equipped to move on land than any vertebrate that came before it. It still had to worry about drying out when it left the water, and it laid soft, permeable eggs. Because of this, it would have been tied to moist environments even when it came ashore, and likely laid its eggs in the water just as its fish ancestors had done. Similarly, this animal probably couldn't regulate its own body temperature. That ability would be left to much later generations of warm-blooded tetrapods.

What made dry land so appealing to tetrapods and their ancestors in the first place? Access to food might have been one reason. Much as invertebrates had preceded vertebrates in their origins, they also beat them onto land. By the time our pioneering tetrapod was leaving its tracks in the mud, invertebrates had already been on land for at least forty million years. Indeed, by this time they had already made three separate incursions onto terra firma: the insects, the arachnids (spiders and scorpions) and the myriapods (centipedes and millipedes). All three of these groups evolved in the water. Which of them was the very first to venture onto land remains unclear, but what is certainly the case is that, in the Devonian, there was a whole host of invertebrate prey crawling about on dry land, a rich food source just waiting for a new predator to exploit.

"With the ability to see vast distances across this new terrestrial frontier, tetrapods could take in the world around them to a degree never before possible. Suddenly, it paid to be proactive as well as reactive."

One crucial asset in the tetrapod conquest of the land was their eyes. Early tetrapods like the one on Valentia Island had eyes three times bigger than their fish ancestors – and, crucially, they developed these before they developed legs. Why? Eyes are of limited utility in murky water, but they make all the difference on land. Larger eyes, conveniently positioned atop the head, would have helped our tetrapod see three times further in the air – and ten times further than it could underwater – as it raised the top of its head, crocodile-like, above the surface. With these to guide it, our tetrapod could have snapped at millipedes and other crunchy invertebrates that strayed too close to the water's edge.

These eyes would have given our tetrapod an enormous advantage. A predator with short-range vision has to traverse a large area in the hope that prey will cross its path. But armed with large eyes positioned to spot prey above the water, our little Devonian predator could save all that effort by scanning a wider area before zeroing in on its target. Once their eyes made them aware of the bounty to be had on shore, it was only natural that proto-tetrapods would develop more robust fins and eventually legs to help them access this glut of food, which was beyond the reach of predators confined to the water.

Some scientists even think that spending more time on land and hunting terrestrial prey caused tetrapods to revolutionise their cognition as well as their bodies. In water, it's hard for an animal to see more than one body length in front of it. Because of this, fish are highly reactive predators. They just snap at whatever suitable food comes within range. But with the ability to see vast distances across this new terrestrial frontier, tetrapods could take in the world around them to a degree never before possible. Suddenly, it paid to be proactive as well as reactive. This might have been the spark that led to the development of forward planning and strategic thinking, abilities that would reach their pinnacle of expression in our own species, nearly 400 million years later.

Much as the temptation of invertebrate prey might have pulled the first tetrapods out of the water, a further push factor might have been predators of their own. Bottom-feeders like *Bothriolepis* mightn't have been much of a threat, but there was always a bigger fish in the Devonian. We know from fossils found elsewhere that far larger and more fearsome placoderms plied the waterways at this time. The armour plates of these terrifying fish extended into vicious shears in their mouths, with which they could slice through almost any prey. As if these killers weren't scary enough, Devonian waters also still played host to the dreaded sea scorpions. Predators like this would have easily been large enough to make a meal out of a metre-long tetrapod like the creature that crawled ashore on Valentia Island. Perhaps this provided further impetus for the first tetrapods to spend more time on land, where they were beyond the reach of their aquatic nemeses. Large, land-based predators had yet to evolve at this time, and so the land – for all its difficulties – offered a relatively safe haven.

Whatever their motivations, creatures like the Valentia Island tetrapod represent a milestone in the history of life on Earth. As primitive as this animal may have been, it would go on to become the progenitor of a tetrapod dynasty that would come to dominate the land and skies. Its distant descendants would develop harder skins and tougher, waterproof eggshells, completing the transition to a fully terrestrial lifestyle. Later still they would develop endothermy, warm-bloodedness, the ability to maintain their own body temperature, and so free themselves from relying on their environment to keep warm. The primitive legs and feet on which our tetrapod waddled on the mud would eventually give rise to sturdy pillars of flesh and bone that would carry the largest creatures ever to walk on land, and one day form wings with which pterosaurs and (later) birds and bats would go on to conquer the skies. Freed from the need to paddle their owner through the water, the digits of the forelimbs would one day form fingers, dexterous instruments with which to express the genius of mankind, one of untold lineages of tetrapods – from the smallest hummingbird to the largest whale – that can trace their descent to creatures like this, sprawling awkwardly from side to side on the mud of the mid-Devonian.

One day, its grandchildren of generations beyond count would find these tracks and look back in wonder at their primordial ancestors, those pioneering tetrapods without which none of this – and none of us – would be possible. In these tracks, we have a hallmark from the genesis of our own evolutionary story.

The world of our Devonian tetrapod was not to last. Around twenty-six million years later, the Devonian would give way to a new age. The Carboniferous had arrived – and, as we shall see, a host of weird and wonderful creatures came with it.

3

Sharks, Shells and Monsters: Carboniferous Ireland

From the murky depths of a tropical swamp, one of the most fearsome predators on Earth watches its prey. Peering through the peat-stained water, its eyes latch on to its target; a small tetrapod has chosen the wrong stretch of river in which to lay its eggs. Though comfortable on land, it still needs water to reproduce. This is where it faces its greatest risk.

In a second, the surface of the water is shattered as the predator erupts out of the river. Huge tusk-like teeth sink into its victim. As quick as it struck, the predator wheels around; like many creatures in this strange swamp forest, it cannot survive out of water indefinitely. It thrashes its way back into the water, taking its wriggling prey with it. Within moments, the tumult on the water's surface fades to a ripple, a trail of blood the only residue of the carnage.

The forest resumes its normal rhythm, the whir of insects' wings the only noise permeating the fern fronds ...

No period in Earth's history has had a greater impact on Ireland's formation than the Carboniferous. It began at the end of the Devonian around 359 million years ago and lasted for 60 million years. This was a critical time in the history of life. On land, in the air and in the water, new groups of animals were arising which would go on to change the course of life on Earth right up until the present day. And given the ubiquity of Carboniferous rocks here, it's perhaps not surprising that some of these weird and fascinating creatures have been unearthed in Ireland. Indeed, the Carboniferous has yielded some of Ireland's most important (and impressive) fossils.

A quick glance at any geological map will reveal the significance of the Carboniferous to the Ireland we know today. Most of these will show a vast belt of blue stretching from Dublin to Galway, ballooning across the Midlands before spreading its tentacles deep into Ulster to the north and Munster to the south. This is Carboniferous limestone, which forms around half of Ireland's bedrock. The lime from which this stone takes its name plays a crucial role in nourishing the calcium-rich, well-drained pasturelands of the Irish interior. Without the Carboniferous, we probably would not have the beef and dairy industries for which Ireland is renowned today.

But it is on the west coast that the limestone finds its most poetic expression, in the haunting karst landscape of the Aran Islands and, in particular, The Burren of County Clare. Here, the topsoil was stripped away by glaciers during the Ice Age and the actions of man that followed it. What's

"This was a critical time in the history of life. On land, in the air and in the water, new groups of animals were arising which would go on to change the course of life on Earth right up until the present day."

left is a vast plain of silvery limestone, furrowed by grikes, natural trenches in the stone hollowed out by water over the millennia. This is now home to one of Ireland's great ecological treasures. The grikes of the Burren form natural plant pots for a unique flora, where Arctic, Alpine and Mediterranean flowers all intermingle, latching onto the boulders and filling the spaces between them. Around 70 per cent of Ireland's native plants can be found here. The limestone pavement is lent colour by the pink of the bloody cranesbill, the vanilla and gold of the mountain avens, and the royal blue stars of the spring gentian, each hue giving the karst its visual flare.

Much of this limestone is built from the hard parts of long-dead creatures. Their soft flesh might be long gone, but the calcium carbonate that made up their shells and skeletons still nourishes Ireland's grasslands today; a continuum of life stretching back more than 300 million years. During the Carboniferous, Ireland lay around ten degrees south of the equator, like New Guinea does today. The limestone belt that wraps around the country was then the bottom of a warm, shallow sea. It is the creatures that dwelt below these azure waters that would one day form the bedrock of The Burren. If you know what you're looking for, you can still see their remains ridging and corrugating the limestone.

These are the leftovers of a once thriving ecosystem. Corals were abundant, branching out across the sea floor as they still do in tropical waters, or forming great cylinders as can be seen fossilised on the Sligo coast today. Theirs are some of the most common fossils found in the region. Trilobites still patrolled the sand, as they had done for hundreds of millions of years. Crinoids – cousins of starfish and sea cucumbers – lived a more static life, latching onto the seafloor and snaring tiny prey that passed by. With their long stalks terminating in a flower of tentacles, they would have looked more like plants than animals. Sponges, caressing the sea from below like bulbous, furrowed fingers, took an even easier approach. These simple creatures got all the food they needed from the water passing through the pores in their body, a feeding mechanism that has seen them survive for nearly 600 million years. They shared this space with shelled creatures such as brachiopods and bivalves, the latter being kin to the oysters, clams and mussels that still pepper the beaches of our Atlantic coast. Like the sponges, the fact that they've changed so little in all that time attests to their success.

Stranger creatures also employed shells to keep themselves safe in the Carboniferous seas. And sometimes, their remains can turn up in the most unlikely places. The spectacular fossil of one such animal was found in a block of limestone in a wall in Tuam, County Galway, in 2017. It was shaped like a drinking horn, broad at the base before curling around to the tip. This, however, was no horn but a large shell. It belonged to an enormous snail called *Phanerotinus* that lived on the Carboniferous sea bed around 340 million years ago. In life it would have looked even more spectacular than the fossil suggests. The shell, which curled around like a Danish pastry, was fringed with spiny flanges running up and down its length. These saw-tooth protrusions served as anchors, preventing the snail from sinking into the seabed. Given this, it probably lived a sedentary lifestyle, straining all the food it needed from the water around it, or from the nutrient-rich mud on the seafloor. Gastropods (snails and slugs) were common in the Carboniferous seas. This giant was one of the largest gastropods in the ancient world; the Tuam shell measured around eighteen centimetres across at its widest point, and other *Phanerotinus* found elsewhere in Ireland were even larger. Fossils of this kind are extraordinarily rare; only fifteen such giant snail shells have been found worldwide, all of them in a belt of Carboniferous rock bisecting Ireland and Britain. As well as Galway, the fossils of this giant gastropod have been found carved like Celtic swirls into rocks in Roscommon, Limerick and Westmeath.

Even this great snail, though, was dwarfed by some of the more mobile shelled giants that plied our Carboniferous seas. Remains of that creature emerged from rocks at Castle Espie, County Down; great cylinders of fossilised stone, with strange striations running across them. These were among the largest fossils ever found in Ireland. Strung together they would have formed an enormous, conical shell that would have been as long as a person – or perhaps even longer. The owner of this was called *Rayonnoceras*, and it was one of the largest – and probably most alarming – creatures to patrol Ireland's warm, shallow Carboniferous seas.

Rayonnoceras was an enormous cephalopod, a member of the same family that includes octopuses, squids and cuttlefish. It would have looked like one too; protruding from the end of the giant shell would have been a ring of writhing tentacles, and probably two bulbous eyes like most cephalopods have today. These strange-shelled cephalopods were some of the top predators in the prehistoric seas, a menace from a time before the rise of the fish.

The giant shell, known as an orthocone, would have been divided into chambers. The oldest was where the hatchling *Rayonnoceras* began life, gradually growing into larger and larger chambers as the creature got bigger. The older chambers, carried around like tokens from a past life, still likely served a purpose: air trapped within them probably acted as buoyancy, helping this giant raise and lower itself in the water. Special deposits within the chambers also provided balance, preventing the creature from keeling forward and helping it stay horizontal. *Rayonnoceras* probably lurked near the sea floor. Here it would lunge at trilobites and maybe fish, snaring them in its ring of tentacles before passing them to its beak to finish them off.

Invertebrates like this did not reign unchallenged in the Carboniferous seas. In these warm, tropical waters, fish certainly thrived as well. But what kinds of fish? The extinction event that brought the Devonian dealt a huge blow to the placoderms, the great dynasty of armoured fish that dominated the oceans at that time. As they declined, the stage was now set for the rise of another dynasty, one that would go on to haunt oceans across the world right up to the present day.

In 2017, a tiny fossil tooth was found in 320-million-year-old rocks in County Clare. It was triangular in shape and flanked by miniature clones of itself to form a three-pronged weapon, about the size of a five-cent piece. Even someone who knew nothing of fossil teeth could guess its owner to have been a shark.

Sharks are among the most ancient creatures in the sea. They had already existed for at least eighty million years by this point. But in Carboniferous seas shorn of their armoured competitors, the sharks diversified like never before, entering a golden age in their long history. The sharks eschewed the bony plates of the placoderms for a lightweight skeleton made of cartilage, the same substance that forms your ears and nose. This allowed them to evolve into the fast, streamlined predators that still terrify the popular imagination, becoming some of the most agile fish in the sea. It also helped them stay afloat and cover vast distances across the ocean far more efficiently than the bony fish they shared the seas with. This, coupled with a supremely streamlined shape and an array of senses sharpened to detect any prey the oceans had to offer, meant you had the recipe for a new breed of apex predators, ready to stake their claim on the Carboniferous oceans.

The Clare shark was up to seventy centimetres long – and a voracious carnivore. Prehistoric sharks came in a weird and wonderful array of shapes and sizes. Cartilage rarely fossilises though, and so all too often the only evidence they left behind them were their teeth. These, though, can tell us a lot about how a shark lived. The Clare tooth is in the classic cladodont mould, the three blades designed to get maximum purchase on struggling prey. This shark likely prowled the warm, shallow waters of the Carboniferous, sinking its teeth into smaller creatures that were swallowed whole.

Sharks were not the only fearsome fish swimming in Carboniferous waters. Of all the rocks dating from this time, the most productive when it comes to fish fossils have been found in more northern counties such as Derry and Armagh. Carboniferous deposits from the former contained the scales and terrifying teeth of a true monster, one that could have eaten a small shark, like the Clare specimen, for a snack. Its name: *Archichthys*.

Archichthys belonged to a family of fish called the rhizodonts. They were among the top predators of the Carboniferous. The rhizodonts were lobe-finned fishes, cousins of the creatures that had given rise to tetrapods back in the Devonian. They counted among their ranks some of the largest freshwater fish that ever lived, predators that would have rivalled modern killer whales in size. These giants could have made mincemeat out of any other creature that entered their murky domain.

Archichthys, a medium-sized member of the family, may have grown over two metres long, and was first discovered in Ireland's Carboniferous rocks. It probably shunned the open ocean in favour of the murky rivers and lakes that strung their way through the fetid swamps of the Carboniferous. Instead of the razor-sharp cladodont dentition of contemporary sharks, this creature was armed with even more fearsome weaponry: huge, tusk-like teeth, long and curved, protruding from immensely powerful jaws. Once these grabbed hold of a victim, there was no escape.

Resting on its broad, fan-shaped fins, *Archichthys* could have lurked with infinite patience beneath the water, perhaps even with its head protruding menacingly above the surface. It was well equipped to ambush its prey, be it the sharks, acanthodians and other lobe-finned fish it shared its habitat with or even tetrapods that came too close to the water's edge. And with powerful lobe fins strong enough to help their owner crawl on land, some scientists even speculate that their predations may not have been limited to the water. Horror of horrors, this fish could probably beach itself like a modern killer whale, sinking its fangs into its victim before dragging it back to the depths to be shaken and torn to pieces. In all rhizodonts, the lateral line was exceedingly well developed compared to most other fish, helping them detect moving prey in the gloom.

Life in Ireland was certainly not confined to water during the Carboniferous. As the period wore on, lush, tropical forests coated much of the land. The first trees might have evolved in the Devonian, but it was during the swampy, humid conditions of the Carboniferous that they really started to come into their own, reaching a level of diversity and structural sophistication they'd never had before. The *Archaeopteris* trees that typified Devonian forests were long gone by now. In their place, the swamps of the Carboniferous were dominated by enormous clubmosses, up to forty metres tall. These lycopod trees would have looked truly bizarre by today's standards, with bare trunks covered in diamond or honeycomb-shaped scales peeling off into a tangled mass of fronds at the very top. Ferns and horsetails also diversified greatly at this time, and developed into tree-like forms that would have towered over their more modest living counterparts.

The menagerie of micro-organisms that disintegrate dead trees in our modern forests had yet to evolve in the Carboniferous. Because of this, when a tree died, instead of slowly disintegrating into the soil, it simply compressed into peat on the forest floor. Over time, layers and layers of this dead plant matter built up to form coal. Ninety per cent of our coal had its origins in this period. The effects of this are still keenly felt today; were it not for the Carboniferous, there would have been no Industrial Revolution. The modern world would not have been possible were it not for these swamp forests more than 300 million years ago.

It is from this coal that the Carboniferous – meaning 'coal-bearing' – takes its name. And it is after the coal that would be its legacy that this habitat was also named: the coal forest. At sites such as Coalisland (County Tyrone), Arigna (County Roscommon) and the Leinster coalfield that straddles Counties Carlow, Laois and Kilkenny, we have places where the remains of Ireland's prehistoric coal forest still survive – as well as some of the country's most remarkable fossil sites.

If the plants in the coal forests were unusual by today's standards, the animals were even more alien. During the

Carboniferous, land animals started to get big. This was the age of the monster arthropods, a time when insects, arachnids and myriapods (centipedes and millipedes) attained terrifying proportions. From the remains of swampy Carboniferous forests around the world have emerged fossils of scorpions larger than house cats, dragonfly-like predators as big as crows and – most alarming of all – millipedes that would have been longer than a person. The latter would have been the largest herbivores on land at this time.

"In the Carboniferous, life took to the air for the first time."

To date, none of these giant arthropods have been uncovered in Ireland. But sometimes small fossils can be just as valuable – if not more so. Such was the case near Doolin, County Clare in 1991, when a tiny specimen, only twenty-one millimetres long, emerged from Carboniferous rocks around 315 million years old. It was the impression of an insect, with most of the body obscured by the intersecting wings. When it was found, this was the oldest insect fossil in Western Europe. It represented yet another milestone in the history of life on Earth. In the Carboniferous, life took to the air for the first time. By 325 million years ago, insects had become the first creatures on Earth to evolve powered flight. The flying reptiles, birds and bats that would follow the insects into the air many millions of years later already had the forelimbs which would become their wings. Insects, the true pioneers, had to evolve their wings from scratch.

How they achieved this is still not fully understood. Their wings might have evolved from flat, stiff appendages affixed to the body. These would have allowed the insect to make gliding descents from high points. In time, these proto-wings became longer and more flexible, enabling their owner to beat them in order to steer its descent and eek more and more distance out of its glides until, eventually, insects' wings as we now know them finally emerged.

The Doolin specimen in particular signifies another important leap forward in the evolution of flying insects. This is one of the oldest examples of an insect that could fold its wings back over its body. Prior to this, all flying insects could only hold their wings out to the sides like dragonflies still do today. But being able to fold its wings allowed the Doolin insect – which belonged to the same family as crickets and cockroaches – to enter and explore smaller nooks and crannies than would have been possible before. This would have given it a big advantage when it came to finding food, escaping predators or finding a safe place to lay its eggs.

The evolution of flight would change the course of life on Earth forever. Prior to flight, insects were rare in the fossil record, outnumbered by arachnids and myriapods. But wings allowed insects to travel further, find mates, escape predators and access new food resources that they never could before. Herbivorous insects could now browse on the very highest branches, while a new generation of winged carnivores emerged to hunt them. As a result, the insects exploded in diversity, becoming one of the greatest evolutionary success stories the world has ever seen. They have since survived every extinction event the Earth could throw at them, and today comprise over a million species spread across every continent (by contrast, mammals, birds and reptiles make up fewer than 30,000 species between them). Millions of years after the Carboniferous, the first flowers arrived on the scene. They would avail of the pollinating potential of winged insects to spark a revolution among plants, resulting in the wonderfully colourful flora we see today. And it might well have been the insects that tempted reptiles, birds and bats onto the wing, eager to feast on the flying bonanza in the forests around them. The genesis of all of this can be traced back to those first flying insects in the Carboniferous.

Arthropods were not the only group of land animals to survive the Devonian and thrive into the Carboniferous. Tetrapods – the descendants of the creature that dragged itself ashore on Valentia Island – also flourished during this time. As with many other groups, the tetrapods had been hit hard by the extinction event that brought the Devonian to an end. But survive they did, as specimens such as a fossil jaw bone uncovered in County Derry confirm. Ireland's oldest tetrapod footprints might date from the Devonian, but our oldest tetrapod bones do not appear until 325 million years ago in the Carboniferous, yet another impressive fossil find to emerge from Doolin, County Clare. Tetrapods blossomed into a range of shapes and forms during this time, including this four-legged, newt-like creature that could fit in the palm of your hand.

By the late Carboniferous they had given rise to the amphibians, that great order of creatures that counts frogs, toads, newts and salamanders among its living members. Amphibians are nowhere near as predominant as they once were; in most habitats around the world today, they find themselves dwarfed by reptiles and mammals. But the latter had yet to evolve by this time, and reptiles were still rare. So, in the wet, humid conditions of the Carboniferous, the amphibians enjoyed a gilded age of their own. In this green new Eden, the amphibians would expand to occupy a range of niches they never had before – and, in some cases, grow to formidable sizes.

Among the world's most important collections of prehistoric amphibians was dug out of the Jarrow Colliery in Castlecomer, County Kilkenny. At around 314 million years old, this is one of the oldest coal-swamp faunas in the fossil record. The coal in which the bones were interred was formed from the compacted ferns and other plant life that filled up the Carboniferous forest. Due to the conditions they lived in, fossils of Carboniferous amphibians are extremely rare; the acidic peat of the time disintegrated bones. These precious remains help us build up a picture of a long-lost ecosystem where, for the very first time, amphibians were the dominant animal group.

Because they breathe through their skin, and need to remain moist, amphibians – even though they can spend time on land – are often most at home in the water. Among the specimens unearthed at Castlecomer were some species clearly adapted for an aquatic life. *Urocordylus* was among them. This animal is unique to the coal measures of Castlecomer, having been found nowhere else on Earth. It was modest as far as Carboniferous amphibians went, being only around twenty centimetres long. The vast majority of its body was made up of an extraordinarily long tail, which was flattened to give its owner maximum propulsion in the water. With its four slender limbs affixed to a small trunk, this animal would have looked much like the salamanders that are still around today.

A slightly more striking inhabitant of the waterways would have been *Keraterpeton*, whose exquisite skeletons are among the most common fossils from Castlecomer. Its overall body shape was similar to a newt, one of the few amphibians we still have in Ireland today. However, its most striking features were the two 'horns' jutting out from the back of its flattened skull. *Keraterpeton* was the first in a family of highly specialised amphibian predators to possess such protrusions. It's thought that, in tandem with the flattened skull, they acted as a hydrofoil, helping the animal to exploit the current and rise from the riverbed to snatch at its prey. As in earlier tetrapods, eyes surmounting the skull would have helped it spot small fish or invertebrates from below.

By this point in their history, amphibians (and, therefore, tetrapods) were not solely confined to the waterways. Many of the niches that are held by reptiles in tropical parts of the world today were occupied by amphibians in the Carboniferous. Among the strangest of Castlecomer's amphibians was *Ophiderpeton*. At around seventy centimetres long, this creature had lost its legs altogether. If you saw it slithering about on the forest floor, you would immediately think it was a snake. But snakes would not evolve for another 200 million years. *Ophiderpeton* and amphibians like it had just converged on the same body plan as the snakes in order to live the same lifestyle. While their tetrapod ancestors had striven to evolve the legs that would make walking on land feasible, creatures like *Ophiderpeton* lost them again, probably to help them tunnel through the masses of rotting ferns on the floor of the coal forest. They were snakes before snakes.

The resemblance was more than superficial. Like snakes, *Ophiderpeton* had an extremely wide gape, helping it swallow prey wider than its own narrow head and body. Also like snakes, forward-facing eyes would have helped it zero in on prey directly ahead of it, judging the distance before a well-placed strike. Recurved teeth, just like those of a python, helped prevent prey from escaping once *Ophiderpeton*

[53]

had grabbed hold of its victim. This animal probably lived in burrows, pursuing the arthropods (insects, spiders, centipedes) that milled about in the leaf-litter. With its long, narrow body, unimpeded by legs, it was well equipped to go to ground after its prey.

With so many smaller creatures scurrying about in the swamps, it should come as no surprise that there were also larger predators here too. The biggest creature to come out of Castlecomer had a skull up to thirty-five centimetres long. Broad at the base, its skull elongates and gradually tapers to a rounded tip. It looks to all the world like that of a crocodile. But even these ancient reptiles had yet to appear in the fossil record at this point. The top predator in this prehistoric swamp, and the owner of the fearsome skull, was another amphibian: *Megalocephalus*.

Where *Ophiderpeton* stood in for snakes in this weird ecosystem, *Megalocephalus* filled the niche that crocodiles and alligators would eventually evolve into. Nothing of this animal has been found anywhere in the world other than its skull, so we're left to guess at what the rest of its body looked like. It was probably crocodilian in form, reaching about one-and-a-half metres long, including webbed feet and a flattened tail used to sweep it through the water. It would have dwarfed all but the very largest amphibians living today.

The jaws of *Megalocephalus* would have been lined with sharp, needle-like teeth, perfect for piercing the fish that probably made up the bulk of its diet. As in earlier tetrapods, a lateral line would have helped it detect the movements of its prey as it swam through the murky waters of the forest. Smaller amphibians with which it shared the waterways might also have fallen victim to its powerful bite.

Megalocephalus might have haunted the waterways of the coal forest, but amid the hollowed-out tree trunks that littered the forest floor lived the most remarkable amphibian of them all. It was called *Dendrerpeton*, meaning 'tree-creeper', because its remains have so often been found in tree hollows. These probably served as lairs, cosy crevices in the forest in which to sit out the less active parts of the day and escape the unwanted attention of predators.

If other ancient amphibians of Castlecomer had their living analogues in snakes and crocodiles, *Dendrerpeton* looked most like a lizard. It had a long tail, short body, sprawling legs and a large snout. A jaw full of sharp teeth would have helped it snap up insects, smaller amphibians and other prey it came across. Like in *Ophiderpeton*, these teeth were raked back to prevent prey from escaping.

This creature was still very much an amphibian. It could not lay solid eggs, and so was tied to moist environments to reproduce. The miniature *Dendrerpeton* that wriggled out of these eggs then had to complete a larval stage, just like every other amphibian. And yet, *Dendrerpeton* and its immediate forebears still signify another fascinating turning point in evolutionary history. Of all the strange amphibians found at Castlecomer, here was one that probably spent more time on land than it did in the water. The robust leg and ankle bones of *Dendrerpeton* confirm this. Seventy million years before, the Valentia Island tetrapod had ambled awkwardly onto land. *Dendrerpeton* could now crawl in comfort on its stout limbs through the humid coal forests of Carboniferous Ireland. *Dendrerpeton* also had an ear structure better adapted for hearing in the air rather than the water – one of the first creatures on Earth to possess such a trait. Life on land had come a long way from the lobe-finned fish that first dragged themselves ashore in the Devonian.

Dendrerpeton and creatures like it were among the first of a new dynasty of amphibians, the temnospondyls, that went on to dominate swamp habitats the world over, and cling on for nearly 200 million years to come. Despite this, though, the golden years of the amphibians were numbered. As the Carboniferous drew to a close, the world was struck by yet another extinction event: the Carboniferous Rainforest Collapse, around 307 million years ago. A shift in the Earth's climate devastated the Carboniferous coal swamps – and all the unique creatures that lived in them. As a new, dryer world emerged from the retreat of the rainforests, amphibians, which need wet conditions, were hit hard. So too were the arthropods; less plant life meant less oxygen suffusing the atmosphere, the fuel which enabled the great millipedes, scorpions and insects of the time to attain their monstrous sizes. All of these families would survive, but never again would they achieve the dominance – and sheer scale – they enjoyed in the coal forests of the Carboniferous.

However, from the ashes of devastation was born opportunity immeasurable. An exciting new order was about to rise.

Scurrying about in the Carboniferous swamps was a new group of animals, the amniotes. These small, lizard-like creatures had a crucial advantage over the amphibians they shared the coal forest with: they laid hard eggs, and so could survive in dry conditions fatal to amphibians. At last, tetrapods could leave moist habitats behind them. In the dryer world that emerged from the Carboniferous, it was the amniotes that were set to take over.

Early in their history, the amniotes splintered into different strands. One would eventually give rise to mammals, including our own lineage. Another was the ancestor of the reptiles. Wrapped in water-proof scales, reptiles would do well in this arid new world. Among their descendants in many millions of years would be the most famous reptiles of all …

4

Ireland's Dinosaurs

S ome fossil hunters travel the world in search of the find of a lifetime. But for others, a trip to the local beach will suffice.

In the case of the late Roger Byrne, a school teacher from County Antrim, it took just two trips to his local stretch of volcanic beach at Islandmagee to etch his name into Irish paleontological history. It was here that Roger pried two pieces of fossil bone from between the boulders of black basalt and white limestone that festoon the Antrim coast.

To the undiscerning eye, these fragmentary fossils look scarcely different from the stones with which they once kept company. But Roger Byrne's eyes had been sharpened by years of fossil hunting amid the layer of Jurassic rock that winds its way along the northeast coast of Ireland. These slivers of bone – six and ten centimetres long – remain the only evidence of dinosaurs ever found in Ireland. That most famous family of extinct creatures had a presence here, around 200 million years ago.

It can be hard to build up a picture of any animal's life from two splinters of leg bone, but thanks to more complete fossils found elsewhere, and the combined fruits of decades of analysis and research, we now know more about the mighty dinosaurs than ever before. And with this, we are equipped to travel back in time to explore how Ireland's lost dinosaurs looked, hunted and lived.

Around 299 million years ago, the Carboniferous – that gilded age of amphibians that would go on to form the bedrock of much of modern Ireland – came to an end. Amphibians as a group survived till the present day, but they would never again dominate to the degree they did in the Carboniferous. Instead, as the world moved into the Permian period, cooler and dryer conditions saw the great coal swamps go into retreat. The warm, wet conditions in which creatures like *Dendrerpeton* once thrived began to contract.

The world was now ripe for the reptiles. With solid, waterproof scales and hard eggshells, the reptiles could divorce themselves from water to a degree their amphibian predecessors never could. They were well placed to exploit the new, dryer landscapes that opened up in the Permian. And exploit them they did, sharing the new habitats with the proto-mammals that, much later, would give rise to our own lineage. Sadly, Permian fossils are a rarity in Ireland. What Permian rocks we do have were mostly laid down in deserts or salt lakes. In such harsh environments, animal remains are scarce.

Then, around 252 million years ago, the most devastating mass extinction in Earth's history shook the planet. Known as the 'Great Dying', it saw up to 90 per cent of species die out as volcanic gasses smothered the planet. Life on Earth was brought closer to ending than ever before. But from the ashes of the Permian a new dawn was set to rise. The Mesozoic, the golden age of the giant reptiles, was about to begin. This would see new groups of reptiles dominate life on Earth like no groups of animals had done before. Among them were the greatest reptiles of them all, the dinosaurs.

The Mesozoic era, or the Age of the Dinosaurs, can be divided into the Triassic, the Jurassic and the Cretaceous periods. In the ecological chaos that followed the Great Dying, the Triassic saw the various surviving lineages of reptile diversify to fill the roles left vacant by the mass extinction – and vie with each other for control of the planet. One of these pretenders left its footprint imprinted at Scrabo Hill, County Down – a rare Irish relic from this time period. However, as the Triassic gave way to the Jurassic around 200 million years ago, one family of reptiles stood out above all others, having achieved supreme domination of the land that would last for more than 100 million years to come. The reign of the dinosaurs had dawned.

The dinosaurs first emerged in the Triassic, around 240 million years ago. At this time, the landmasses of the world had coalesced into a single supercontinent, Pangaea, dominated by arid deserts. By then, many groups of more ancient reptile had come and gone. Those that survived dwarfed the earliest dinosaurs. We're used to thinking of dinosaurs as towering giants, but the first members of the family were in fact small predators, about the size of a dog. They were as likely to be the hunted as the hunter. But these early dinosaurs had a few trump cards that would see them succeed in the evolutionary arms race that ensued.

Among these characteristics were special bones in their hips and ankles. Their legs were planted beneath their bodies at all times instead of sprawling to the side like most other reptiles. This made it easier for them to walk on two legs, making them more nimble and agile than the cumbersome reptiles they competed with. As the dinosaurs moved into their heyday during the Jurassic and Cretaceous, those same legs, positioned straight underneath the body, enabled them to bear weight far more efficiently than any of their reptilian forebears.

This meant that dinosaurs could get big – bigger than any land animals before or since. The sauropods, that magnificent family of long-necked, plant-eating dinosaurs, were the largest creatures ever to walk the Earth. The largest land mammal ever weighed in at around fifteen tonnes. But the largest sauropod weighed more than three times as much – and could have gotten even bigger. Egg laying could also have been a factor. A mammal's size is limited by the size of the foetus it must carry in its womb. Egg-laying dinosaurs had no such constraint.

"Ireland's dinosaur remains – though tiny and few in number – are still very important to science."

Dinosaur size was abetted by another secret of their success: air sacs throughout the body, just as in modern birds. These helped to reinforce hollow bones, lending them the strength needed to carry a dinosaur's great mass while keeping weight down. Another advantage was when it came to breathing. A complex network of air sacs, integrated into the respiratory system, meant that dinosaurs had oxygenated air running through their lungs at all times – even when breathing out. This highly efficient system – still found in birds today – helped them stay lively and active when their reptilian rivals had run out of gas. It may have been a reason why dinosaurs survived (and thrived) into the Jurassic when their reptilian and proto-mammal nemeses had perished.

This is where we pick up the story of Ireland's dinosaurs. It is the early Jurassic, around 200 million years ago. With most of their competition on land obliterated by an extinction event at the end of the Triassic, dinosaurs had taken centre stage. This was an exciting time in their long history, when many of the familiar dinosaur families were starting to take shape. In their shadows, our earliest mammal ancestors – small, shrew-like animals – scurried to safety wherever they could.

Dinosaur fossils from this early in the Jurassic are rare, and so Ireland's dinosaur remains – though tiny and few in number – are still very important to science. They are also among the most westerly dinosaur bones found anywhere in Europe.

The early Jurassic was a time of enormous change, for the planet as well as its creatures. The giant supercontinent of Pangaea, that once held all of the world's terra firma in one giant landmass stretching from north to south, was splitting in two. Ireland, along with the rest of Europe, went north. There were no ice caps at the poles, and so sea levels during the Jurassic were much higher than they are today. As such, much of modern Europe (including Ireland) would have consisted of warm, tropical islands of various sizes, scattered across a shallow sea.

Dinosaurs might have begun life as small predators, but by the end of the Triassic they had become partial to plants too and certainly, by the early Jurassic, plant-eating dinosaurs were abundant. One such herbivore was the owner of the six-centimetre fragment of femur found by Roger Byrne at Islandmagee on 13 January 1980. Though tiny, scientists are still able to confirm what family of dinosaurs it belonged to. This was a thyreophoran, an armoured plant eater. The particular species is harder to tell for certain, but *Scelidosaurus*, a well-known thyreophoran from early Jurassic rocks in England, is the best bet.

Scelidosaurus would have been around four metres long, maybe one metre high at the hips, and weighed in at just over a quarter of a tonne. Its back legs would have been significantly longer than its front legs – a legacy of descent from bipedal, predatory ancestors. This animal, though, would probably have been too front heavy to move about on two legs, and so was reduced to all fours once more.

The head of *Scelidosaurus* was tipped by a short, horny beak, with which it would have cropped the vegetation it fed on. Behind the beak were jaws lined with leaf-shaped teeth. This dinosaur only partly chewed its food, storing it in its cheeks as it was sliced over and over again by the teeth. It was probably a selective feeder, picking off the fresher leaves of the ferns and conifers on its Jurassic island home. Grass did not exist in the Jurassic. Flowering plants had probably evolved by this time, but were nowhere near as prevalent as they are now; a Jurassic forest or meadow would have been a monotony of greens, reds and browns, altogether lacking the rich colours to be seen in a temperate woodland today. Deciduous trees had yet to arrive on the scene; oak, ash and the other giants that make up the canopy of our modern woodlands were nowhere to be found. Instead, our *Scelidosaurus* probably inhabited a world of dry, low-lying shrubs, where ferns filled the role that grass does today. The forests of this time were made up of pines, ginkgoes and cycads, with tree-ferns reaching up to fill the space between them. *Scelidosaurus* remains are often found in marine deposits, leading some scientists to suspect that they may even have had a taste for seaweed.

If our *Scelidosaurus* only partly chewed these plants, how did it digest them? Once again, the more complete remains of other plant-eating dinosaurs provide the answer. Like modern birds, it seems that many plant-eating dinosaurs used stones to help them grind down their food. Small stones, known as gastroliths, were swallowed and kept in the stomach. These then acted as a mobile mill, grinding up plant matter as it passed through.

Were you to lay eyes on *Scelidosaurus* as it appeared in life, its most striking feature would have been its impressive suit of armour. This animal would likely have been panoplied from its head to the tip of its tail in rows of bony scutes protruding from the skin. Bony plates on its skull, curling into a pair of rear-facing horns, completed its formidable defences. The powerful tail, meanwhile, could have been swung freely at any predator that got too close.

While smaller dinosaur herbivores of the day relied on speed to escape predators, the thyreophorans took an altogether different route: impenetrable defence. *Scelidosaurus* likely wasn't a fast runner – it was too heavily armoured for that – but it didn't need to be. In life, its bony scutes would have formed living chainmail against any predators it might have come across. A biting predator would have found it hard to get purchase on skin studded with protruding bone, and could suffer severe injury in the process. Teeth could have been lost in the attempt. Less armoured prey would have been more appetising.

Scelidosaurus was among the very first of the armoured dinosaurs. As impressive as it was, its defences were meagre compared to those that would follow in the hall of fame of dinosaur defence. As creatures like *Scelidosaurus* pioneered dinosaur armour, predatory dinosaurs – the theropods – were forced to up their game. This set off an arms race that would ensue for over 100 million years – and produce some of the most iconic dinosaurs in the process.

As the scutes of early Jurassic thyreophorans became obsolete, later members of the family evolved weapons to defend themselves. The famous ankylosaurs would replace the chainmail of their early Jurassic forebears with full plate armour. Sheets of fused bone enveloping the upper body were virtually impenetrable, while a heavy tail club could cripple a tyrannosaur that got too close. In some species, heavy spikes on the shoulders and hips added another layer of protection.

The ankylosaurs were some of the most heavily armed herbivores that ever lived. They can likely trace their descent from the more modest thyreophorans that came before them, creatures just like the one whose bone was found by Roger Byrne on an Antrim beach.

Defence, though, might not have been the only reason *Scelidosaurus* covered itself in scutes from head to tail. In life, an impressive suit of armour might also have served as a status symbol. Perhaps a male with more impressive armour might have made for a more attractive mating prospect. If so, this new selective pressure – coupled with the evolution of larger and larger predators – might have supercharged the forging of more and more elaborate suits of armour as the Mesozoic wore on. Early forms, like our *Scelidosaurus*, might have maxed out at around four metres long, but later members of the family would grow to over twice as long – and more than ten times as heavy. Creatures like the one that left six centimetres of leg bone behind at Islandmagee were the forerunners of generations of armoured titans to follow.

Scelidosaurus had good reason to armour itself in the perilous Jurassic landscape it called home. On 15 April 1981, Roger Byrne would pick out another piece of bone among the boulders of the Antrim coast, larger and darker than that of *Scelidosaurus*. This fragment cannot be positively assigned to a particular species. However, palaeontologists were still able to discern the family of dinosaurs its owner came from: the theropods, two-legged carnivores, the top land predators of the Jurassic.

Later members of the theropod clan would include some of the most infamous dinosaurs of all, from the deadly *Allosaurus* and gigantic *Spinosaurus* to the legendary T. Rex. At maybe two to three metres long, our Antrim theropod didn't quite measure up to the enormous predators that would follow it. We can't tell from the one bone found whether this animal was fully grown, or only a fraction of the monstrous size it would attain in adulthood (though in the early Jurassic, theropods rarely grew larger than five metres long). Still, enough evidence has been gleaned from more substantial theropod remains – and comparisons with their living relatives – to help us build up a picture of how Ireland's Jurassic theropod might have behaved.

No group of dinosaurs was more diverse than the theropods. They varied immensely in shape and size, from smaller than a chicken to larger than an elephant. Most ate meat, some caught fish, and others fed entirely on plants. But across most of the family, the basic theropod form remained largely consistent. A deep, narrow head played host to rows of sharp, recurved teeth. This sat atop an S-shaped neck, much like many large birds today, itself affixed to a short trunk. Past the hips stretched out a long tail, which served as a counterbalance. Most theropods were bipedal, stalking the landscape on two legs. This in turn would have freed up their front limbs to play a part in the hunt, giving them a distinct advantage over any predator confined to all fours. With their flexed knees, drumstick shanks and three-toed profile, their legs and feet were like a chicken's writ large.

Every predator needs weapons. In the case of our theropod, these would have been its teeth. While arms tipped with sharp claws might have grabbed onto prey, this would only have been a precursor to the lethal bite to follow. Flattened serrated blades would have been driven home by powerful muscles in the jaw and neck. These teeth would have been pretty uniform throughout the mouth, and tell us a lot about how these animals hunted. Theropod dinosaurs lacked the dental sophistication of modern mammalian carnivores. For the most part, they probably couldn't lock onto their prey like dogs, nor deliver precise, suffocating bites like a big cat. Instead, a theropod's razor-sharp teeth, serrated fore and aft, would have sliced deep into the flesh of its victim, causing severe bleeding, shock or even evisceration. If the victim survived the first onslaught, infection could well have finished the job.

We can imagine our Jurassic theropod, crouched on its heels, waiting from the cover of the cycads to launch a surprise attack. On a large prey item this would have been a hit-and-run manoeuvre, inflicting as much damage as it could while minimising the risk of injury. Once the initial attack had done its job, the theropod moved in again for the final act.

Such a hunting technique may have enabled theropods to take down prey larger than themselves. They were undoubtedly aided by the highly efficient breathing system to which they (and all other dinosaurs) owed at least some of their success. It also suggests that theropods were active, warm-blooded killers, in contrast to their cold-blooded cousins the crocodiles, which must bask in the sun in order to build up enough energy to launch an attack. The fastest theropods could run as fast as a racehorse, and even some of the larger kinds could hit forty-five kilometres an hour.

Smaller theropods that, in turn, took smaller prey – mammals, fish, baby dinosaurs, even insects – had more conical teeth, designed to puncture and grab onto these bite-sized meals. If our Jurassic theropod did indeed reach its maximum size at two to three metres, perhaps this would have been the sort of fare it would have dined on. There is evidence that some theropods dug mammals out of their burrows; even underground, our distant ancestors weren't safe.

Just as modern wolves will target prey as small as a mouse and as large as a bison, it's probable our Jurassic theropod wasn't fussy either. When dinosaur flesh was in short supply, lizards or small, scurrying mammals would have sufficed. And if injury, disease or another predator had done the hard work for it, this animal – like almost all carnivores today – would not have been beyond scavenging. This could explain why so many theropod footprints have been found along prehistoric watercourses. Maybe our Antrim theropod patrolled the shoreline of the Jurassic sea for dead animals washed up on shore, or waited to ambush prey that came down to the local river to drink.

The social life of theropods has long been a topic of debate. Is there any proof that creatures like our Jurassic theropod hunted in groups? Some clues come in the form of parallel trackways; footprints left by theropods walking side by side have been found for both large and small species. Mass graves add further evidence. While some of these might just be different individuals accruing at the same site one after the other, it's possible at least some died (and, thus, lived) together. Pack hunting, of course, allows predators to take down much larger prey, or benefit from the hunting success of a pack member when their own efforts end in failure. The price of this, of course, is having to share the rewards with the rest of the pack. This may not have been the well-coordinated, communal hunting shown by wolves today. Instead, it could just have been a case of hungry predators coalescing on a weak or injured animal, as is seen in modern Komodo dragons. Once the kill was made, it could have been every theropod for itself.

Even if they did hunt in groups, there is plenty of evidence to suggest that relations between theropods were far from cordial. Gouges and other head wounds inflicted by those serrated teeth are common on the faces of theropods throughout the Mesozoic. These are the legacy of vicious fights between members of the same species, where head and face biting were the main tactics used. It's thought such conflict was how dominance was established in a pack, or disputes over food or territory resolved.

We like to think of predatory dinosaurs forever on the run, fighting each other and tormenting the docile plant eaters they shared the Jurassic landscape with. In reality, they probably would have spent much of their time at ease, dozing in the shade or under cover like big cats do today. Our thyreophoran probably had to slice its way through ferns and cycads for hours each day to take in the calories it needed. But our theropod could have made a kill, eaten its fill in one sitting, and spent much of the rest of the day sleeping it off. If large enough, it could have gone days or even weeks between big meals.

All was not sleep and carnage in the life of a carnivorous dinosaur. For all its undoubted ferocity, our Jurassic theropod would also have had moments of beauty, and maybe even tenderness. And at certain times of year, theropods might have been dapper dancers as well. Unusual trace fossils attributed to theropods suggest that these animals might have had communal display areas – known as leks – just like modern, ground-dwelling birds such as grouse. Here, males would congregate to strut their credentials, hoping to entice the onlooking females in for a coupling. The males might have raised their heads and tails to the sky to make themselves as imposing as possible, maybe fanning their arms and strutting to reveal any colouring they had to its fullest extent. In the excitement they left scrapes embedded in prehistoric stone. Scientists have interpreted this as 'nest scrape displaying', a behaviour common today in birds that nest on the ground (as almost all theropods did). In the thralls of courtship, males scrape the dirt with their feet, showing the females that they can excavate the nest site they will later need. If he was a male of breeding age, perhaps our Jurassic theropod did something similar in his bid to woo a mate.

"All was not sleep and carnage in the life of a carnivorous dinosaur. For all its undoubted ferocity, our Jurassic theropod would also have had moments of beauty, and maybe even tenderness."

Like his living avian cousins, it's likely that he would have drawn upon every attractive feature he could to win a female's affections. What might they have been? Scientists suspect that theropod dinosaurs might have been boldly marked in the manner of modern predatory animals, with (for instance) striping or spots to help break up their outline in the undergrowth. The heads of many theropods were adorned with miniscule horns, ringlets and other protrusions that would have helped a male advertise his genetic fitness. And thanks to exceptionally well-preserved fossils emerging from Mesozoic deposits around the world, we can't rule out that our theropod had another weapon in his courtship arsenal: feathers. They're more prevalent in theropods than any other dinosaur family. This is not to say, though, that all theropods were feathered beasts. Whether our theropod was scaly from head to toe, enveloped entirely in fluffy down or

[69]

only possessed simple quills on its neck, arms and tail, we'll probably never know for certain. But if it did have feathers, they could have assumed any of the myriad amazing hues to be seen in the living avian gallery around the world today. Long before birds used feathers for flight, it's likely that dinosaurs were using them to keep warm – and as a canvass on which to paint themselves with colour. Living birds use their bright, attractive plumes to win the hearts of the usually more modestly coloured females. It's possible theropods were no different. Far from being ugly, bloodthirsty brutes, these beasts would have been elegant, graceful predators, possessed of a dangerous beauty.

It's also possible that this display would have been augmented by mating calls – but palaeontologists now think these would have been wholly different from the blood-curdling roars attributed to theropods on the silver screen. Like birds, theropods probably didn't have vocal chords as we know them. Scientists can only speculate on the exact noises they could have made. But it's thought that they kept their mouths closed and made deep, resonant sounds, similar to those produced today by large flightless birds such as ostriches and cassowaries, as well as their crocodile cousins. If anything, our theropod's signature call might have been closer to the coo of a pigeon than the roar of a lion.

"We like to think of the dinosaurs as long gone, consigned to school books and museum exhibits the world over. But they're all around us today."

Of course, the ultimate goal of courtship is reproduction. Nesting behaviour for theropod dinosaurs is now well documented. It's thought that theropods laid ten to twenty eggs per clutch. Larger species would have been too heavy to incubate their eggs, and they probably laid them in a mound of earth and rotting vegetation like modern crocodiles do. The expectant mother probably crouched nearby, ready to see off any nest-raiders that might be on the prowl. Smaller theropods, though, likely sat on top of their eggs to keep them warm, just like living birds. At least some theropods are thought to have strung their eggs in a ring so they could incubate them without sitting directly on top of them. We now know that different dinosaur species even laid different coloured eggs, in yet another similarity with birds. How much care the chicks received when they emerged from those eggs remains up for debate. Both crocodiles and birds are well known for the parental care and protection they afford their hatchlings. Crocodile mothers guard their young in their earliest weeks, while almost all birds (with some notable exceptions, such as the cuckoos) feed their chicks , or at least lead them to food. Perhaps theropod parents behaved in a similar way.

The many traits theropods share with birds is no coincidence. Of all the dynasties of dinosaurs that came and went during the Mesozoic, the theropods are the only one with a living legacy. We like to think of the dinosaurs as long gone, consigned to school books and museum exhibits the world over. But they're all around us today. In fact, if you're reading this outside, you're almost certainly being watched by a theropod right now.

The Jurassic forests of Europe would provide a nursery for another landmark in the history of life on Earth. Here, successive small theropod dinosaurs would use their extensive feather-covered arms and legs to glide between trees, until eventually they – like the pterosaurs and insects before them – mastered powered flight. By the end of the Jurassic, the very first birds had arrived. With more refinement over the millions of years that followed, their body-mass shrank to ease their transition to life on the wing. A heavy, toothed jaw was replaced by a lightweight beak; the bony tail was lost altogether, substituted by feathers.

These primitive birds continued to develop and thrive in the Cretaceous, outliving their theropod cousins as the Mesozoic came to a cataclysmic end 66 million years ago – the only family of dinosaurs to do so. And, of course, they are still with us today, forming a core branch of Ireland's natural heritage. Every bird you see, from the tiniest goldcrest to the largest mute swan, every raucous herring gull, soaring buzzard and swooping swallow, is a theropod dinosaur. All of them can trace their descent from feathered theropods, terrorising small creatures in the fern and cycad forests of the Jurassic. When that blackbird or robin in your garden cocks its head to get a look at you, you might well find yourself locking eyes with a dinosaur.

The dinosaurs were the superstars of the Mesozoic era. But they were certainly not the only family of reptiles to reach their apogee during this time. The Jurassic rocks of Antrim bear witness to this. While the dinosaurs were achieving their potential on land, a perhaps even more remarkable reptilian revolution was taking place in the oceans.

5

The Sea Dragons of Ulster

By the early Jurassic period, 200 million years ago, the dinosaurs' dominion over the land was absolute. Above them, the skies were replete with pterosaurs, flying reptiles filling the niches that would one day be inherited by the birds. And in the warm, shallow seas of the Jurassic, another reptilian success story was playing out.

Evidence of this has been found in the pockets of Jurassic rock that dot the rugged coast of County Antrim. It was here in 1991 that the jumbled, truncated skull of a long dead marine reptile was uncovered, a specimen that has since gained infamy as the 'Minnis Monster'. There were three great dynasties of seafaring reptiles that swam in the Mesozoic seas. This skull – as well as ribs and vertebrae weathered out of the Antrim coast – belonged to the oldest of the three, the ichthyosaurs.

The ichthyosaurs first took to the seas around 250 million years ago, making them older than even the dinosaurs. By the time the Minnis Monster was patrolling the waters where the Glens of Antrim now stand, they had already developed the classic ichthyosaur form, a dolphin-like shape for which the family is famed. A short, sturdy body was topped and tailed by a long, snapping snout at one end, and vertical, shark-like tail fluke at the other. Like fish before them, and dolphins yet to come, ichthyosaurs had developed a tall dorsal fin that stood erect halfway along the spine. This provided stability, preventing the animal from keeling over as it powered through the water. Beneath this, front feet had long since given way to flippers which, as in dolphins and sharks, helped with steering, the bulk of the propulsion coming from the side-to-side swiping of the powerful tail. With this, and a torpedo-shaped body built for speed, ichthyosaurs could pursue their prey through the water at up to forty kilometres an hour.

Ulster's ichthyosaurs maxed out at just over two metres long (although some species grew much larger, rivalling the great whales of today). As such, they were similar in size to the common dolphins and harbour porpoises that still occasionally make an appearance off the Antrim coast. Unlike modern dolphins and whales, ichthyosaurs never shed their hind limbs entirely (these were, though, reduced in size to minimise drag). Their presence is only a minor blemish in what would have been a silhouette eerily reminiscent of a dolphin, a shark or even a tuna. In this, we can see a truly remarkable example of convergent evolution: nature arriving at the same basic body plan in fish, then in reptiles and (much later) in mammals. The laws of hydrodynamics that dictate the form of dolphins on Ireland's Atlantic coast today applied just as much to Ulster's marine reptiles 200 million years before.

More fleshed-out ichthyosaur remains from elsewhere have shown that their resemblance to dolphins was more than just skin deep. A 2018 analysis of a 180-million-year-old ichthyosaur specimen from Germany, with soft tissue structures intact, revealed that, like modern whales and dolphins, ichthyosaurs were darker on the top than on the bottom – an adaptation that later marine reptiles would also develop. It also seems that ichthyosaurs even had a layer of blubbery fat beneath the skin. This would have acted as insulation, helping them maintain a steady temperature and hunt even in cold water. Skin impressions show that ichthyosaurs even lost the scales of their lizard-like ancestors, developing smooth skin reminiscent of that of whales and dolphins. This would have reduced drag and made swimming even easier.

Developing such a body presented ichthyosaurs with a problem when it came to reproduction. Most reptiles reproduce on land, typically by laying eggs. Even modern sea turtles still have to crawl ashore to deposit their eggs. Like the dolphins they resembled, ichthyosaurs could not do this. With limbs repurposed as paddles, they simply no longer had the equipment with which to move about on land. But reptilian eggs cannot be laid in water. How, therefore, did ichthyosaurs give birth?

The answer to this question came in the form of some remarkable fossil evidence. Smaller ichthyosaurs were occasionally found in the stomachs of larger ones. Palaeontologists at the time chalked this up to cannibalism, the old devouring the young. That was until a beautifully preserved female ichthyosaur was found in Germany with a fully developed baby still emerging from her birth canal, the two having died together and become locked in stone for over 100 million years. This specimen confirmed that, in order to completely surrender themselves to the seas, ichthyosaurs had had to jettison that most ancient of reptilian traditions. Instead of laying eggs, they gave birth, at sea, to live young. These babies would have been born tail first. Although much like fish in locomotion, ichthyosaurs were still air-breathers, with nostrils on the top of the snout. A lengthy labour could see a baby drown if it emerged from its mother headfirst.

In life, the Minnis Monster would have been equipped with long, thin jaws lined with sharp teeth. With these, it was well poised to pursue the range of small prey the Jurassic seas had to offer. There were certainly fish and squid to be savoured, much as there are today. And as the Jurassic rocks of Ulster reveal, prehistoric oddities floated in these ancient seas as well. Most iconic were the ammonites; with their distinctive spiral shells, these are among the best known of all prehistoric creatures. In life they would have hung suspended in the water, reaching tentacles out to snag their prey. The coiled shells of the ammonites would have allowed them to be more stable than the straight-shelled nautiloids that came before them. Belemnites abounded here too. These would have looked a lot like modern squid. They had an internal shell, like a bullet casing, contrasting with the circular, swirling shells of the ammonites.

Jurassic ichthyosaurs could have hunted them all. Modern dolphins, which fill the same ecological niche in today's

seas that ichthyosaurs once did, are masters of echolocation. They use the feedback from complex clicks to track down their prey. Ichthyosaurs had no such apparatus (although they

> "The early Jurassic was the golden age of the ichthyosaurs."

did have the solid ear bones needed to pick up the vibrations of prey swimming in the water). Instead, they relied on the largest eyes of any vertebrate to pick out prey in the gloom. It's likely that ichthyosaurs hunted their small prey in much the same way that modern dolphins do, lunging through schooling fish at speed, snapping at them with their long beaks. Cephalopod hooks found in ichthyosaur stomachs confirm that squid were on the menu. Belemnites might have been too; some palaeontologists think that ichthyosaurs simply vomited up the indigestible shell. New discoveries continue to give us even greater insights into ichthyosaur diets. In 2020, Jurassic-aged rocks in Italy revealed the first evidence of ichthyosaur scavenging, suggesting that they might occasionally have fed on dead creatures (including other ichthyosaurs) on the seabed.

The early Jurassic was the golden age of the ichthyosaurs. But they were not the only marine reptiles to be found here. At the same time the Minnis Monster was pursuing fish with lightning speed through the tropical seas of Ulster, a new dynasty of sea dragons had also laid claim to the oceans of the early Jurassic. Fossil vertebrae and ribs found at Cave Hill, overlooking Belfast, and Islandmagee further up the coast, confirm that the long-necked plesiosaurs also once made their home here.

Plesiosaurs first appeared at the end of the Triassic period, following the ichthyosaurs into the oceans. By the early Jurassic, 200 million years ago, they too had arrived at their iconic form. This was a radically different solution to underwater living than the ichthyosaurs. Instead of a fish-like shape, the plesiosaurs developed four long flippers affixed to a rotund body, terminating in a relatively short tail. This was countered at the other end by an exceptionally long neck, sometimes as long as the rest of the body combined. At the top of this was a short head jammed with thin, interlocking teeth.

The neck is the plesiosaurs' defining feature. In more modern times it would serve as inspiration for the Loch Ness Monster and other lake monsters. Believers remain adamant that relict populations of these marine reptiles still cling on in remote water bodies around the world. Unlikely – but thanks to remarkable fossil evidence, we can still glean insights into how the long-dead plesiosaurs of Ireland once looked, swam and lived.

Let's start with that neck. We now know that the swan-like pose of the Loch Ness Monster would almost certainly have been beyond the Cave Hill plesiosaur. The neck would have been far too stiff to be curled in such a manner. Plesiosaur necks had up to seventy-six vertebrae, more than that of any other animal before or since. They needed to be inflexible in order to limit drag as the animal flew through the

water; bend too much and the neck could veer its owner off course. In fact, having such a long neck posed some problems for underwater living. As well as drag, there were also the questions of breathing and swallowing, not to mention the small issue of pumping blood to the brain. Such an awkward adaptation must have offered its owner significant advantages to make it worthwhile. In modern seabirds, a long neck can actually reduce drag when swimming in a line – or at high speed. This was likely also the case for plesiosaurs in our prehistoric waters.

A long neck also came in handy for feeding. While plesiosaurs were big bodied, their triangular heads were often tiny. Perched atop that neck, the plesiosaur could dart its head in and out of a school of fish or squid while keeping its imposing body at a distance. Its long, thin profile would have caused minimal disturbance in the water, leaving the prey none the wiser until it was too late. A long neck would also have allowed its owner to scan a large area of ocean with minimal effort, and grab at prey while keeping its body still, helping the plesiosaur save energy. With such endowments, a plesiosaur could wait in stasis like a crocodile, ready to snap at any suitably small prey that strayed too close. It could also have reached into snags of coral and other crevices beyond the reach of other predators. At least some Jurassic plesiosaurs were able to point their long necks downward to a high degree, suggesting they raked and sieved their food from the seafloor with their intermeshing teeth. The thin, pointed teeth of plesiosaurs were probably less adept at dealing with shelled prey than those of ichthyosaurs, perhaps helping these two great families of marine reptiles avoid competition.

Soft tissue impressions show us that, like the ichthyosaurs, at least some plesiosaurs had a small, vertical fin on the end of their tail. However, unlike ichthyosaurs, the main means of propulsion came from the flippers. Because of this, plesiosaur locomotion would have been entirely different to the side-to-side swimming of the ichthyosaurs they shared the warm, shallow seas of Ulster with. This animal would have 'flown' through the water, in a way totally unlike any living creature. Even sea turtles, their closest living analogue among marine animals, don't swim by using all four flippers at once. But computer models have shown that this would have been the most efficient method of swimming for the long-dead plesiosaurs. The fore and hind flippers raised and lowered in opposing pairs; a graceful, elegant motion. The hind flippers would flap between the whirlpools of water stirred up by the front flippers. In this way, the plesiosaur could make use of its own wake to save energy – the only animal in the Jurassic ocean to do so. Topping out at around nine kilometres an hour, the long-necked plesiosaurs would not have been quite as fast as the ichthyosaurs, and they didn't need to be. Their four flippers allowed for excellent manoeuvrability when snapping at schools of fish or squid beneath the waves.

Too much buoyancy would have been a problem for all marine reptiles – but plesiosaurs developed an ingenious solution to this. Swallowed stones, known as gastroliths, have been found with many plesiosaur specimens. Like modern birds, these may have helped the plesiosaur – which could not chew – to grind up the food passing through its stomach. Their extra weight could have been an added benefit, preventing the animal from floating to the surface.

Plesiosaurs might have looked and moved differently to ichthyosaurs. But the demands of underwater life saw them converge on some of the same solutions. Like ichthyosaurs, it seems likely that plesiosaurs were countershaded – bright on the bottom, darker on top. Also, like ichthyosaurs, plesiosaurs likely had smooth skin to reduce drag in the water. A steady body temperature – perhaps maintained by a layer of fat beneath the skin – helped them live an active lifestyle. And they too gave birth to live young at sea, divorcing themselves from the land entirely. It is thought that young plesiosaurs cleaved to the shallows, only venturing out into the open ocean once they matured.

While ichthyosaurs gave birth to up to eight small babies at a time, the fossil evidence suggests that plesiosaurs, like modern whales and dolphins, gave birth to one, large pup, nearly a third the size of its mother. Other marine animals that reproduce in this manner tend to take care of their new-borns, and some palaeontologists think that plesiosaurs might have done the same, perhaps living in pods like modern whales or dolphins. This behaviour, though, remains speculation.

At just a few metres long, the Cave Hill dragon was at the smaller end of the plesiosaur scale. The group evolved a range of shapes and sizes to fill different niches in the Mesozoic seas, from one-and-a-half-metre minnows to ocean-going giants ten times that size.

Ichthyosaurs and plesiosaurs continued to ply their trade in the seas and oceans of the world for millions of years. Then, 145 million years ago, the Jurassic gave way to the Cretaceous, the final act of the Mesozoic era. It was a time of giants. On land, the horned and armoured dinosaurs reached their zenith as new predators like the tyrannosaurs emerged to hunt them. In the southern continents, the long-necked sauropods reached sizes unsurpassed by any land animal before or since. In the air, giant pterosaurs attained wingspans of ten metres or more, becoming the largest creatures ever to fly. Below them, more modest flying creatures thrived in forests that were now full of flowers, injecting vibrant colours into the flora for the first time. These woods were replete with feathered oddities: birds that looked like dinosaurs, dinosaurs that looked like birds, and some that blurred the boundaries between the two.

In the seas, meanwhile, the plesiosaurs would persist right up until the end of the Cretaceous, although they would never be as diverse as they were in the Jurassic. Their necks grew to almost ridiculous proportions as they too reached their largest sizes. The ichthyosaurs, though, had had their heyday in the Jurassic. This oldest and most superbly adapted family of marine reptiles, having flourished for tens of millions of years, began to dwindle as the Mesozoic era wore on. By the late Cretaceous, around ninety-three million years ago, they were gone altogether.

Why they disappeared, having been so successful for so long, is still a mystery. Some scientists chalk it up to ructions in the marine ecosystem. Around ninety-three million years ago, an extinction event decimated marine invertebrates – including the squid and other cephalopods on which ichthyosaurs fed. Such loss of food could have been devastating for a marine predator, and sent the last ichthyosaurs tumbling towards extinction. Others think their demise was due to wider changes to the ocean ecosystem. The Cretaceous saw the emergence of streamlined, fast-swimming fishes (including new forms of shark) that could match the ichthyosaurs for speed. These not only made for more difficult prey but – in the case of larger fish – more efficient predators of young ichthyosaurs.

In short, the days of the underwater pursuit, so perfected by the hydrodynamic, torpedo-like ichthyosaurs during the Jurassic, were over. Instead, the Cretaceous seas were now ideal for a new breed of ambush killers, with long sinuous bodies better suited to lying in wait before launching at an unsuspecting victim. The bones of just such a predator emerged from the Ulster White Chalk rocks of County Antrim; vertebrae that, in life, formed the backbone of a mosasaur.

Of the three great tribes of Mesozoic marine reptiles, the mosasaurs were the last to take to the waves. As a group, they first burst onto the scene about ninety million years ago. They were essentially lizards, distant cousins of the monitor lizards (such as the legendary Komodo dragon) that still thrive in rainforests and tropical waterways around the world, as well as snakes. The ancestral mosasaur would have looked a lot like a modern lizard. It probably only ventured into the water to feed or escape the jaws of a hungry theropod dinosaur. But by the late Cretaceous, these marine lizards had become wholly aquatic, leaving the land altogether. With ichthyosaurs extinct and plesiosaurs in decline, the oceans were in need of a new clan of apex predators. The mosasaurs duly obliged.

Although a few vertebrae are not enough to draw a complete picture of what our Irish mosasaur was like in life, we know a lot about this remarkable group of lizards from more complete specimens found around the world. Mosasaurs evolved into many different species in their conquest of the global oceans, leaving their fossils on every continent (including Antarctica). They were big. Even the smaller kinds were rarely less than three or four metres in length. The largest, at over twelve metres long, were some of the most formidable predators the oceans have ever seen.

Almost all mosasaurs, though, retained the long serpentine shape of their lizard ancestors. The four limbs gave way to flippers which, as in ichthyosaurs, were primarily for steering. Propulsion instead came from the long, flattened tail with which the animal slithered through the water. Beautifully preserved fossils with soft tissue outlines show us that, instead of tapering to a point, a mosasaur's tail ended in a sharp, downward-pointing fin. With this, they could get more power out of each sweep of their tail – and tear through the water with devastating speed.

Topping it all was a long, narrow head bisected by powerful jaws. Contained within them, mosasaurs had two sets of conical teeth, the second embedded on the roof of the mouth. This would have helped them gain extra purchase on slippery, struggling prey. And like a snake, a hinge in the jaw allowed it to expand, helping the mosasaur wolf down large chunks of flesh. Equipped with such weaponry, mosasaurs were more than capable of dealing with any prey the Cretaceous seas had to offer – including other mosasaurs. Smaller species hunted fish and swimming molluscs such as ammonites, and were themselves hunted by larger mosasaurs. Some had a broad, powerful snout strong enough to crush the shell of a sea turtle. Others had robust facial bones, suggesting they used their heads to ram into their prey at speed like modern killer whales, stunning it before moving in to finish it off with a lethal bite. And fossil evidence suggests that mosasaurs of the same species were quite capable of turning their fearsome weaponry against each other, perhaps in contests over food, territory or a mate. Scientists think they used their teeth and jaws in a similar way to modern crocodiles. It's tempting to imagine these enormous marine lizards thrashing about in the surf, jaws locked, as long, elegant tails whipped the ocean into a milky foam.

Finer details of mosasaur life and appearance can also be discerned from the fossils they left behind. It seems that, like the ichthyosaurs and plesiosaurs before them, they gave birth to live young at sea. Remarkable discoveries in recent years have even revealed their colouring. Just like apex predators of the ocean today (the killer whale and great white shark) mosasaurs were likely countershaded; brown or black on top, pale (maybe even white) below. Cast in monochrome, the mosasaur could mask itself against the gloomy ocean depths from above and bright sunlight shimmering through the surface from below. Viewed from the side, it would have been almost invisible in any kind of murky water – until it was too late. A darker back may have served another purpose; dark colours suck in sunlight, helping the animal warm its body at the surface between dives. Unlike the older marine reptiles, mosasaurs retained their scales rather than developing smooth skin.

To help them in tracking down their prey, mosasaurs likely had well developed sight and hearing. But it's thought they could also draw upon another sense, a legacy of their lizard ancestors on land: taste. Like modern lizards, mosasaurs possessed a Jacobson's organ on the roof of their mouth. And, like them, they might have had a long, forked tongue with which to direct particles from the water into it. This way, mosasaurs could 'taste' their way to their next meal by latching onto any promising particles floating in the current. The fork at the end of the tongue served as a navigational device, steering the murderous jaws of the mosasaur in the right direction.

Mosasaurs might have needed those jaws for defence as well as attack. They were just one of many predators that prowled the Cretaceous seas. As if mosasaurs weren't enough to worry about, there were enormous predatory fish to contend with. And then, as now, none were more terrifying than the sharks.

Sharks had been patrolling the oceans long before mosasaurs arrived on the scene. But they had come a long way from the more modest creatures that left their teeth embossed on Ireland's Carboniferous rocks, more than 200 million years before. In Cretaceous waters teeming with large prey, sharks could get big. From the Hibernian Greensands formation of Antrim, older than the Ulster White Limestone, emerged a terrifying, triangular tooth in the classic vein of a predatory shark. Its owner: *Cretoxyrhina*, one of the most fearsome sharks that ever lived.

"Sharks of this genus could grow truly enormous; at around ten metres long, the largest species rivalled the largest living fish, the whale shark, in size."

Cretoxyrhina would have been similar in shape and form to that most chilling of modern marine predators, the great white. It probably would have shared the darker back and white belly of its modern counterpart, perhaps even the same empty black eyes. Averaging about five metres long, it would have been as big as a great white too – and could have gotten even bigger. Like that shark, *Cretoxyrhina* probably lurked at a depth, ready to lunge with great speed at prey lounging on or near the surface. Large eyes would have helped it pick out its victims from below, while jaws that could protrude forward from the mouth helped it bite deep into its prey. Powering through the water with its crescent-shaped tail, it may have been one of the fastest sharks ever, able to lunge at its prey at up to seventy kilometres an hour. Even creatures flying above the sea weren't safe; bite marks found on a pterosaur suggest this monster might have leaped clear of the water to snatch prey on the wing.

Cretoxyrhina cruised Cretaceous seaways worldwide, ready to sink its conveyer belt of razor-sharp teeth into plesiosaurs, turtles and other predatory fish. Small or juvenile mosasaurs were certainly on the menu as well. It is incredible to think that this tooth unearthed in County Antrim could have been dislodged, millions of years before, in a tussle between a killer shark and an overgrown lizard.

Antrim's Hibernian Greensands would yield yet another shark tooth, wholly different from the blade of *Cretoxyrhina*. This tooth was pillow-shaped, and furrowed rather than serrated. Seen out of context, you'd struggle to identify it as a shark's tooth. And yet a shark's tooth it was. It belonged to a *Ptychodus*. Sharks of this genus could grow truly enormous; at around ten metres long, the largest species rivalled the largest living fish, the whale shark, in size. However, unlike *Cretoxyrhina*, this was no hyper-carnivore; teeth of this design were unsuited to tearing through flesh. Instead, while *Cretoxyrhina* caused carnage on the surface, *Ptychodus* likely hugged the seabed. Here, its unusual teeth were put to use crushing the shells of the enormous molluscs that studded the sand.

Despite the challenge to their reign posed by the sharks, it was ultimately the mosasaurs that ruled the oceans until their reckoning – and the reckoning of all the great reptiles of the Mesozoic – arrived from space. Sixty-six million years ago, an asteroid smashed into the modern Gulf of Mexico, leaving a massive crater, one 180 kilometres in diameter, that has lasted till the present day. The force of this impact was incredible; fifteen kilometres wide, and travelling at twenty kilometres a second, the asteroid slammed into Earth with a million times more energy than the largest nuclear bomb ever tested. The impact on Earth's atmosphere was devastating. The collision blanketed the planet in a layer of ash and dust, blocking out the sun and grinding photosynthesis to a halt for months on end as the world descended into darkness. As plant life died, herbivores starved. Next to go were the carnivores, once the glut of scavenged meat had been exhausted. In the ecological chaos that ensued, up to 80 per cent of life on Earth died out.

This event, known as the K-T extinction, brought the Mesozoic, the Age of the Dinosaurs, to a dramatic end. Having dominated life on land for 160 million years, the non-avian dinosaurs died out. The impact also spelled the end for the giant pterosaurs, who finally relinquished the skies to the birds. Ocean ecosystems were also devastated; ammonites and belemnites were confined to the fossil record. So too were the last of the great marine reptiles, the mosasaurs and plesiosaurs, following the ichthyosaurs into oblivion.

It took millions of years for life to recover. But from the shadow of this catastrophe emerged a new world of opportunity. The stage was set for the rise of the mammals. Free from their saurian oppressors, these small, furry creatures – our own ancestors – found themselves in a world ripe for the taking. And having been miniscule for so long, they could now produce giants of their own, some of whom would go on to leave their bones in the bogs and caves of Ireland.

In Part Two, we'll fast forward nearly sixty-six million years to meet the incredible beasts of the Ice Age.

Bray Head, County Wicklow, where some of Ireland's oldest trace fossils have been found.

The Valentia Island trackway, made by an early tetrapod some 385 million years ago.

Phanerotinus, the giant snail that lived on the floor of Ireland's Carboniferous sea.

A drawing of *Dendrerpeton*, one of the remarkable amphibians that lived in the coal forest of Castlecomer, County Kilkenny.

The Burren, County Clare. This stunning karst landscape was formed from the remains of sea creatures that lived during the Carboniferous, over 300 million years ago.

Islandmagee, County Antrim, where dinosaur and plesiosaur remains have been unearthed that date back to the Jurassic.

Ammonite fossil from the Jurassic period of France. Two hundred million years ago, creatures like this shared the seas of Ulster with ichthyosaurs and plesiosaurs.

Engraving of a giant Irish deer skeleton. Note the massive antlers, that could stretch up to 3.6 metres from tip to tip.

The Gap of Dunloe in County Kerry, carved out by glaciers during the Ice Age.

The woolly mammoth. This prehistoric giant once roamed the Pleistocene plains of Waterford and Cork.

The muskox, whose remains have been found in County Antrim.

The Norway lemming, one of the smaller beasts to emerge from Ireland's Ice Age bone caves.

Now synonymous with Africa, the spotted hyena once terrorised the Ice Age grasslands of Munster.

The brown bear was the largest of Ireland's Pleistocene predators.

Rutting red deer, County Kerry.

The ancient woodlands of Killarney National Park. At one time, around 80 per cent of Ireland was covered in forest.

PART II

The Beasts of Ice Age Ireland

Where the Purple Mountains and MacGillycuddy's Reeks meet in County Kerry sits the world-famous Gap of Dunloe. Winding its way through the border of these two mountain ranges, the Gap is hemmed in by sheer slopes on all sides, towering into the firmament. Its floor is puckered with little lakes, festooned together by the River Dunloe. Further up, the slopes of the valley are strewn with boulders, cast off by Ice Age glaciers as they moved through here thousands of years ago. The space between the boulders is filled out with ferns and grasses that whip and billow in the wind funnelling through the Gap, the slopes grazed by free-ranging sheep. Above them, streams cascade in waterfalls down rocky outcrops that descend in terraces to the valley floor. The Gap terminates in the vast bowl of the Black Valley, studded with conifers and scattered farmhouses. Looking back, you take in a pristine, V-shaped view through the mountains, all the way to the distant Atlantic.

Glaciers would look out of place in the Gap today. But it was their action that carved out the magnificent valley that hikers now flock to. Were it not for the ice, there would be no Gap – nor many of the other spectacular mountain valleys and passes that texture the surface of Ireland.

Luckily, the Ice Age left more than a magnificent landscape as its Irish legacy. Buried beneath bogs and in caves across the country, tantalising clues about what life might have been like here have also emerged. Together, they paint a picture of the remarkable fauna that made its home in an Ireland long gone: a perplexing potpourri, combining beasts that today would look more at home on the Siberian tundra or African savannah. Among them were now-extinct giants, the largest creatures ever known to have shaken the ground in Ireland. All came and went in the long saga of life in Ice Age Ireland, a drama that played out over thousands of years. Some of these beasts coexisted with each other, some didn't. But all left their remains behind, pieces of the ecosystem of which they were once a part.

6

The Coming of the Ice

From the glacial valleys of Kerry to the drumlin belt that wraps around Ulster, no singular event in Ireland's long history has shaped the land we now know more than the Ice Age. Its influence is wrought in our mountains, glens and lakes. It was the ending of the Ice Age that sundered Ireland from Britain, forging an island identity still integral to its people to this day. The *Eiscir Riada*, a ridge of gravel running from Dublin to Galway that was deposited by melting glaciers, would form a natural barrier between the feuding medieval dynasties that sought to control Ireland. It also provided a convenient highway through the bogs of the Midlands, connecting the east and west coasts since time immemorial. The fertile soils requisitioned from glaciers in retreat left a rich substrate for agriculture. In places like County Meath, this nourished a rich Neolithic culture that would give us some of our most revered historical landmarks, notably Newgrange. Through this, the Ice Age has woven itself into Irish history, culture and our modern economy. Even our place names can trace their genesis to the Ice Age.

Any village or townland beginning with 'drum' derives from the Irish *droim*, for drumlin, one of the 20,000 low hills stamped on our landscape by the glaciers.

We were left with more than just a magnificent landscape by the Ice Age. Some of our most spectacular fossil evidence dates from this time too, including the antlers and bones of the most impressive beasts ever to set foot in Ireland.

To discover where these creatures came from, we need to wind the clock back much further – sixty-six million years. The demise of the non-avian dinosaurs left a world ripe for conquest. Never again would reptiles hold dominion over the planet. Not only were the dinosaurs gone from the land, but the pterosaurs were shorn from the sky and giant marine reptiles emptied out of the seas. This left a myriad of different niches for new creatures to exploit. The time of the mammals had come.

> "The Ice Age has woven itself into Irish history, culture and our modern economy."

These little, furry creatures had spent over 100 million years in the shadow of the dinosaurs, cowering away in tree holes and underground burrows. Now they were set to take over the world. Free from the predation and competition of the giant reptiles, the mammals blossomed into a multitude of new forms, from hornless rhinos to rival the dinosaurs in size to sabre-toothed apex predators.

It was a fascinating and underappreciated period in the history of life on Earth – and tragically, it left next to no fossil evidence in Ireland. There are precious few rocks here that date from this golden age of the mammals. Instead, there stretches an almost entirely barren record of life on this island for over sixty million years.

The mammals' march to global dominance would see them overcome many challenges. But one of their greatest tests came between 2.6 million–11,700 years ago. Science knows this as the Pleistocene epoch. To the popular imagination, it's known as the Ice Age. And this is where the fossil record for life in Ireland picks up again in earnest.

Although the Pleistocene began around 2.6 million years ago, the planet is thought to have been getting slowly colder for some time before that. The decisive factor was a slight tilt in the Earth's axis and a wobble in its orbit. In the cosmic scheme of things, such movements are miniscule. But they had a massive impact on life on Earth. They combined to take the Earth ever so slightly further from the sun, reducing the amount of summer sunshine received by the northern hemisphere. The result: colder and colder summers, year after year.

Eventually, temperatures got too low to melt the snows from the previous winter. These snows built up season after season, until they consolidated into ice, and ice amassed into glaciers. It was these glaciers that would fashion the Ireland we now know. The Ice Age had arrived.

These changes were not confined to Ireland. Glaciers hording so much of the world's water meant that forests around the world went into retreat, drained of their lifeblood. Global sea levels also plummeted. It's no happenstance that many of Europe's most exquisite Ice Age fossils have been dredged up from the bottom of the North Sea. Back then, it was a grassy plain grazed by prehistoric giants. Meanwhile, the Bering land bridge connected Alaska to Asia, allowing both animals and people to transfer between Eurasia and the Americas.

We're still in an Ice Age now. Far from being a ubiquitous blanket of ice, the Pleistocene was cyclical in nature. Long bouts of freezing conditions were broken by bursts of warm weather, when the glaciers retreated and life could flourish more easily again. All of human civilisation has arisen during just one of the many warm periods that divide the glaciations, a fleeting purple patch of around 10,000 years. Since the dawn of the Pleistocene, there have been about twenty glacial cycles. They have varied in length and severity, but in general, each cycle has consisted of around 90,000 years of glaciation (known as a stadial) followed by a warmer spell (interstadial) of around 10,000 years, give or take. And by this model, the current warm snap has just about run its course.

Some scientists reckon that man-made global warming will prevent the great glaciers ever again spreading south of their polar strongholds. Whether or not this is the case will have to be seen over the next few thousand years.

7

Ice Age Ireland

Twenty-one thousand years ago is a flash in the pan in the history of planet Earth. But back then, Ireland would have been unrecognisable.

A map of Europe at this time would show a great protuberance erupting out of Belgium and France, swallowing Britain and Ireland in the embrace of the continent. The glaciers seeping out of the Arctic Circle and across Eurasia had absorbed enough water to drop global sea levels by 120 metres. There was no Irish Sea. As a result, modern Ireland is but a rump of its Pleistocene predecessor. All around our coasts, up to forty kilometres of what is now seabed would have been dry land during the height of the Ice Age. If you were to stand where you are now, 21,000 years ago, you'd more than likely find yourself pulverised by thousands of tonnes of ice bearing down on you. This is because, back then, Ireland was blanketed in glaciers almost from top to bottom.

But Ice Age Ireland was not a frozen dead zone for the duration of the Pleistocene. As the ice ebbed and flowed over the millennia, warmer spells saw the glaciers surrender more and more of the landscape. In the wake of the retreating ice, the land opened up into a vast, verdant plain carpeted with grasses, daisies and sorrel docks. The occasional ragwort might have added a dash of dull yellow in this sea of muted green. Yet more plant species took hold in the lakes that pitted this scarred landscape, a tantalising source of nutrients beneath the surface of the water. Forest, the default habitat in much of post-Ice Age Ireland, was a rarity back then. As conditions improved, cold-resistant trees like juniper and eared willow might have formed thin woodlands. Occasionally, conditions might even have allowed temperate woodlands to take root. But for the most part, Pleistocene Ireland – that is, the parts that weren't buried in ice – was an open, grassy landscape. This was ideal for grazers – and the predators that fed on them.

"If you were to stand where you are now, 21,000 years ago, you'd more than likely find yourself pulverised by thousands of tonnes of ice bearing down on you."

Even at their zenith, there were parts of Ireland the glaciers couldn't touch. Much of this zone lay south of a line running from Limerick to Wicklow – although some of our most intriguing Pleistocene fossils have been found further north as well. In any case, there were times and places when ice-free oases allowed living things to cling on – among them, giants.

8

One Big Tooth

As we have already seen, the glaciers did not hold a monopoly over the Pleistocene. Nor was Ice Age Europe just an endless expanse of grassy steppe. As the temperature of the planet seesawed with the wobble in the Earth's orbit, there were times when forests were able to gain a foothold once again – and forest creatures with them. But the forest creatures of our deep Pleistocene past were of a different vintage to the ones we find today – and a vastly different scale.

One remarkable, if contentious, piece of evidence that might speak to the nature of these long-lost giants washed out of the Twisel River in Holywood, County Down in 1990. It was a massive tooth, grooved and ridged like that of a modern elephant. Baffled, the young brothers who found it showed the tooth to their father. He in turn presented it to the Ulster Museum in Belfast, where it has remained ever since. Its original owner: *Palaeoloxodon*, the straight-tusked elephant.

The elephant family that has limped into the twenty-first century is a pitiful vestige of a once mighty dynasty, with branches that flourished across Africa, Eurasia and the Americas. Having first evolved from small, pig-like creatures, the elephants grew to become one of the most successful lineages of mammals. Today's elephants are largely beasts of the tropics. But their deceased cousins made their homes in a vast array of habitats from rainforests and swamps to frozen steppes and temperate woodlands. Armed with diverse configurations of trunks and tusks, they were well equipped to exploit almost every environment that their great expansion brought them into contact with.

The success of the elephants was (literally) writ large in their tremendous size. The straight-tusked elephant would have been a magnificent example of this. Standing four metres tall at the shoulder, the largest bulls would have tipped the scales at up to fifteen tonnes, half as big again as their African counterparts of today. *Palaeoloxodon* was not just the largest animal in Pleistocene Europe. It was one of the largest mammals ever to walk the Earth.

This giant had an incredibly long trunk and huge tusks (up to three metres apiece) jutting like javelins from its upper jaw. With these, the straight-tusked elephant could have prised leaves from branches up to eight metres above the ground. A long tongue is also thought to have helped in this endeavour. In eclipsing the reach of all other herbivores of its time, it could avoid competition and thrive across Europe right through to westernmost Asia.

Its massive tusks now adorn museum collections across Europe. But what else can we tell about how the animal looked and behaved in life? Like modern elephants, it was mostly hairless, wrapped in a wrinkly grey hide. The tusks for which it was named were not completely straight, curving slightly at the tips, but still a far cry from the corkscrew tusks of the mammoths (see page 106). Its remains are found in areas that were once verdant woodlands, with ample supplies of water and a temperature similar to that of Europe today.

This gives us some idea of what the habitat in Holywood might have looked like around 130,000 years ago, an approximate age given for the massive tooth. Another clue comes from the DNA gleaned from *Palaeoloxodon* remains. Its closest living cousin is not the Asian elephant, as might be expected, but the African forest elephant, the smaller of the two elephants found in Africa today. Remarkably, this speaks to multiple exoduses of the elephant family out of their ancestral home in Africa, and a sundering of savannah and forest elephants stretching back much further in time than had previously been thought. The straight, streamlined tusks of today's forest elephants help them move unencumbered through their rainforest home. Perhaps the eponymous tusks of *Palaeoloxodon* served a similar purpose in the distant past.

The authenticity of the Holywood specimen remains controversial. Instead of being embedded in substrata that could be readily dated, the giant tooth kept company with an assortment of broken bricks and pottery before being pulled from the Twisel River. This makes its actual age difficult to pin down, and even casts doubt on whether it is genuinely Irish in origin. But if it is, and the circumstances of its finding were mere coincidence, then it serves as a tantalising token from the giants that might once have thrived across the plains and forested valleys of an Ireland long gone. We know from fossil finds elsewhere that the straight-tusked elephant shared the woods and waterways of Europe with a menagerie of other enormous beasts: hippos, rhinos and lions to name a few, all markedly different from their living counterparts. Did these creatures colonise Ireland too – and leave mementos behind? Who knows what's still out there, waiting to be found?

Despite its imposing stature, the days of the straight-tusked elephant were numbered. The fair weather in which it thrived was not to last. Colder days were coming; the ice sheets would return to Europe and to Ireland, laying waste to all before them. Their ever-present travelling companion on their crusade across the continent would be the tundra; windswept, treeless grassland, not a place in which a hairless elephant could thrive. Conditions became too cold for most trees; forests went into retreat. This, and possibly human hunting, would see the demise of the mighty *Palaeoloxodon* as much as 50,000 years ago. Dwarf forms persisted on Mediterranean islands for much longer, but elephants of the scale of the one whose tooth was found in the Twisel River were doomed. As we shall see, the creatures that took its place would be of an altogether different form. For the most part, the Ireland of the Ice Age would belong to beasts with wool and fur, hardy enough to survive in a cold, merciless world.

9

The Giant Irish Deer

A roar echoes through the frosted autumnal valleys. A young stag, a challenger, casts his head skyward, his bellow suffusing the cold air with mist. His huge antlers embrace the pale light of the late morning, amplifying their splendour, as they cast many-fingered shadows across the mountain slope. The challenger has been nurturing them for months on the rich forage to be had on the plains of Pleistocene Ireland. He is ready at last.

Incensed, his opponent approaches as a herd of females looks on with half-interest between bouts of grazing. The two stags size up. For the dominant stag, this is usually enough to cement his supremacy. Not today. The challenger is his match. They can only come to blows.

Deposed after a long tussle, the loser limps to the side of a lake. His flanks are now mantled with blood, seeping from gouges left by the antlers of his usurper. Exhausted, he desperately seeks the succour of the water. In his thirst, he ignores the soft, boggy ground he treads on, slowly gumming up around the ankles. Dark mud swallows his front hooves as he leans in to lap up the cooling elixir. Extracting them will not be easy. But he is none the wiser as he slakes his thirst, burying his muzzle in the lake.

The peat bogs of Ireland have provided warmth and income to farmers for centuries. But many did not know that the turf they harvested was made up of long dead plant material, built up, compacted and solidified into peat. And contained within it was a record of Ireland's botany stretching back thousands of years.

It wasn't just plant remains that became entombed within Ireland's bogs, as generations of farmers also found out. Hacking sod after sod of turf from the bogs exposed the peat-blackened bones of Ice Age beasts. Most spectacular of all were massive antlers, each as long as a person. Tempted to the verges of prehistoric lakes by fresh forage or the promise of a soothing drink, their owners may have become trapped in the mud. But in its deadly munificence, the bog polished and preserved all: hooves, bones, teeth and antlers. And it is the antlers that are the hallmark of Ice Age Ireland's most famous denizen: *Megaloceros*, the giant Irish deer.

These enormous antlers – the largest to ever adorn the head of any mammal – were first unearthed from Ireland's bogs in the late sixteenth century. At first, the remains were believed to be those of a moose, and so the term 'Irish Elk' was born. But this is misleading on two counts. Far from being confined to Ireland, we now know the species ranged right across Eurasia as far east as Russia and China. Nor was it an elk. Despite the similarly palmated antlers, the Ice Age mega-beast that emerged from Ireland's bogs was no elk, but a deer – one of the largest that ever lived. Its living

"These enormous antlers – the largest to ever adorn the head of any mammal – were first unearthed from Ireland's bogs in the late sixteenth century."

relatives, such as the fallow and red deer, still haunt Ireland's forests and mountains today. As spectacular as they are, theirs is but a shadow of the splendour of their prehistoric cousin.

Despite its domain stretching right across Eurasia, Ireland's peat bogs have yielded more specimens of this spectacular animal than anywhere else on Earth. Bones and antlers have been excavated all over the country. Ballybetagh Bog in the Dublin Mountains is the most prolific source of remains for this species in the whole of Europe. Over 100 specimens have been uncovered at this one site. Other fossils have emerged at Downpatrick in County Down, Lough Gur in County Limerick, Whitechurch in County Waterford and Ballyoran Bog in County Cork.

Upon seeing a giant Irish deer skeleton – such as the three exquisite examples that greet visitors at Dublin's Natural History Museum – you're immediately struck by the vast antlers. In life (as in death) they served to draw attention to their owner. We know from analysis of their skulls that giant Irish deer stags had much smaller scent glands in proportion to their body size than deer alive in Ireland today. They did not rely on scent to attract the affections of the opposite sex – and they didn't need to, with antlers that stretched up to 3.6 metres from tip to tip. In the deer that survive into the twenty-first century, antlers are allometric; the larger the deer species, the bigger and more elaborate the antlers. The giant Irish deer was the epitome of this.

As with modern deer, the antlers were shed and re-grown each year – at immense nutritional cost to the owner. Antler is the fastest growing of all mammalian tissues; living deer can add up to ten centimetres to their antlers every day in the build-up to the mating season, or rut. There's no reason to assume our giant Pleistocene deer were any different. A rich diet was needed to achieve this – and even then, it took a massive toll on the stag's body. This can be seen today in living deer, whose bone density contracts by up to 60 per cent as more and more calcium and minerals are redirected to their antlers. Weakened bones are then more likely to snap at just the time of year when stags come to blows.

For a successful *Megaloceros* stag, however, it was clearly a good investment. His antlers advertised his fitness, health and readiness to reproduce. Bigger antlers indicated more genetic vigour. This made a male more attractive to prospective mates. In this way, reproductive pressure endorsed the development of bigger and bigger antlers over time, as only the most well-endowed males passed on their genes.

Scratch marks on many antlers indicate that they were not just for show. These immense appendages – like their more modest counterparts on living deer – were also used in ritualised combat. Stags would show off their antlers in a bid to intimidate rivals. The inferior male was the one that gave way. If stags were evenly matched, however, the issue could only be settled through violence.

Every component of the antlers was honed over generations to abet this contest. The prongs of the antlers – known as tines – served different roles in the duel. Those closest to the head locked against those of the rival stag, forming a platform through which the contestants could test their strength. The curving, rapier-like tines that terminated the antlers were offensive weapons, designed to maim the neck or flank of an opponent. Seeing two such huge sets of antlers locking as their roaring owners wrestled for supremacy would have been one of the most impressive sights of Ireland's Ice Age plains.

Weighing around forty kilogrammes, these antlers were an enormous burden for their owner. Stag skulls had to be heavily reinforced to prevent them splitting down the middle from the weight of all this extra bone. The pronounced hump on the male's shoulders anchored an extensive network of ligaments. These helped the stag hold his head aloft and display his antlers proudly.

Fully grown, a giant Irish deer stag stood almost two metres at the shoulder, measured three metres long and weighed around 600 kilogrammes, making it a lightly-built beast even factoring in its impressive dimensions. It was still a massive animal – three times heavier than the largest red deer stag in Ireland today. Females, though still huge by the standards of modern deer, were slightly smaller.

Ancient cave art found at sites in southern Europe gives us even more evidence of what the giant Irish deer looked like. The coat was mostly pale, with darker markings on the head, neck and shoulders. The cave art also shows the larynx, the bulging Adam's apple also present in modern deer stags. Coupled with those immense antlers, this would have been a very striking giant.

The broad muzzle of the giant Irish deer suggests a beast suited to open, grassy terrain. Silica-induced scratch marks on its teeth confirm that it fed almost exclusively on grass. All this adds up to a creature of the open plains. Certainly, the stags' antlers would have been a huge encumbrance in dense forest. *Megaloceros* may have been the most cursorial deer that ever lived; its build and even colour suggest that it was made for cantering across grasslands.

Late Ice Age Ireland served up just the kind of environment this giant needed to survive. When the deer had its Irish heyday during the Woodgrange Interstadial (around 13,000 years ago) the landscape was dominated by grasses, sorrel dock and daisies. This was just the sort of nutritious forage the giant Irish deer needed to sustain its large body and calorie-guzzling antlers.

Modern deer segregate into gender-specific herds for most of the year outside the rutting season. It's likely that the giant Irish deer did the same. It is thought that while the does (females) went to higher ground to graze, stags preferred to feed in the rich, wet pastures found close to lowland lakes. This is supported by the fact that many stag skulls have been recovered from prehistoric lakebeds. In late summer, when the stag's antlers were at their most spectacular, the rutting season began in earnest. This was when the stags tried to justify the immense calorific cost of their antlers by winning access to the herds of females. After a pregnancy of about thirty-six weeks, the doe would have separated from the main herd, probably searching out the shelter of a copse of trees – a rare commodity on the plains – to give birth. This was when the fawn would have been most at risk from Ireland's Ice Age carnivores, the wolves, bears and hyenas that stalked the plains. He would have had to be able to walk almost instantly to keep pace with the herd – and run if necessary. However, if he survived into adulthood, his massive antlers would have made him a daunting prospect for any predator.

As impressive as the giant Irish deer was, it cannot claim the top spot as largest beast to roam Ireland's Ice Age plains. The number one honour belonged to an even more imposing mega-beast.

10

The Woolly Mammoth

In 1715, construction workers building a flax mill in Drumurcher unearthed some massive and unusual bones. Among them were strange, grooved teeth reminiscent of those of elephants – the last creature you'd expect to find in rural County Monaghan.

This would not be the last time such gargantuan remains were uncovered in Ireland. In 1859, huge bones were paraded through the streets of Dungarvan, County Waterford, by workers who had uncovered them at a limestone quarry in the nearby Shandon Cave. These bones, and those found in Drumurcher, dwarfed those of any wild animal living in Ireland at the time. So, what did these monstrous remains belong to? The undisputed icon of the Ice Age: the woolly mammoth.

In the intervening years, subsequent fossil finds confirmed that the mammoth ranged across Ireland. As well as the Shandon mammoth and the bones at Drumurcher, mammoth remains were unearthed in Castlepook Cave, County Cork, part of which was christened Elephant Hall, dating from around 35,000 years ago.

What do we know about how this Ice Age giant looked and behaved in life? Thankfully, more complete specimens found elsewhere help provide some answers. The woolly mammoth was around the same size as a living African elephant, with large bulls standing up to three-and-a-half metres at the shoulder and weighing in at up to six tonnes. It was one of many mammoth species to populate the northern hemisphere, after the mammoth family split from their elephant cousins and spread out across Eurasia and beyond.

The woolly was not particularly large as far as mammoths went. Its direct ancestor, the steppe mammoth, was even larger. And the Columbian mammoth – one of the largest of all the Pleistocene giants – held court on North America's great plains until the end of the Ice Age.

Although not the biggest, the woolly was without doubt the most successful of the family. It was among the most advanced elephants ever to evolve, diverging from the steppe mammoth in Siberia before colonising the entire northern hemisphere. It ranged all the way from Ireland through the entirety of Europe, Russia (the most complete remains

[109]

being exquisitely preserved frozen mammoths found in Siberia) and North America almost from coast to coast. The species survived untold cold and warm snaps over hundreds of thousands of years. During its long reign, it usurped *Palaeoloxodon* as the dominant elephant in Europe. The fact that it thrived for so long makes its ultimate disappearance all the more puzzling.

The mammoth might have been similar in size to a modern elephant, but there were important dimensional distinctions between the two. Mammoths had relatively shorter hind legs, leading to a distinctive sloping back topped by a shoulder hump, as well as a shorter tail, smaller ears and shorter trunk than modern elephants. All of these were adaptations for living in a much colder environment, as smaller extremities minimise heat loss. Woolly mammoths also possessed an insulating layer of fat around eight to ten centimetres thick beneath the skin, as well as their iconic woolly coat. This comprised two layers: a longer outer layer around ninety centimetres long and a shorter, denser undercoat. It's believed that the outer layer was shed and re-grown each year as winter set in, leaving the mammoths less 'woolly' during the relative warmth of an Ice Age summer. This multi-layered solution was highly effective at fighting the fierce cold of the icy Eurasian plains, and is still employed by animals living in colder climes, such as the muskox.

Recent evidence indicates that the mammoth's adaptation to the cold was more than skin deep. Soft tissues preserved in frozen Siberian specimens show that mammoth haemoglobin (the oxygen-carrying component of blood) contained an anti-

"They played a huge part in shaping the world around them, creating the largest terrestrial habitat ever seen."

freezing agent. This enabled them to function in sub-zero conditions fatal to many other animals. As if all this weren't enough, mammoths even had a valve covering their anus to prevent the cold getting in the other end.

The woolly mammoth was also endowed with the most complex tooth structure of any elephant. Like those of their living cousins, mammoth teeth consisted of very thin, closely-spaced plates coated with enamel – perfect for grazing. Armed with these, the mammoths could tackle the toughest grasses and other vegetation on the plains. Mammoths grew twenty-four teeth throughout their lifetime. As older teeth were worn down, others emerged to replace them, forming a conveyer belt of grass-guzzling bricks to last a lifetime (over sixty years). Mammoths needed such hardware. A large individual had to put away up to 300 kilogrammes of grass a day just to survive. This meant eating for up to eighteen hours out of every twenty-four.

Although their bones may have been found in caves, mammoths were beasts of the open plains. They played a huge part in shaping the world around them, creating the largest terrestrial habitat ever seen: the mammoth steppe, a vast belt of open, wind-swept grassland stretching the length of Eurasia, across the Bering land bridge into North America. It played host to dozens of species of herbivores – and the predators that tormented them. But the mammoth was the lynchpin in it all. Mammoths were living snowploughs, exposing grass for a catalogue of smaller grazers to feed on. This in turn promoted fresh growth that perpetuated the steppe ecosystem over thousands of years.

To help them in their constant quest for food, mammoths made use of their iconic spiral tusks. At over three metres long, these vastly exceeded the tusks of modern elephants. Living elephants use their tusks to break branches and unearth roots. Tell-tale marks on mammoth tusks suggest they too were used as tools, shoving snow out of the way to expose the grass beneath (much of the wear on mammoth tusks is on the underside as a result of this process).

The finer aspects of mammoth family life can be inferred from a combination of fossil evidence and comparisons with their modern cousins, the Asian (in particular) and African elephants. These species are well known for their matriarchal societal structure. A typical family group comprises female relatives (sisters, mothers, daughters, aunts and nieces). Females remain within the same herd their whole lives while males leave at adolescence.

Fossil finds of mammoth herds indicate that they too cherished this family unit. As in modern elephants, it was headed by a matriarch, often the eldest female. In modern elephant society, the matriarch's strong leadership and vast experience accrued over decades is vital for the family's survival. It is she who must direct the herd to food or water when the greenery of the savannah has been stripped bare and rivers run dry. Mammoth matriarchs would have fulfilled a similar function on the Pleistocene plains of Ireland, guiding their dependents to fresh grazing and more sheltered terrain when the savagery of an Ice Age winter began to bite. To do this, the matriarch called upon memories stretching back half a century or more to secure the survival of the herd. Like elephants, it's possible that mammoths never forgot.

In contrast to the close-knit family life of the females, adult male elephants live a more solitary existence. Typically leaving his herd when he comes of age (ten to fifteen years old), a young male may join a bachelor group or live alone entirely. He may feed or drink with females at certain times of year, but aside from mating, this will be his only interaction with the predominantly female herds.

Once again, all evidence from the fossil record suggests that mammoth bulls conducted themselves in a similar manner. Larger tusks indicated a fitter, stronger bull. As with the great antlers of the giant Irish deer, this sexual bias fuelled the development of the mammoth's gargantuan tusks over generations. As with modern elephants, it's thought that mammoth bulls entered musth, a temporary state of testosterone-fuelled aggression that saw them competing to mate. Modern elephant bulls employ their tusks when fighting for access to females, and it would be remiss to suggest that the massive spiral tusks of bull mammoths were not used in combat. A particularly visceral example unearthed in Nevada shows how two Columbian mammoth bulls became entwined within each other's tusks during such a tussle, eventually dying in this fatal embrace.

Their contrasting lifestyles might also explain why the majority of mammoth fossil finds are of male individuals (69 per cent of mammoths found in Siberia, for instance, were male). Travelling alone, mammoth males – particularly inexperienced youngsters who had just left their families – were more likely to fall through the ice or get stuck in rivers, bogs or sinkholes, their remains then preserved for thousands of years. Female mammoths, led by a matriarch with intimate knowledge of the terrain, were better able to avoid such pitfalls.

Beyond a certain size, mammoths would have had little to fear from most predators, though younger mammoths in Ireland may occasionally have been targeted by wolves, bears and hyenas. Their counterparts on the European continent would also have had to contend with the massive cave lion, as well as modern humans and Neanderthal man. However, just like modern elephants, mammoth herds would have been fiercely protective of their young. Most predators would have sought out an easier meal.

11

Giant Goats and Reindeer: The Other Herbivores of Ice Age Ireland

Every mating season, in the rolling tundra that weaves around the Arctic Circle, the whisperings of the wind are broken by a sequence of sickening thuds, like boulders being smacked together at speed. At first, you would think these sounds must be man-made. But then you pick out the grunts of a beast filling the space between the thuds, sounding the charge for the next clash of heads. It is this collision of skulls that reverberates across the snow-flecked hills. It is the courtship carnage of one of the Arctic's most charismatic denizens: the muskox. We know from a single skull and teeth found in Aghnadarragh, County Antrim that this sound could have been heard more than a kilometre away on the icy steppes of Pleistocene Ireland. At 75,000 years old or more, these muskox remains are among the most ancient of all Pleistocene fossils found in Ireland. At that time, the area around Aghnadarragh would have been a cold, harsh landscape, a domain the muskox shared with the mammoth.

Muskoxen are essentially goats – on a whole other scale to the ones you'd find on any farm today. The males are formidable creatures, weighing more than a quarter of a tonne. And when they come to blows over control of a harem of females, the forces involved are bone-shattering. As with most males that win mating rights through brute force, violence is usually a last resort; strutting their credentials is often enough to sort the superior bull. But, if the male oxen are of equal calibre, a brutal contest ensues. This is not the wrestling match of deer. The horns of the muskox are too short to get a purchase on the weapons of his opponent. He has no tines to lock his nemesis in place, creating a platform through which their strength can be assessed. Instead, this is a highly ritualised collision course. The bulls back away from each other, swaggering as they go, before charging head on. The boss, where the two horns meet, bears the brunt of the

impact. Moving at full speed, the power involved is like a car being driven at nearly thirty kilometres an hour, straight into a brick wall – and it may have to be repeated up to twenty times before the issue is resolved. Fortunately, their brains are shielded from the brunt of the impact by ten centimetres of horn and nearly eight centimetres of solid bone. Eventually one will concede, retreating with his long, shaggy coat trailing behind him as he yields the herd to the victor.

That coat is key to the muskox's survival in today's Arctic much as it was essential on the cold plains of Ice Age Ireland. Like the mammoth, the muskox possesses a double-layered coat. A shorter denser layer is embraced by a looser outer layer that envelops the ox in a curtain, lending grace to its burly form. A compact body also helps the animal retain vital heat in its cold, harsh domain. As if that weren't enough, horizontal pupils in its eyes even act like sunglasses, reducing the glare from light reflected off snow and ice.

All is not testosterone-fuelled fury in the life of the muskox, however. They are very protective of their own, facing down every threat together. In the Arctic Circle of today – just as in Pleistocene Ireland – wolves are the main threat. If the attacker is alone, the oxen form a line, a formidable wall of horns ready to descend as one. If cornered by a pack, though, this strategy leaves them open to attack from the rear. This is when the muskoxen adopt their famous defensive circle. The most vulnerable members of the herd (young, sick, injured) are shielded by a schiltron of healthy adults. Brave outliers will sometimes sally forth to charge the threat, testing their nerve against that of the predator, but never ranging too far from the safety of the formation. By joining forces like this, the oxen are much more effective at fending off predators than the reindeer they share the tundra with, whose first instinct is to flee.

While muskox fossils are rare, reindeer remains have been found in Counties Clare, Cork, Waterford and Sligo. Their Irish heyday might be long gone, but reindeer still cling on in the Arctic to this day. When they coalesce into herds numbering hundreds of thousands during migration, they form one of the great wildlife spectacles of that region.

"Broad hooves serve as perfect snow shoes, easing their movement across rough, uneven terrain."

The features that make the reindeer such a hardy survivor in the present Arctic served it well in Ice Age Ireland too. Female reindeer sport their own antlers, the only female deer to do so, although they're somewhat smaller and less elaborate than those of the males. They help their owner clear snow to get at the greenery buried underneath – and then protect it from any hungry mouths that might have eyes on it. Should this not be enough to keep their body ticking over, reindeer can slow their metabolic rate to shrink the number of calories they need. In long, cold winters, this can help them hang on for one more day without sufficient food – and make every last calorie count.

In both genders, exceptionally broad hooves serve as perfect snow shoes, easing their movement across rough, uneven terrain. And should the deer have to circumvent a stream oozing from a melting glacier, those broad feet can double as a quartet of paddles. The light outer coat of the reindeer (which leaves no stamp on the snow when the animal sleeps, as all of its body heat stays locked in) even helps it float.

That coat is at its darkest during the summer months, when the males boast the heaviest antlers for their body size of any deer living today. As with the giant Irish deer, these

serve to entice females and make formidable weapons when it's time to face off against a rival stag. Fights beneath the midnight sun can be fatal.

In Ice Age Ireland, the large herds of rutting reindeer likely drew the hungry eyes of the region's predators. A reindeer stag would have offered a much softer target than a giant Irish deer or certainly a mammoth – particularly if he'd injured himself in his bid for mating rights. Though they rarely stand their ground like muskoxen, reindeer aren't completely defenceless against the predators of the frozen wastes. Their eyesight can venture into the ultraviolet, beyond the scope of human vision, lighting up a bleak snow-scape in vivid, shimmering colour. Against this, an advancing wolf is stripped of any camouflage, allowing the deer to take evasive action once a threat has been sighted.

Reindeer might be at their most spectacular in summer. Come the winter, though, sunlight is in short supply. This is when the reindeer's coat takes on the cooler accents the deer is better known for. Communicating with other members of the herd can become difficult in permanent darkness, particularly when a need to keep warm forces the deer to keep their mouths shut and heads bowed against the wind. An ingenious adaptation helps in this regard: a tendon slipping over a bone in the hind legs produces a clicking noise that helps the deer stay in touch, even in the worst blizzard conditions. This way, they can commune without exposing their lungs to the freezing air of the tundra.

As with all Ice Age animals, keeping warm was paramount. And in this regard, reindeer had (and still have) several advantages over their counterparts in warmer southern climes. Notably, they are the only deer with their entire nose covered in fur. This makes sense, given how the extremities of the body provide an outlet through which heat can be shed; many a human nose has been lost to frostbite in the colder parts of the world. The nose also has 25 per cent more capillaries (minute blood vessels) on its surface than a human nose. These facilitate more blood flow to the nose, keeping it warm in the coldest conditions. (Maybe there's more to Rudolph's red nose than Christmas myth.) The reindeer's adaptation to the Arctic is more than skin deep; a chamber in the nose, like quarantine for cold air, warms it up before it reaches the lungs.

Both muskox and deer belong to the order of even-toed ungulates. But what of the other branch of the family, with odd-toed feet? Thanks to advances in radio-carbon dating, we now know it was represented among Ireland's Ice Age fauna too.

Remains unearthed in Waterford's Shandon Cave, dated at around 28,000 years old, confirmed the presence of another grazer on the Ice Age plains of Ireland: the tarpan, or Eurasian wild horse.

Horses have since become synonymous with human habitation in Ireland, an integral part of rural life for centuries. But thanks to the Shandon specimen, it's clear that they have a much longer history here, arriving well before the first people. Having evolved in North America about 2 million years ago, early horses crossed the Bering land bridge and spread out across the steppes of Eurasia. It is here that you can still find the world's last truly wild horse, the now endangered Przewalski's horse.

This species – coupled with other offshoots of the family, such as the zebra, as well as feral horses that have reprised the natural state of their ancestors – gives us an idea of how the now extinct tarpan would have lived. As with many grazers, the family herds would have been predominantly females, all monopolised by a dominant stallion. His task was to fend off any rival stallions with designs on the herd. Unlike the reindeer or muskox, he had no horns or antlers to help in this endeavour. This would have forced him to use his teeth and feet should it come to a fight, rearing up to rain sharp hooves on his opponent or grab a mouthful of his neck. Every now and then, the Ice Age plains of Waterford must have borne witness to vicious duels of this nature.

Human handlers could later attest to the tarpan's ferocity. Unlike the mammoth or the giant Irish deer, the tarpan managed to survive into modern times, only fully succumbing to extinction in the early twentieth century. Sometime after the Ice Age ended, the tarpans of the Eurasian steppe were domesticated (some believe them to be the ancestors of all domestic horses). Records left by men foolhardy enough to try to tame a tarpan attest to how vicious these wild horses could be. They would bite and kick ferociously, since the docility of modern horses had yet to be bred into them.

The tarpan lasted long enough to be captured in grainy, black-and-white glory; just a single image, of an animal of questionable purity. This, and paintings in France's Chauvet and Lascaux caves, gives us an idea of what this wild horse looked like in life: an altogether shorter, scruffier creature than most modern horses, with a short, frizzy mane and black stripe running down the back. Stocky of build, the tarpan had a large head relative to today's horses. In modern equine nomenclature, its coat was dun (brownish grey, or tan, with a black tail and mane).

Modern horses are affectionate, highly social creatures. It's likely the tarpan was no different. A significant portion of their day would have been given over to grooming each other, gently running their teeth through the manes that bisected their necks. Much of the rest would have been spent grazing. Like all modern horses, tarpans were active animals, covering many kilometres each day in search of fresh forage. Although the stallion oversaw the defence of the herd, it might have been the dominant mare who led them to water and fresh grazing. Unlike deer, horses don't have a four-chambered stomach to help them eek every ounce of nutrition out of the grass. As a result, the tarpan's digestion was much less efficient than that of the ruminants with which they shared the plains, forcing them to eat a lot more to get the same benefit.

The big game – mammoths, horses, deer – might have been the star attractions of an Irish Ice Age safari. But when it comes to surviving a harsh climate, there are some advantages to being small. So, it should come as no surprise that, between mammoths and muskoxen, horses and giant deer, there were smaller herbivores here during the Ice Age too.

One of these more modest vegetarians is still with us today. This hardy survivor remains a charismatic member of Ireland's modern fauna. It is one of the few truly native mammals we have, with a deep heritage here written as much in myth and legend as in the bones it has left behind: the Irish hare.

There are two species of hare in modern Ireland. The Eurasian hare, introduced from abroad, has a small landholding in northern counties. But the native Irish hare has a nationwide presence. This is not its only claim to its well-deserved forename. Genetic analysis indicates that the Irish hare is a distinct subspecies of the continental mountain hare. (The biggest difference between the two is that our hare doesn't turn white in winter.) This speaks to its ancient heritage here, cut adrift from genetic reinforcements to the west. Our hares boast descent from ancestors that once scurried to safety amid the legs of the giant deer. It's perhaps sad, then, that the main lagomorph (long-eared, hopping mammals of farms and meadows) to spring to mind in Ireland today is not the hare but the rabbit, which arrived much later.

Rabbits may be fair-weather colonists of verdant fields, but our native hares are made of much tougher stuff. The extremities are especially densely furred, and the hare can even restrict blood flow to these to retain heat if need be. The thick fur that sees the Irish hare through our current winters was likely needed even more back then. Especially thick fur on the feet helped distribute its weight when crossing snow. Mountain hares also have shorter ears than other hare species, minimising heat loss in the cold of winter. Like their living counterparts, our Ice Age hares would have fed with their backs to the wind to soften its impact, and employed their furred boots to swat away snow and expose fresh grazing.

Hares can also adapt their diet to suit the vegetation available to them. They have tough saliva that can neutralise a plant's chemical defences. But even this might not have been enough to guarantee a daily feed in winter, meaning many lean days crouching for cover. Unlike rabbits, hares don't dig burrows. While their descendants have trees to retreat to, our Ice Age hares probably had to make do with rocks or bushes where they could find them, or the occasional juniper if they were lucky.

Leverets (baby hares) would have had to grow up fast in a tough Pleistocene environment. Then, as now, mortality would probably have been high. Hares spend longer developing in their mother's womb than other lagomorphs, ensuring they're better prepared for the harsh world that awaits them. Unlike rabbits, they don't have the benefit of being born in the relative safety of a burrow, and so have to be able to see and move almost immediately.

"Our hares boast descent from ancestors that once scurried to safety amid the legs of the giant deer."

They can hit speeds of seventy kilometres an hour. In the Pleistocene, they would have needed this to escape the interests of a wolf or Arctic fox.

Spring would have seen the hares show their aggressive side. The madness of the March hare was likely no less potent in the Pleistocene than it is now. Duals for mating rites would have been like a microcosm of the more earth-shaking clashes between the stags on the steppes around them. Though more modest, the boxing matches between hares were certainly more athletic. Unlike the other herbivores of the plains, this behaviour would not have been the sole province of the male hares. In living hares, the larger females often initiate the trouble – to see off an overly amorous male, or even to test his credentials for fatherhood. The agility needed to best the female in a boxing match may one day be called upon by his offspring to evade the predators of the plains.

Still smaller grazers made their home in Ireland at this time. By far the most successful order of mammals in the world are the rodents. Rodents make up over 40 per cent of all mammal species and have made every habitat type above water their own, from the tropical rainforest to the man-made jungles of concrete and glass. And between the litany of massive bones left in the wake of the great Ice Age herbivores of Ireland, scientists have uncovered the tiny remains of rodents unique to the tundra today: lemmings.

There were two species of lemming to be found in Pleistocene Ireland, the Norway and the Arctic lemming. As its name suggests, the Norway lemming is largely confined to Scandinavia today. The Arctic lemming, meanwhile, is found only in the polar regions of Russia. They also differ in their colour. Both species boast a black-and-tan coat in summer. But while the Norway lemming retains this year-round, the Arctic lemming, the true cold-weather specialist, turns white in winter to help conceal itself in the snow.

Both species were superbly adapted for Ice Age life. The same rules for survival that shaped mammoths still apply to the lemmings: short extremities (ears, nose, tail) keep heat in, and long fur also traps warmth close to the body. Their long claws are perfect for digging their way through fresh snow drifts, or failing that, through soil now hardened by frost. They're highly accomplished burrowers, with separate sleeping quarters and latrines laced together by a labyrinth of tunnels. Lemmings don't hibernate. Stowed away in their underground domains, they stay active throughout the year, snug while larger creatures above are exposed to the worst of the winter weather. They can even feed underground, nibbling away at roots and tubers without exposing themselves to predators or the crushing hooves of horses or deer.

This likely made them as successful on the Ice Age plains of Ireland as they are in the Arctic and sub-Arctic regions of today. The fossil evidence suggests that, while other species were absent during the worst of the Ice Age cold snaps, the lemmings were still here, weathering them out in their subterranean citadels. In contemporary Ireland, they say you're never too far from a rat. Back then, lemmings might have held that honour. In so doing, they were one of the keystone species of the Ice Age ecosystem. Lemmings, in their vast numbers, provided food for a host of different predators. They exerted an immense toll on the vegetation, which they both spread (through droppings) and helped keep in check.

In another similarity with the mammoths with which they once shared the plains, female Norway lemmings live in family groups – sisters, mothers, daughters and grandmothers. They form a united front against any wandering male that ventures into their tunnels, biting and assailing him with ruthless aggression. Inevitably, some males retreat in the face of this vicious onslaught. But those tough enough to withstand it are rewarded with the opportunity to mate with every female in the group.

Like many other rodents, lemmings excel at reproduction. Both genders are ready to breed within three weeks of being born. Females can churn out three litters of up to nine young every summer – and they don't stop there. They are willing and able to breed throughout the polar year, one of the few species to do so. Many of their offspring naturally succumb to the vagaries of tundra life: predation, exposure, lack of food or water. But enough inevitably survive to kick the population into overdrive, in a cycle that comes to a head every thirty or forty years. When this happens, the lemming population is so dense that they are forced to do more and more foraging above ground. This leaves them exposed to the talons of owls or the jaws of the Arctic fox.

With too many of them now in competition for the same resources, the lemmings are forced to migrate in search of pastures new. Without any clear sense of destination, motivated only by an impulse to find food and space unburdened by swollen numbers of lemmings, they depart in a writhing mass across the tundra. They let no obstacles stand in their way. They circumvent mountains strewn with boulders, and cross fast-running streams and lakes in an incredible feat of endurance for such small creatures. Many, though, die in the attempt.

This dispersal can lead to one of the most perverse phenomena in the natural world: mass drownings. Instinctively, the lemmings tend to gravitate to the lower ground when they migrate, following the path of least resistance like a river. When they reach the coast, the sheer mass of lemmings behind them forces them into the sea, where they drown. This is not a spontaneous act of suicide, as was falsely believed in the past. But it does restore balance to the lemming population, bringing their numbers back below a healthy threshold. The lemmings that survive go on to colonise new territory, helping the species rapidly expand its range.

Perhaps, all those millennia ago, the coastal waters of Ice Age Ireland were periodically strewn with flotillas of dead lemmings, killed by their desire to stay alive.

12

The Predators of
the Plains

On the mammoth steppe of a Munster long gone, a herd of horses stands to attention. The scent of danger hangs in the cold air. From across the grassy expanse, the threat lumbers into view. And it's not alone.

The chase begins. The horses start to scatter. Their tormentors have selected their victim. They have pursued the herd across the plains for hours. It's a game of stamina now, a war of attrition starting to tip in favour of the hunter as its victim tires.

Crushing jaws slam home, grabbing a mouthful of hide around the belly. Pained and panicked, the horse prances, kicking in all directions to dislodge its attacker. One on one, it might succeed. But this predator hunts in a pack. Another member of the clan closes in to secure a second foothold. The urge to survive lends a desperate energy to the horse, its muscles now laced with adrenaline.

Burdened by two attackers, the horse desperately ploughs on. But the landscape is against it today. The rest of the herd is out of sight. A hoof catches the ground at an angle. The horse stumbles. Now, it's on the deck – and surrounded, as the rest of the clan closes in. Within seconds it's buried in its attackers, a feast of which little will be spared. Anything left will be carried off, back to the den for the rest of the family. But for now, the hunters content themselves with their prize. Whoops and yelps saturate the breeze. A sinister laugh weaves into the evening chorus.

From mammoths to lemmings, there was an abundance of prey on the plains of Ice Age Ireland. And wherever you find prey, predators are never far away. So, what kind of hunters plied their trade here thousands of years ago?

Once again, the Ice Age bone beds of Munster provide the answer. Amongst the jumble of bones dragged out of Castlepook Cave in Cork was an incomplete skull, of a different order to the giant deer and mammoth remains with which it shared this dark abyss. It belonged to one of the most formidable predators of the Pleistocene: the spotted hyena.

Spotted hyenas are, today, synonymous with the savannahs of Africa. Here they are the commonest large predator, antagonising the lions and leopards they share the grasslands with. They would seem wholly out of place in Ireland today – even more alien than the other predators that once roamed here. But the hyenas of the Pleistocene ranged far and wide, even terrorising the tundra north of the Arctic Circle. They were among the hardiest hunters of their time. And around 35,000 years ago, we now know they were hunting their Ice Age contemporaries on the plains of County Cork.

Together with the woolly mammoth, the hyena gave an African accent to the primarily Arctic fauna that called

Ireland home during the Ice Age. Pleistocene Europe was home to many creatures with living counterparts in Africa. Where mammoths stood in for elephants and wild horses for zebras, Europe also had its own varieties of lion (the cave lion) and rhino (the woolly rhino). All of these were different from their living African kin, but the spotted hyenas that ran down Ice Age herbivores in Ireland were of the same species as those whose wails haunt the Masai Mara to this day. And it is from them that we can build up a picture of hyena life in Pleistocene Ireland.

Indeed, it could be argued that spotted hyenas in Ireland had it better than their relatives elsewhere in Europe. Much as modern hyenas feud with lions on the African grasslands, in Europe the same dynamic existed with the much larger cave lion. But in Ireland, the hyenas found an outpost at the edge of Europe that the cave lion never reached. We can even see living echoes of this in Africa today. In Zambia's Liuwa Plains National Park, for instance, hyenas assumed the mantle of top predators as the local lion population was all but eliminated by poaching.

We probably have hyenas to thank for the build-up of Ice Age bones at Castlepook. It is to here that the butchered remains of kills would have been dragged to feed the rest of the family. Dimples found on a mammoth bone in the cave provide further evidence for this, perfectly matching the dimensions of a hyena's canines. This suggests that they made their dens underground much as modern hyenas do in Africa and that, like them, they lived in tight-knit clans.

The clan lies at the core of hyena life. Female hyenas tend to remain within the same clan all their lives, while males leave to join a new clan when they come of age. Atypically for mammals, it is the females that lord it over the males.

Female hyenas are larger and more aggressive, and even the highest-ranking male in the clan defers to the lowliest female. Status in the clan is largely hereditary, to the point where cubs can be sure to inherit a place in the pecking order just below that of their mother.

Keeping tabs on this complex social order (which may include up to 130 hyenas per clan) requires phenomenal brain power – more than that of their great rival, the lion. Hyenas are far removed from the dumb brutes they have classically been portrayed as. Much as with primates, a larger brain was required to help them comprehend and manoeuvre through the rigid class structure that pervades the clan.

Their intellect also manifests in the intricate variety of calls they employ, each serving a different purpose within the context of clan life. On the savannah of today – and doubtless on the Pleistocene steppe – they are among the most vocal predators around. The laugh might be the most infamous, but most impactful is the long, haunting whoop, used to keep in touch with clan-mates in the pitch darkness. In an age long gone, this would have been one of the signature sounds of Ireland's frigid twilight.

As well as a large brain, hyenas are also renowned for another exceptionally big organ: their heart. In proportion to body mass, it's twice as heavy as that of the lions they share the savannah with today. And it provides the hyenas with the devastating stamina they need to run down prey across the grasslands. With their incredibly sensitive noses, they can follow a scent trail that's more than three days old.

Famed as scavengers, hyenas – thanks in no small part to that massive heart – are among the most accomplished killers on the African plains. Working together, they can run down and overpower prey much larger than themselves.

Once within striking distance, their primary weapon can be brought into play – a truly devastating bite. It's among the most powerful in the entire animal kingdom: 1,100 pounds per square inch.

Once the prey is down, that bite really comes into its own. Hyenas are capable of eating almost everything on a carcass – bones, hooves, teeth and all. They're aided in this endeavour by exceptionally potent stomach acids. These break down the meal once it's been pulverised at the front end.

> "Working together, they can run down and overpower prey much larger than themselves."

The evidence from Castlepook Cave suggests our hyenas dined on mammoth and giant Irish deer. Fossil finds from the continent indicate that wild horses and the woolly rhino were also among the hyena's favoured prey. This behaviour mirrors that of their modern relatives, for whom zebras are among the preferred fare. Although woolly rhinos never made it to Ireland, wild horse remains have been discovered in County Waterford. Perhaps the primordial battle between horse and hyena – a constant feature on the African savannah today – might once have played out on the wind-swept steppes of Ice Age Ireland.

Hyenas differ from lions in that they don't ambush their prey. They lack the powerful back legs with which to pounce on their victims from cover. Instead, theirs is a pursuit of attrition. They're far from the fastest animal on the plain, but that massive heart ensures they can keep running when their prey is crippled by fatigue. Huge nostrils help keep their lungs full of oxygen throughout the chase, and longer front legs help make for excellent long-distance running ability. Teamwork is also key. When they're closing in on a target, one or more hyenas snap incessantly at its heels. Eventually, the prey is compelled to turn and face its attacker. This is when it's embraced in a double envelment, as other hyenas seize the moment to grab it by both flanks, pinning it down. Reinforcements soon arrive to help finish the job. Unlike the clean, finessed kill of a big cat, a hyena hunt can be an exceptionally gruesome massacre. It's not uncommon for the victim to be eviscerated alive.

The carcass can provide utility long after the meat and marrow are exhausted. The bones and horns of dead prey provide a perfect grinding stone for hyena cubs to sharpen their teeth and strengthen their jaws. Remarkably, the profusion of antlers in Ice Age den sites suggest these fulfilled a similar role for Europe's hyenas thousands of years ago.

Despite their hunting prowess, it's likely that Ireland's hyenas succumbed to the temptation of scavenging whenever a carcass was up for grabs. We know from denning sites across Europe that hyenas fulfilled this essential, if unsavoury, role on the steppe, recycling the corpses of mammoths and other huge herbivores. Hyenas today often commandeer carcasses from other carnivores when they have size and numbers on their side. It would be remiss to think that their Ice Age cousins were above such behaviour. With their corrosive stomach acids, they could have ingested rotting flesh that other carnivores would have (literally) turned their noses up at.

Hyenas didn't have it all their own way here. There were other carnivores with which they shared the Ice Age plains of Ireland. Among the bones to surface from Pleistocene cave sites across the country were fearsome jaws, longer and narrower than the broad, bone-crushing accoutrement of the hyena. This more canid profile betrayed its owner, the ancestor of the dogs we still cherish today. It is a creature that, unlike the hyena, managed to cling on in Europe after the Ice Age ended – the grey wolf.

That wolves formed a thread in the tapestry of Ice Age Ireland should come as no surprise. They are among the top predators on the tundra to this day. In Ireland, they lasted long enough to encounter people – and leave a permanent impression upon our culture. But long before they were revered (and feared) by the first people who came here, they numbered among the great predators of our deep Ice Age past. Their mournful howls duelled with the whoops and laughs of the hyenas for control of the Irish night, long before human ears could hear them.

The grey wolf was (and remains) the largest and most fearsome of the canine clan in Europe. It is also amongst the most successful of all mammalian predators. Even now, when their once vast domain has been truncated by human incursion, wolves still patrol a huge stretch of the northern hemisphere.

Unlike the matriarchy of hyenas, a wolf pack is presided over by a dominant pair. Breeding rights are reserved solely for this duumvirate. The other pack members are typically their offspring. They stick around to help in the rearing of their younger siblings, gaining experience in both parenting and hunting that will serve them well should they ever leave to establish packs of their own. The number of wolves in the pack – and the survival rate of their offspring – is determined by the abundance of prey in their territory.

It is during the time when the pups are at their youngest and most vulnerable that the wolves cease their howling, so as not to give away their den's location to other predators on the plain. It is likely that they feuded with spotted hyenas, for denning sites as well as food. Big predators often feel an instinctual antagonism, and will kill each other if they can. The build-up of wolf bones at hyena dens across Europe suggests the latter may even have fed upon the former. Successive generations of hyenas and wolves may also have made their

homes in the same caves, leading to an accumulation of predator (and prey) remains at these sites.

Bonds of blood are important to wolves, which depend upon each other for survival. The howling for which they are so famous serves to bind them together: a shared symphony through which they express dominion over their territory and fortify their commitment to the clan. The most visceral expression of this is the hunt. Though formidable on their own, wolves amplify their killing prowess when they work together. The bigger the pack, the larger the prey they can take down. In Ice Age Europe, as in the northern tundra of today, reindeer would likely have been the main target. Pursuing this smaller, swifter prey might also have helped the wolves limit competition with hyenas, which focused on the larger beasts of the plains – both dead or alive.

Like hyenas, wolves are pursuit predators, tiring their victims into submission. This is where numbers are critical. A reindeer can outpace a wolf in a straight race. But the wolves work in relay; when one member of the pack tires, another surges forth to replace it. They form a cycle of pursuit that prevents the prey from slowing down. Gender dynamics add another dimension to the chase; lighter, swifter female wolves are best employed in the pursuit, while the bulkier males are more effective at bringing down the exhausted prey. The snows of Ice Age Ireland would have offered little hindrance to hunting wolves. Their large feet help distribute weight in such a way that they do not sink into snow when running. Blunt claws, though useless for seizing prey, add extra grip on slippery ground. Slight webbing between the toes gives them even more purchase on the snow.

Coupled with ruthless determination – which can see them cover more than seventy kilometres a day in search of food – wolves are also master tacticians. They can adapt their approach based on the situation at hand. Sometimes, for instance, the pack will split up to engulf the prey in a pincer movement, with some wolves driving the victim into an ambush set by the others. They can also make tactical use of the terrain to their advantage. Light snow, for instance, favours the wolves; they know that heavier reindeer are likely to become bogged down if they try to run through it. In winter, therefore, the wolves will try to chase the reindeer into just such conditions. In summer, wolves have been observed taking a different tack, forcing their prey into dried-up riverbeds where the uneven surface causes them to stumble and fall.

"Bonds of blood are important to wolves, which depend upon each other for survival."

The constant contest between reindeer and wolf served to strengthen both species in the long run. Any reindeer ill equipped for the harsh reality of Ice Age Ireland were soon weeded out by the wolves – just as wolves which were unable to sustain themselves on the steppe were left catching their breath by the reindeer. A harsh winter, when their prey is under the most stress, can yield a bumper crop for wolves; it is in winter that they enjoy their best hunting.

Hunting in winter would also have meant the wolves did not have to yield their prize to another predator, the largest to roam Ireland's Pleistocene plains.

Formidable as wolves and hyenas are, one-on-one they would have had to concede to the brown bear. Weighing up to 350 kilogrammes, the brown bear was the powerhouse among Ireland's Ice Age predators. Bears are solitary – they don't go in for pack hunting. They don't need to. Despite their bulk, they are capable of devastating bursts of speed – nearly fifty kilometres an hour. Modern bears can take down bison, suggesting they would have tackled the reindeer, horse and maybe even giant Irish deer that once grazed the mammoth steppe.

Like other Ice Age predators, brown bears had a formidable bite, but they also came equipped with weapons denied to both wolves and hyenas: a quintet of sharp claws at the end of each incredibly powerful forelimb. In modern bears, a blow from this is enough to cave in the spine of a deer. There's no reason to assume that their Ice Age counterparts were any less ferocious on the hunt. Although capable of tackling adult deer, it is likely that our Ice Age bears – just like their relatives today – would have targeted fawns, separating them from their mothers in the chaos of the chase before closing in.

Size and power also come in handy when scavenging. Bears aren't as well built for the chase as wolves are. It's likely that Ice Age brown bears would have been happy for smaller predators to do the hard work, before sweeping in to steal their prize. In places where they still share the same habitat, this can lead to vicious confrontations between bears and wolf packs. Occasionally, wolves have to yield

their kill to a determined bear. Conversely, a pack of wolves working together can prove a match for a bear, especially if they provoke it from several angles, dragging it into fruitless pursuits in different directions. Using this tactic, a desperate mother bear can be sundered from her cub, leaving it exposed to attack from another member of the wolf pack.

Brown bears are not obligate carnivores. Up to 70 per cent of their diet isn't even meat. So even if they shared a taste for reindeer or giant Irish deer fawns, wolves and bears could still have coexisted – if uneasily – in Pleistocene Ireland. While the wolves focused their energies on tackling game, the broader tastes of the bear (enabled by plant-grinding molars) allowed for a more diverse diet: grass, berries, fish, insects, nuts. Fuelled by an appetite that knows no end, bears can eat continuously when the going is good, chomping through up to 20,000 calories worth of food a day and gaining more than a kilogramme in weight in the process. Wherever there was food – any food – in Ice Age Ireland, you could be sure a brown bear was not far away. Some bears today have even developed a taste for shellfish, which their huge claws can unearth and pry apart with surprising tenderness and dexterity.

Bears need to be such voracious eaters to put on the weight that will see them through the winter. Ireland's brown bears would have hibernated through the coldest months of the year, re-emerging to gorge on new growth in the spring, just as their living counterparts do. Having found or excavated an underground den in which to see out the snows, the bear's body temperature dips while its heart rate plummets to as few as ten beats per minute. They don't eat, drink or excrete. They occasionally stir from this torpor; as such, it is not *true* hibernation. But they still remain dormant until the call of spring (and the bounty of food it promises) teases them from their den. When our Ice Age bears returned to the plains it would have been with renewed hunger; they would have lost up to 30 per cent of their bodyweight, and would have needed a meal fast to avoid starving entirely.

"Though dwarfed by its Ice Age contemporaries, the Arctic fox was extremely hardy."

Surviving so long without food was highly taxing on the bears' bodies. Brown bears burn up to 4,000 calories a day during hibernation. Then, as now, some bears simply never wake up. It's possible that some of the bears entombed in the caves of Ireland met this silent death, ebbing away for want of food as they slumbered beneath the snow.

Ireland's brown bears are long gone, becoming extinct around 3,000 years ago. However, modern genetic evidence suggests their legacy lives on far beyond our shores, their blood flowing through the veins of the closely related polar bear. The two species occasionally interbreed in modern Alaska, where their ranges overlap. Perhaps the same thing happened in the Alaska-like conditions of Ice Age Ireland.

Of course, any habitat can only sustain so many large predators. Modern ecosystems also have a smattering of smaller carnivores skulking about in their shadows. Ice Age Ireland was no exception. Amongst the bear, wolf and hyena remains unearthed in the Ice Age caves of Munster was another carnivore, probably better adapted to the Ice Age than any other: the Arctic fox.

Though dwarfed by its Ice Age contemporaries, the Arctic fox was extremely hardy. Living Arctic foxes can comfortably survive the sub-zero temperatures that dominate Eurasia's frozen wastes. Their small size (smaller than the red foxes that patrol our suburbs today) makes it easier for them to burrow into winter snows. As well as size, the Arctic fox differs from its red relative in having a shorter muzzle and ears, both of which help to lock in heat. The furry soles enveloping its feet serve the same purpose. An especially bushy tail doubles as a warm, wraparound blanket.

Another dramatic distinction – one for which the Arctic fox is most famous – is the pelage, the coat colour. In high summer, the fox is an attractive blend of browns and greys. This helps it melt into the sparse, mottled plant-life of the tundra. But when the vanguard of winter arrives, the foxes' body reacts to the drop in temperature by turning a stunning pure white; a perfect camouflage against the ubiquitous Arctic snow. By doing this, the fox can blend into its environment throughout the year.

As such, its coat is a vital accessory in its hunting strategy. In the Arctic of today – and in an Ireland long gone – lemmings are among its main sources of food. Fox populations wax and wane in sync with the cyclical explosions of lemmings. The rodents are easier to catch when they abandon their burrows en masse. In winter, when the lemmings are shielded by a layer of snow, the fox must follow its ears and nose to the source, before catching its prey with a precise and often spectacular pounce. Like their red cousins, though, Arctic foxes are adept at making the most of every resource available. They can tailor their diet to suit the season. In summer, for instance, cliffs heaving with nesting seabirds – and their eggs – make for good foraging.

Winter, as for most animals, can mean leaner times ahead for the foxes. This is when they are most likely to shadow the Arctic's apex predator, the polar bear. The foxes can range over huge distances in the hope of polishing off scraps from the carcasses of seals or beluga whales brought down by the bears. It's likely this same strategy served Ireland's Ice Age foxes well, as they lingered in the wake of wolf and hyena packs to pick over what was left. Remains of deer, horses or even mammoths would have been a vital food source. Anything excess would have been buried for future consumption; prescience was prudent in such an unforgiving world.

Ireland's Pleistocene remains also included the bones of an even smaller predator. It was the most diminutive to stalk the Ice Age plains, but no less fearsome – and in an Irish context, perhaps the most remarkable of all.

This tenacious killer is as at home stalking the meadows of twenty-first century Ireland as it was in the grasslands of our distant past. It's so small it can be hard to make out from any distance, unless it is standing on its hind legs to survey its surroundings. Sometimes, its presence can be gleaned by a sudden scattering of rabbits in a field, shattering the tranquillity of the scene. Their tormentor is only around one tenth their weight – but that's no help to a rabbit once the stoat binds itself, snake-like around its neck, before delivering a killer blow to the back of the head. With a fatal click, the rabbit collapses. Victorious, the stoat undulates out from under its kill, before beginning the arduous task of carrying it back to the den.

Even if they left no fossil traces behind them, the blood of our stoats is enough to mark them out as something special. DNA analysis has confirmed that, like the Irish hare, the Irish stoat is a subspecies all of its own, unique to this island and the Isle of Man. And as with the Irish hare, this indicates that they have a long heritage here, stretching back far longer than any of the other mammalian predators that currently stalk our countryside. Red foxes, badgers and pine martens might have settled here in the wake of the Ice Age, but the stoat was here before them all, a menace to small mammals in a tangle for life and death no less dramatic than the one playing out between the Ice Age giants that overshadowed them.

Rabbits were not present in Ice Age Ireland. Instead, our Pleistocene stoats might have had to make do with lemmings. A long, narrow body made them just as suited to a subterranean pursuit. A more lasting trophy from a hunt may have been the burrow of its vanquished prey, commandeered by the stoat as a den in which to see out the cold winter nights.

13

The End of the Ice Age Giants

The conditions that made this unique assemblage of animals possible were not to last forever. By the end of the Pleistocene around 11,700 years ago, the great ice sheets that had once locked so much of Europe in their embrace were drawing back. With this, massive amounts of water were released into the environment once again, coupling with warmer weather to allow forests to flourish. This not only affected the flora of Europe but also the geography. Sea levels began to rise. At various times throughout the Ice Age, Ireland had been affixed to the rest of Europe. But by about 12,000 years ago, as the Irish Sea filled in, Ireland was finally severed from Britain. The last of our Ice Age beasts were marooned in the North Atlantic.

The shift from steppe to forest did not suit many of the creatures that made their home in Ice Age Europe. Muskox and reindeer, for instance, followed their preferred habitat on its retreat back into the far north. The wild horse was more resilient, holding on in Europe until finally succumbing to extinction only a hundred years ago. Bears and wolves adapted well to the new, forested Europe. The spotted hyena, however, did not, and so a fearsome predator that once ranged across Eurasia is now confined to the African grasslands.

Even more than these localised extinctions, the end of the Ice Age heralded the great dying of many of the world's most spectacular megafauna. The woolly mammoth, giant Irish deer, cave lion and woolly rhino would vanish not just from Europe but from across the world. This pattern would be repeated elsewhere, with North America losing its Columbian mammoths, sabre-toothed cats, short-faced bears and a menagerie of other Ice Age giants. As far away as Australia, the winding down of the Pleistocene would spell doom for the truly amazing fauna that once lived there, from giant lizards and three-metre-tall birds to the terrifying marsupial lion.

The two members of Europe's megafaunal community to leave the most lasting mark on Ireland were the woolly mammoth and giant Irish deer. The woolly mammoth doesn't appear to have been here by the time the Pleistocene ended, but the exact cause of the species' demise on a global scale has been the subject of intense scientific debate.

One possible culprit is climate change. Verdant forests would gradually replace the mammoth's preferred habitat – steppe – throughout most of its range. As such, the climate change theory holds that the demise of the Ice Age ultimately spelt doom for the mighty mammoth.

This is not without its faults. The mammoth had survived dozens of warmer and colder periods over the course of millennia, none of which had caused it to disappear entirely. Even with the Pleistocene coming to an end, there still were places (notably in Siberia) where the kind of open grassland mammoths thrived on could be found. Thus, climate change does not provide the definitive smoking gun.

Another theory points the blame at man. Sites throughout the New and Old World indicate that mammoths crossed paths with human hunters. Stone spear points have been found with mammoth remains, the bones showing clear signs of butchery. Furthermore, a warming climate at the end of the Ice Age would have facilitated the spread of humans, bringing them into contact with relict populations of mammoths. So maybe the spread of man across Eurasia and North America led to the decline of the mammoths, as they were hunted for food by an expanding human population.

This theory too runs into difficulty. Sites like these are relatively rare. This suggests that mammoths, although hunted occasionally, were not always regular fare for Ice Age man. That's not surprising – taking on a highly dangerous, six-tonne animal with stone-tipped spears would have been a risky procedure. So, although mammoths were hunted by humans, it seems unlikely that they were slaughtered in such numbers as to go extinct throughout their whole domain.

Ultimately, it's possible that a combination of these factors was responsible for finishing off the woolly mammoth, with climate change playing the biggest part. As the Ice Age ended, a species that once ranged right across the northern hemisphere was gradually driven back by the spread of man and rapid shrinking of the mammoth steppe as a result of a warming world. By 10,000 years ago, the woolly mammoth was effectively extinct throughout most of the vast swath of Eurasia it once called home. The last mammoths on Earth persevered on Wrangel Island off the coast of Russia until around 4,000 years ago when they followed their brethren into oblivion. It's humbling to think that when our distant ancestors were raising Newgrange, there were still mammoths wandering the planet, even if it was half the world away. By the time of their demise, Wrangel Island's mammoths had

succumbed to island dwarfism. Large animals marooned on a small island often shrink in response to the limited food available to them. At around two tonnes, the last mammoths were a fraction of the size of the beasts that once swaggered across the Ice Age plains of Waterford and Cork.

The extinction of the giant Irish deer, meanwhile, was inextricably linked to the end of the Ice Age itself. The species still thrived on Ireland's open grasslands right up until the end of the Pleistocene, sharing its habitat with the smaller red and reindeer as well as the brown bear, wolf, hare and stoat. But this wasn't to last. The demise of the species in Ireland was caused by catastrophic events thousands of kilometres away. Around 12,700 years ago, as the world began to warm up, the great ice sheets that carpeted much of North America started to melt. The central portion of the eastern North American ice sheet was reduced to a lake of frigid water, far larger than the Great Lakes still found in that region today. This was so enormous that the thin strip of ice containing it inevitably gave way.

The breach occurred at roughly the spot of the modern Saint Lawrence River (between the Canadian province of Ontario and New York). It unleashed a monumental amount of cold water and ice into the North Atlantic, greater than the flow of all the rivers in the world today combined. This sudden infusion of cold water interfered with the Gulf Stream that brought warm waters to Europe from the tropics. It would have a catastrophic impact on Ireland's climate.

Ironically, just as the rest of the world was warming up, Ireland found itself sinking into severe cold once again. Without the warming influence of the Gulf Stream, summer temperatures fell by an average of twelve degrees Celsius, shaving a whole month off the growing season for many plants.

For a herbivore like the giant Irish deer, which needed vast quantities of forage, any disruption of plant growth patterns was devastating. The quality of vegetation deteriorated rapidly. Soils already depleted through overgrazing from the large herds of deer were further drained by melting snow, surface run-off and rain, leeching off much of their remaining nutrition.

Fertile grazing lands across Ireland became fragmented. And with their ravenous appetite for grass fuelled by the need to re-grow antlers each year, the deer kept overgrazing these last remaining pockets of productive soil. Over the centuries of this localised environmental catastrophe, the giant Irish deer found it harder and harder to put on enough fat reserves to last through the harsh winters. What little remaining forage was buried under thick snow. Season after season, more deer died than were born. Cut off from their kin on the continent by the filling in of the Irish Sea, the population was unable to replenish itself. The giant Irish deer finally vanished from Ireland about 10,600 years ago. At the same time – and for the same reasons – the reindeer also disappeared, rendering Ireland a deer-less landscape until the return of the red deer (by the hand of man) as recently as 5,000 years ago.

Although this prolonged cold snap may have spelt doom for the species in Ireland, elsewhere the giant Irish deer still clung on. The gradual change in Eurasia's landscapes, however, proved its final reckoning. Inevitably, the spread of forests vastly reduced the available feeding territory for this specialist grazer. It could no longer find the quantities of grass it needed to sustain such a bulky body. Its iconic antlers were also utterly unsuited to the new, more forested Europe. Stags would have found their movements severely restricted in dense undergrowth. Deprived of the space and sustenance they needed to survive, the last giant Irish deer, clinging on in that Ice Age redoubt of Siberia, followed their Hibernian kin into extinction around 7,000 years ago. As with the mammoth, human hunters might also have played a part.

"Over the centuries of this localised environmental catastrophe, the giant Irish deer found it harder and harder to put on enough fat reserves to last through the harsh winters."

The time of the giant Ice Age beasts was over. But an even more remarkable animal was about to take centre stage in Ireland, one that would leave an indelible mark on our landscapes and wildlife right up to the present day.

PART III

Life in the Human Age

14

The Coming of Man

Castlepook Cave in County Cork has proved a goldmine for Ice Age fossils over the years. Bones of mammoths, wolves, reindeer, hyenas and the giant Irish deer have all been uncovered here. And in 2021, one of these bones would rewrite the history of humanity in Ireland forever.

The bone in question, a reindeer femur, had been unearthed in the cave way back in 1972. But on closer examination, the bone was found to have cut marks – scars that could only have been inflicted by the stone tools of human hunters. Once dated, the bone was found to be 33,000 years old.

This proved a bombshell. Until this discovery, the oldest evidence for human habitation in Ireland was a butchered bear bone from County Clare, dated at around 12,500 years old. As such, the Castlepook specimen pushed back the date for human arrival in Ireland by more than 20,000 years.

With their coming, a revolutionary new chapter in the history of life here was about to begin.

The long history of life in Ireland has seen many amazing creatures come and go over millions of years. But then, around 33,000 years ago, came the most remarkable animal of all.

Anatomically modern humans – us – had travelled a long way, over a very long time, to get here. Primitive humans evolved in Africa over the course of the Pleistocene, slowly acquiring the features we still see in ourselves before finally arriving at our own species, *Homo sapiens*, between 200,000 and 300,000 years ago.

What would follow would be multiple exoduses out of our African cradle as modern humans slowly spread across the globe. Over tens of thousands of years, these intrepid explorers added Europe, North America and even Australia to their list of conquests. Thanks to the evidence at Castlepook, we now know Ice Age reindeer hunters arrived in Ireland around 33,000 years ago. This drastically changed our understanding of human history in Ireland and in Western Europe as a whole.

By the time the Mesolithic (Middle Stone Age) people arrived here, 10,000 years ago or so, Ireland was already an island, sundered from Britain by the rising of the Irish Sea. As such, these people almost certainly arrived here by boat. The precise location of this first landing is unknown, but the prolific Stone Age remains concentrated in the northeast of the country suggest an influx of people from Scotland across the narrow stretch of sea to Ireland's northeast coast.

Over the millennia that followed, successive waves of invaders and settlers came to shape the geopolitical and cultural landscape of Ireland – Neolithic farmers, Celts, Vikings, Anglo-Normans, Scottish and English planters – gradually building up the Ireland we know today. Each of them left their own thumbprint on our heritage. And each would help contribute in their own way to the landscapes we now see in Ireland – and the fauna that inhabit them.

The people who left their marks on the reindeer bone in Castlepook Cave might have been as subject to the laws of nature as the creature they were butchering. But over the thousands of years that followed, man would exert a mastery over the natural world that would allow him to shape his own destiny to a degree no species had before. The onset of modern farming allowed people to free themselves from the vicissitudes of hunting and gathering and grow their own regular supply of food. With this, they could abandon nomadism and settle down. This brought the first permanent settlements, clusters of farmsteads that would evolve into villages. As food production ramped up and the population grew, villages would swell into towns, and towns into cities.

In so doing, they would create an array of new habitats for the wildlife of Ireland to exploit, from the farms that patchwork our countryside to the glass and concrete constructions that make up our modern cities. Some species would find themselves squeezed out of the new, human Ireland – while others thrived in it. Humans have led to the extinction of some of our most charismatic wild creatures. Concomitantly, the fauna that we still cherish today would be significantly poorer were it not for the influence of man. As ensuing waves of humanity made their way to our island outpost on the edge of Europe, they did not come alone. They brought with them a menagerie of creatures that can still be found here today. Some came as stowaways, the pests that naturally followed humans (and the food they provided) in their expansions around the world. Others were brought here deliberately; some for fur, others for food and yet others for sport, providing ideal quarry for hunting. All would escape or gradually revert to their wild state, and so add their own strand to the faunal tapestry we now know as wild Ireland.

This is particularly true of our mammals, many of which were introduced by humans over the centuries. This has even led to some debate over what constitutes an authentically 'native' Irish mammal. Some – such as the grey squirrel, brown rat and feral goat – were clearly ferried here by humans. Others (most notably the marine mammals such as seals and whales, as well as bats) colonised Ireland (and its seas) under their own steam. A handful, among them the Irish hare and stoat, seem to have been here in unchanged form since the end of the last Ice Age.

"Humans would create an array of new habitats for the wildlife of Ireland to exploit."

But this is where things get complicated. Creatures such as the red deer, red squirrel and pine marten are considered native to Ireland, and yet the possibility that their arrival was aided by man cannot be ruled out. This is because remains of these species cannot be found in Ireland past a certain point in time, thereby implying that they were not here before being introduced by human settlers. In the case of both the red squirrel and the red deer, it seems they were present here for a time, became extinct and then repopulated Ireland after being reintroduced by man. It's even possible that some of our mammals were brought here as far back as the Stone Age to fill the forests with food for early human hunters (the wild boar being a good example).

We don't know a huge amount about Ireland's Ice Age people, other than they probably followed herds of migrating reindeer across the vast plains of Pleistocene Europe. Ireland's Stone Age people, on the other hand, left more evidence behind them. It is from this that we start to draw a picture of life in Ireland as it was lived by these early human arrivals.

The Mesolithic people of Ireland had not yet mastered metal or cultivation. But they still possessed an array of sophisticated technologies that enabled them to make the most of every resource available. Chief among these was their mastery of stone tools. Flint, which could be deftly hacked and shaped into fine blades, was particularly prized. Antrim was an attractive spot to these early Irishmen and women, with plentiful flint to fashion their tools from. But as the first people spread out across the country, they often found flint in short supply, so had to broaden their repertoire to include other stone cores from which they could create their axe heads and spear points. With these weapons they were equipped to tackle almost every prey they came across, from trout and salmon in the rivers to the wild boar that thrived in Ireland's post-glacial forests.

They would have woven intricate clothing from the pelts of the animals they killed, necessary insulation in the cold Irish climate. Animal hides would also have been stretched over primitive wooden structures to provide extra warmth for those sleeping inside. Of course, fire would have been another essential tool in their arsenal, a safeguard against the chill of the night and a crucible for cooking food and twilight storytelling. Surely, this was one of the few comforts in what must have been a very tough existence.

We know next to nothing about the language in which these fireside tales were told. (For most of its inhabited history, Irish was not spoken in Ireland; the language would only start developing with the coming of the Celts less than 3,000 years ago. The English language would arrive even later, with the Anglo-Normans, less than 900 years ago.) The gods they prayed to, and what they did to appease them, are likewise a mystery to us. It is thought they might have decorated themselves with red ochre, a natural pigment. Eagle bones found at Mount Sandel suggest the feathers of these great birds of prey were also used as ornamentation. Clearly, these people weren't too wrapped up in the struggle to live not to care for cosmetics from time to time.

Many of their tools and artefacts would have been made of perishable materials such as wood, and so tragically have withered away in acidic Irish soils. Nevertheless, there are many things we can discern about how they lived. Not yet having the permanency of a pastoral lifestyle, these people were nomadic, wandering to wherever the pickings were richest. It's believed they lived in family groups like most nomadic peoples still do today. They would usually set up camp close to a water source – be it a river, lake or the sea, for the latter offered a rich bounty of fish, shellfish and seaweed that would have been accessible throughout the year. Fish would have been caught using harpoons, nets and intricately woven traps. These people were keenly attuned to the seasons and the different bounties that each had to offer, from the glut of bird eggs in spring to the rich harvest of berries and nuts in autumn. Nothing went to waste.

As such, they were well equipped to get all the sustenance they needed from a forested landscape. And as the Ice Age gave way, forest was one commodity that ancient Ireland had in abundance.

15

To a Forest Primeval: Ireland's Lost Woodlands

E very autumn, the forests of Killarney National Park resonate to a deep, guttural roar. The bellow rises in pitch to the point where its maker sounds almost in pain to expel it. Yet persist he does, for silence would only clear the airwaves for his rivals to fill with their own calls. The largest of Ireland's forest denizens is ready to rut once again.

For months, the red deer stags of Killarney have been preparing for the annual autumnal rut. Antlers, fed on rich forest foliage, are now at their peak. Calcium has been siphoned from their bones and channelled into their crowning glory, branching out up to ninety centimetres from their skulls. The stags' manes, embracing their bulky necks, are at full size. Their testosterone levels have peaked, and with it their raw aggression. At up to 225 kilogrammes apiece, they have attained their maximum weight. They are by far the heaviest land animal left in the wild in Ireland.

What results is undoubtedly one of our great wildlife spectacles. Competing stags thrash the undergrowth and rip up grass with their antlers, festooning their tines with vegetation to augment their visual splendour. Splotches of mud add a layer of war-paint to their attire. The stag then shatters the serenity of the forest with his unmistakable roar. Once one starts, others soon take up the challenge until the ruckus of roaring stags drowns out the usual forest patter. The roar of the red deer is adapted specifically to its forest home, a low bellow that penetrates the undergrowth as effectively as the high-pitched bugle of the elk, its North American counterpart, floats over desolate hillsides and prairies. The effect, of course, is the same: to draw the females, the hinds, to the most appealing stags. The stronger the stag, the deeper and louder his roar. A hierarchy is not long forming, with the most impressive males commanding the largest harems.

Usually, their size alone is enough to dissuade any challengers. But inevitably, evenly matched males will coalesce on a harem, and a shouting match will not be enough to settle the matter. This is when the climax of the contest between the stags arrives, as the males lock antlers and duke it out for supremacy. Suddenly, the roaring dissipates as the sound of antlers crashing into each other echoes through the park. The vanquished loser is chased from the scene. Triumphant, the victorious male struts back to his harem, cementing his supremacy with a roar. He resumes his vigil, calm yet ever watchful, ready to see off any other challengers that might emerge from the undergrowth. Undoubtedly, there are echoes here of the titanic tussles that played out on Ireland's Ice Age plains, thousands of years before.

The toll of doing all this is devastating on their bodies. Stags can lose up to 20 per cent of their weight during the rutting months alone, such is the precedence that mating takes over food and other maintenance. The undoubted cost of all this spectacle is the culling of the weaker stags. But the reward for the victors is a priceless opportunity to mate, a chance that might come around once in a lifetime – and, for many red deer stags, never at all.

There was a time when the rutting of Ireland's native red deer could be enjoyed right across the country. The fact that it's now largely confined to Killarney is a stark reminder of the decline of our primeval woodlands over the centuries – and what we have lost in the process.

Ireland's Mesolithic people lived in a heavily wooded landscape. At their height, Ireland's forests covered 80 per cent of the landscape. This primeval Irish forest was broken only by lakes, bogs and the peaks of the highest mountains. It was even said a squirrel could cross from coast to coast without needing to descend to the ground. You could traverse the island without emerging from the shade of this vast, temperate rainforest.

Ancient as they were, the forests of Ireland did not reach that far back into antiquity. They certainly weren't here at the end of the last Ice Age, when the giant deer grazed a largely treeless landscape broken perhaps by the occasional juniper or dwarf willow. But as Europe warmed, and the ice went into its final retreat, trees that had clung on in isolated refugia across Europe started to advance northwards.

Eventually the spreading trees would reach Ireland, probably by way of residual land bridges with Britain that were eventually severed as sea levels continued to rise. Some seeds were carried here by animals; others – such as those of the willow and birch – were so light that they might have been borne on the wind. Among the first trees to reach Ireland after the Ice Age ended was the hardy birch. Together with willows and junipers, they started to coalesce into the first post-glacial Irish woodlands, slowly transforming an otherwise open landscape. Juniper, that hardy holdover from colder times, eventually found itself muscled out.

A tree is an ecosystem all of its own – and birch was no exception. Wherever birch trees went, they brought a whole retinue of fungi with them. Birch is home to more fungi species than any other native Irish tree. They played a vital role in digesting and delaminating rotting trees when they died, in turn releasing more nutrients back into the soil. With this, earthworms, insects and microbes could flourish.

"A squirrel could cross from coast to coast without needing to descend to the ground."

In time, this process boosted the organic content of the soil enough for other trees to colonise Ireland. After the birch came the hardy Scots pine, our redoubtable native conifer, capable of holding its own in all climates and soil types. Soon after came the catalogue of broadleaved trees that would form the backbone of Irish forests for millennia to come: hazel, then elm and of course the mighty oak. Ironically, this next wave would spell doom for the pioneering birch that helped make their colonisation of Ireland possible to begin with. Oaks and elms are ravenous for sunlight, and soon choke up every available inch of space, forming an impenetrable canopy. Birch, however, cannot thrive in the shade, and so the tree that led the broadleaved charge into Ireland found itself increasingly squeezed out of the picture.

One by one, the arrival of other tree species – alder, ash, hawthorn and wild cherry to name a few – would fill out the native flora that made up Ireland's indigenous woodlands. The oaks and other broadleaved giants formed the forest canopy, while beneath them, smaller trees like holly and hazel made up the understorey. Closer to the ground was a herb layer of ferns and flowers, flourishing in the shade and constant humidity created by the towering giants. A carpet of moss on the forest floor completed the picture. In the millennia that followed, more trees (as well as animals) would be introduced to augment the forests we still see today. Sycamore and beech, for instance, probably arrived with the help of man in the seventeenth century.

Within 2,000 years of the Ice Age coming to an end, an open treeless landscape had become a vast, verdant woodland. It was a remarkably speedy transformation – too fast, in fact, to be accomplished by trees alone. Unassisted, trees advance very slowly; a forest can only manage to expand at less than half a kilometre a year under its own steam. It must have had help. A retinue of woodland creatures must have assisted the spread of Ireland's forests – many of which are still with us today.

Every autumn, as green leaves fade to bronze and gold, the forest floor is bombarded with acorns. A single oak tree can release thousands of them. This is the moment the jay has been waiting for. Easily one of our most resplendent woodland birds, it sets to work stashing away enough acorns to last it through the winter. It can carry away up to nine acorns at a time in its throat crop, ferrying them off to a burial site. This can be over ten kilometres away from where the jay found them. A single jay can hide over 5,000 a season. Not only does it have to recall where all of these are buried, but also make sure other acorn aficionados don't dig them up. All this speaks to the remarkable intelligence of these birds, an intellect we're only now beginning to comprehend.

There are acorns aplenty for mammals as well. Jays are joined in this endeavour by red squirrels, one of the most charismatic denizens of our woodlands. Like jays, squirrels also stash acorns to help them outlast the winter, which they spend in nests – drays – high in the canopy. Supremely agile, the red squirrel is perfectly adapted to life in the trees. The joint between the ankle and the heel allows it to turn its feet through 180 degrees without moving its legs, helping it ascend or descend a trunk headfirst. Fatty deposits at the base of the feet act as shock absorbers for leaps of up to two metres between branches, steered by that long, bushy tail. In the early months of the year, the male must employ these tools as he pursues the female on a breathless courtship chase through the treetops.

For millennia, the jays and the red squirrels divided the oak's bounty between them. Inevitably, though, there were some stashes that were overlooked, forgotten in their sequestered bunkers beneath the leaf-litter. But this was no wasted crop; the buried acorns were able to germinate, aiding the spread of Ireland's ancestral forests year on year. As much as the woodland critters depended on the oaks, the oaks depended upon them.

In more recent times, our native red squirrel has found itself sharing its woodland demesne with the grey squirrel, its more robust cousin from North America. The grey squirrel first arrived in Irish woodlands in the early twentieth century, having been imported for its luxuriant silver fur. But the tenacious greys soon escaped their captors and, in Ireland's remaining forests, found a haven much to their liking. Whereas the lightweight red squirrel is more adept in the canopy, the grey squirrel is at ease foraging on the ground. The grey is now the most common squirrel across much of Ireland. It has a more varied diet than the red squirrel, being able to digest unripe acorns. Sadly, this has come at the expense of our red squirrel. Outcompeted by the bulkier grey squirrel, and less immune to squirrel pox carried by its cousin, the red has gone into decline. This is also to the detriment of the forests as a whole; with its penchant for buds and bark, the grey squirrel does more damage to trees than the red.

It's not just in autumn that the oaks and other deciduous trees have food to offer. Living or dead, native trees play host to hundreds of species of insects and arachnids, from the caterpillars that graze on their leaves to the beetles and grubs boring through rotten wood. These, coupled with the nuts and berries offered by the catalogue of woodland plants, provide a feast for forest birds. The woodpigeon is among the largest. It's a true vegetarian at heart, dining on acorns, hazelnuts, beech mast and the flowers of deciduous trees.

Smaller birds have learned to divide the forest's bounty among themselves. The treecreeper, hard to see unless it moves, ascends the trunk vertically, probing crevices with its curved beak for invertebrate prey. Goldcrests (our smallest species) pirouette about the finer twigs in their pursuit of food, a sector they share with coal, blue and long-tailed tits. The larger great tit is excluded from this behaviour by its weight, and so forages further down – including on the ground, where it often keeps company with finches. They have developed an extraordinary array of beaks to deal with the diverse food sources that flourish in the woodland, from the bulky bud-cracker of the bullfinch to the fine, conical bill of the siskin, adept at prying alder seeds from their cones.

The wren finds the bulk of its invertebrate prey at or close to the ground, where its short wings and rounded body let it negotiate the tangled mass of roots and crannies with an ease few other birds can match. The great spotted woodpecker, meanwhile, uses its chisel-like beak and enormously long tongue to extract grubs from beneath the tree bark, a food source beyond the reach of other forest birds.

It is these creatures – some of the forest's smallest inhabitants – that give it voice. Every spring, Ireland's native woodlands come alive with birdsong as the males of different species jostle to establish their territories. Prized real estate is much sought after, and so competition is intense. Our songbirds number among the most boldly marked creatures in the forest, and the males often perch prominently to display their colours with pride. Genetic vigour is writ large in the brilliance of a bullfinch's scarlet breast or the thickness of a great tit's black stripes. In such a tangled and claustrophobic space as this, though, sound is the most effective way of making their presence known – both to females in search of a mate and to rival males. A male that can sing for extended periods has both energy and access to a prime territory full of food. He is also brave enough to betray his location to predators in the forest. All of these attributes mark him out as a suitable mate.

Unlike our voices, which stem from the larynx, bird song emanates from another organ called the syrinx set much deeper in their body. The twin pipes splintering off from this into the bird's lungs can be opened and closed separately, allowing their owner to produce contrasting notes at the same time – with incredible speed. The wren, for instance, can fire out thirty notes a second. This ability, and a brain designed to orchestrate the complicated muscle modulations needed to moderate their vocal apparatus, leads to the extraordinary diversity of birdsong to be heard in an Irish forest. Our woodlands are home to some truly powerful songsters. For its size, the wren produces the loudest noise of any Irish bird; ounce for ounce, its trilling song is ten times more powerful than the crow of a rooster.

This fuses with a myriad of other bird calls to form the dawn chorus, a symphony of interwoven avian melody permeating the undergrowth. Dawn is too cold for most insects to take wing – and too dark to see them – and so makes a poor time to go foraging. The layer of cool air still hugging the earth also makes a fantastic conduit for sound, helping birdsong penetrate further through the tangled mass of branches.

Larger creatures make their home here too. In most Irish woodlands now, the biggest browser is the fallow deer. The red is the only native deer we have – but from the Middle Ages on, it found itself sharing its woodland home with the fallow. Unlike the rapier-sharp tines that surmount the head of a rutting red, fallow deer produce more palmated antlers – like those of the giant Irish deer, but in microcosm. Every year, a fallow stag uses his prominent Adam's apple to produce the guttural belch with which he declares his dominance during the rut. The forests and glens of Dublin's Phoenix Park are a good place to enjoy this natural drama.

Other large herbivores once roamed our woodlands as well. Deer might have browsed the leaves and stripped saplings of their bark, but the tantalising array of food (roots, tubers, fungus) beneath the forest floor provided a feast for the wild boar. These pigs are a staple of woodlands across Europe – and before being hunted to extinction as late as the twelfth century, they could be found rummaging their way through Ireland's woodlands too. The boar was once very common here, traversing the forest in matriarchal family groups called 'sounders'. Like the mammoths thousands of years before them, these would have been led by the eldest female. Boars are natural diggers. A head that accounts for up to a third of the animal's bodyweight is perfect for shoving aside soil, and tusks up to twelve centimetres long in the males make short work of any food (animal or plant) unearthed. They'll eat almost anything – acorns, nuts worms – but are especially fond of truffles, which grow on the roots of oak trees stretching out under the soil, a food source that few other forest creatures can tap into. Weighing in at over 100 kilogrammes, Ireland's wild boars would have been a daunting proposition for all but the largest woodland predators. Where stags had their antlers, wild boars had their armour; a special layer of tissue up to three centimetres thick beneath the skin, designed to shield their organs from the tusks of rival males.

Herbivores of this size would have exerted a big impact on the forest, acting as natural gardeners. By clearing away understorey in their search for food, they served as ecological engineers, opening up space for other plants and animals

to exploit, while preventing the vegetation from becoming overgrown. Their constant shifting of the earth helped recycle nutrients in the soil, feeding into the constant cycle of decay and rejuvenation that defined all of life in Ireland's forests. This process also created convenient pockmarks and trenches for acorns to tumble into and germinate.

Although it might have appeared a ubiquitous blanket of foliage to untrained eyes, Ireland's forests were more diverse than they first appeared. For one thing, the country was not entirely dominated by deciduous woodland. Conifers, in the form of the indomitable Scots pine, colonised Ireland too. They managed to form woodlands of their own – and once housed a natural spectacle which is now sadly lost to us. Where our broadleaved woods still have the autumnal chaos of rutting red deer, Ireland's conifer forests once played host to the bizarre mating ritual of the capercaillie.

It's a sight that can still be enjoyed in isolated pockets of the Scottish Highlands to this day. Every breeding season, the pine forests of the Cairngorms National Park resonate to one of the most bizarre calls in the animal kingdom: the deep, percussive clucking of the male capercaillie. He holds his ivory bill aloft and fans his tale, hoping to entice females to a coupling. The bristling black feathers on his neck add to his splendour. Occasionally, he'll have to put paid to the designs of other males. Then, the ivory bill finds use as a weapon as the two rivals fight it out to the rhythm of beating wings.

Capercaillie are enormous birds; the males are almost the size of a turkey. The females, though somewhat less striking in stature, are no less boldly marked. Indeed, with their complex coat of mottled browns, some would say they are more attractive. While the glossy black plumage of the males is mostly for show, the females' more modest uniform is designed to keep them (and their chicks) hidden on the forest floor.

Although proud and boisterous in the breeding season, capercaillies are retiring throughout the rest of the year. They are a bird that needs specific conditions in which to thrive, favouring Scots pine forests with a healthy understorey of woody species such as bilberry. This provides the shoots, buds and berries the bird feeds on. Tragically, such fare is in very short supply in modern Ireland. From the Bronze Age onwards, Ireland's pine forests went through a long period of almost continuous decline, climaxing during the plantations of Tudor and Jacobean rule. By the end of the 1700s, they had almost completely disappeared – and the capercaillie with them.

With so much prey, it's inevitable that Ireland's forests are home to predators as well. For the myriad of small songbirds, the great fear is the sparrowhawk. Of all Ireland's birds of prey, it is by far the best adapted to hunting amid the undergrowth. Short, rounded wings provide excellent manoeuvrability among the leaves and branches. These can be folded in close to the bird's body to avoid obstruction as the sparrowhawk slips between gaps in the trees. The bird is further aided in this endeavour by its long tail, a versatile natural rudder. This can be fanned or closed with ease, allowing for quick directional changes – vital in a frantic chase through the bushes. Long, thin legs and toes give maximum reach for grabbing prey on the wing, even reaching through dense foliage if need be. Its plumage also plays a part in the hunt; a dark back helps conceal the sparrowhawk in the shadow of the trees, while a barred chest and belly helps break up its outline among the leaves and twigs of the forest.

The sparrowhawk uses the vegetation to maximum advantage: the crags and branches of the trees provide plentiful cover for an ambush. These can shield its approach right up until the final, frantic pounce. Sometimes, the sparrowhawk will even mimic the flight of a woodpigeon, disguising itself in plain sight as it closes in. The tits, finches and other avian songsters on which the sparrowhawk feeds have evolved to counter this. Each has a song all of its own. Once the predator is sighted, however, they emit a short, high-pitched warning call, a signal that transcends species. That's the cue for the forest birds to silence themselves and take cover until the threat passes.

The attributes that make the sparrowhawk such a menace in our forests to this day once served its larger cousin, the goshawk, just as well. This magnificent raptor is almost identical to the sparrowhawk in form – but swollen to twice the size. While the sparrowhawk usually contents itself with prey up to the size of a blackbird, the powerful goshawk can take out birds larger than a pigeon.

"There was a time when even the most formidable red stag couldn't sleep in safety."

The sparrowhawk might have survived the persecution of Ireland's raptors in ages past, but sadly the magnificent goshawk did not. In medieval Ireland it was prized as a falconer's bird, and this status helped keep it safe for a time. But once this pastime fell out of fashion, and Ireland's woodlands went more and more into retreat, our forests were sadly shorn of their apex avian predator.

Forest denizens also have to contend with mammalian killers. Our two squirrel species are rivalled for sheer agility by their great nemesis, the pine marten. It is unquestionably one of the most attractive mammals we have, with chocolate brown uppers giving way to a cream-coloured chest and belly.

The nimble pine marten is more than capable of tormenting all manner of small prey in the forest, from raiding birds' nests to pouncing on squirrels when they descend to the forest floor.

The pine marten has taken to the trees better than any other mustelid (weasel). Alone among the family, it has semi-retractable claws. These, along with large paws with hair between the pads, help it find purchase on the smoothest branches. A long, bushy tail provides a counter balance for all manner of arboreal acrobatics. The athletic marten can leap nearly four metres between branches, making it the only mustelid capable of pursuing squirrels through the canopy. Even if it falls, the marten can land on its feet from heights of up to twenty metres. Though adept at scaling branches, the pine marten makes most of its kills on the ground.

Squirrels and songbirds might live in constant fear, but there is nothing in Ireland's remaining patches of woodland to threaten our forest deer today. This was not always so. There was a time when even the most formidable red stag couldn't sleep in safety. For Ireland's ancient forests were home to yet another predator, one that had survived the extremes of the Ice Age and flourished in this forested new Eden.

The grey wolf is among the most adaptable apex predators in the world today, at home in a huge range of habitats from arid tundra to dense woodland. The reindeer, muskox and wild horses of Pleistocene Ireland might have been long gone, but in the wild boar and plentiful deer of Ireland's new forests, our wolves found a more than adequate substitute. With such game at their disposal, the wolf was able to thrive here as the top native predator. Hares and even rodents, like rats and mice, might have been on the menu too.

Ireland's forests had a diverse cast of mammalian predators. Dogs, weasels and bears were all represented, the brown bear having survived the end of the Ice Age and adapted well to a changing Irish landscape. But what of that other great clan of mammalian carnivores, the cats? Thanks to a few remarkable bones retrieved from a cave in County Waterford, we know that they had a presence here too.

As the ferocious Ice Age felines perished along with the open habitat they once reigned over, the title of top cat in the new, forested Europe passed to the lynx. Ireland was certainly part of its domain. Lynx remains are rare here; the cat did not take to caves as often as bears or wolves, and so its bones often withered in the acidic soil. It's possible, though, that this graceful predator had a presence in our woodlands right up until historical times. In a forest filled with impressive beasts, it would have been among the most striking; a fearsome face crowned with piercing eyes, framed in a dual pair of ruffs like the blades of a double-headed axe. Its silvery coat was peppered with black spots to help break up its outline in the undergrowth. Indeed, the Eurasian lynx has a more variable pelage than any other cat. This, and its supreme adaptability, once helped it range far and wide across the wooded expanse of Eurasia.

A solitary hunter, the lynx would have been a master of moving unseen through the trees. Like a shadow incarnate, it would have cleaved to the dark recesses of the forest, cover from which to surprise a passing hare or deer. The low light of dawn and dusk undoubtedly helped it stay hidden. Where wolves are pursuit predators, lynx – like most cats – are masters of the stalk and pounce. They can crouch motionless for hours at a time, waiting for the perfect moment to strike. Strong legs would have helped it leap up to three metres onto struggling prey, before dispatching it with a suffocating bite to the throat. Its spring-loaded back legs would also have helped it jump onto any larger birds that descended to the forest floor, or poach them mid-air as they tried to escape. Lynx are exceptionally powerful cats; they can bring down prey four times their size. Even smaller predators, like foxes, might have been in their sights.

Given the dearth of lynx remains, we can't say for certain when this magnificent cat met its end in Ireland. The decline of our wolves, though, is much better documented – and altogether more tragic. In it is reflected the fate of Ireland's primeval wilderness as a whole.

Eventually, the human hunters and gatherers of Ireland's ancient forests began to settle down. Campsites became permanent. Homesteads grew into villages and towns. With the Neolithic (New Stone Age) came the first forest clearances, as space was needed for farming and human habitation. Over the millennia that followed, the trees started to recede. With them went the habitat that the wolves – and a whole host of other woodland creatures – depended on. By 1600, Ireland's dense woodland cover was reduced to around one-eighth of the island.

It was from this point on that Ireland's wolves started to come under systematic persecution, the likes of which they had never had to endure before. This was when the wholesale arrival of new people into Ireland brought with them new attitudes about both the wolves and the forests that sheltered them. To the native Gaelic Irish, the wolf was an integral part of the Irish landscape, another thread in the rich tapestry that made up the island's native fauna. While the nobility practiced wolf hunting, this was done for recreation rather than eradication. As a result, wolves remained plentiful in Ireland right through the Middle Ages when they were rapidly disappearing from much of the rest of Europe.

The waves of English and Scottish settlers that started arriving with successive plantations, however, took a different view. Coming from an island largely robbed of its wolves, they were shocked to find the animal still in such abundance in Ireland. Wolves, after all, were a threat to settlers and their livestock. And the remaining forests of Ireland were a bastion not just for wolves but for native rebels who might have notions of reclaiming their lost lands. Profit played a part as much as preservation; in Ireland's oak forests, the new arrivals saw a huge potential export. Timber was needed for ships, buildings and barrels; charcoal for furnaces; tree bark for making leather.

Thus began, almost in tandem, a major phase of both deforestation and a concerted effort to eliminate Ireland's wolves. By the end of the seventeenth century, the remaining forests of Ireland were largely cleared to the point where, by 1711, a once verdant wooded landscape was left denuded. From 1600–1800, Ireland's

"Centuries of clearance and harvesting have taken a heavy toll. Ireland is now one of the least forested countries in Europe."

[172]

forest cover fell from around one-eighth of the country to only one-fiftieth. Some was cleared for farming, some for export to England and Wales. The densest growth was simply burned to rob any rebels of a potential hideout.

As for the wolves, bounties placed on their killing, coupled with the introduction of professional wolf-hunters and organised hunts, saw them eliminated from county after county as the eighteenth century progressed. Their population ebbed and flowed with the horrific wars that rocked Ireland from 1500 onwards, when the surplus of unburied bodies provided a feast for the wolves. With subsequent persecutions, and the devastation of their woodland home, however, the last wolves of Ireland increasingly found themselves forced into the hills until the very last one was shot on Mount Leinster, County Carlow, in 1786.

Ireland's forests have not gone the way of the wolf. But centuries of clearance and harvesting have taken a heavy toll. Ireland is now one of the least forested countries in Europe. Although tree cover accounts for around 11 per cent of our land surface, less than 2 per cent is native woodland. The rest is mostly non-native forestry, consisting of conifers such as Sitka spruce that can thrive in poor soils and reach maturity faster than deciduous trees. These alien woods are no haven for wildlife. Instead, they form a dark, impenetrable void where little understorey – and precious few animals – can thrive. In this coniferous abyss, birdsong can be a rare commodity.

The end of Ireland's primeval forests, however, was not the end for life in Ireland. As the woodlands were pared back, they would find themselves inevitably replaced by farms – and all of the wild creatures that came with them.

16

Life in the Long Grass: Ireland's Farms

From deep within the nettles at the edge of a grassy pasture, a male corncrake begins his long vigil. Having found himself an ideal spot, he starts yammering away in the relentless *crex crex* from which his species derives its Latin name. The sound is easily one of the most unique made by any Irish animal. It was once as foundational to the soundscape of the Irish farm as the roar of the red deer was to the fabric of our forests.

The male corncrake may lack the imposing stature of the red deer stag – but his aptitudes are no less impressive. He has travelled all the way from equatorial Africa to stake his claim to a patch of farm on the banks of the Shannon. For a creature his size, the potency of his voice is amazing. The call of the corncrake can reach up to 100 decibels. By way of comparison, any sound above ninety decibels can lead to chronic hearing damage in humans. It's so loud that the male corncrakes developed a special reflex to protect their own hearing. Every time the male opens his mouth wide, exposing his pink gullet with his cry, the tension in his ear drum changes, temporarily reducing his own hearing to save it from any long-term damage. He might have to repeat it more than 20,000 times each night to draw every female within earshot to him for an ephemeral coupling. And in this treeless expanse dominated by nettles, wildflowers and silverweed, it rings out like a siren to the females. They can hear it up to one-and-a-half kilometres away. Not to be outdone, the other males within earshot also take up his challenge. Soon the field is replete with *creck*ing.

This chorus was once the harbinger of warm days in rural Ireland. Summer had arrived on the farm once again.

The days of Ireland's hunter-gatherers drawing their sustenance from the forests and rivers were not to last. Farming, the domestication of plants and animals for food that began in the Fertile Crescent of west Asia, eventually swept through Europe and found its way to Irish shores. This would have a transformative effect on Ireland's landscapes – and its animals.

It began with the introduction of cattle and cereals on the island. Cattle have been here for over 6,000 years. They would go on to form a cornerstone of Irish life for centuries. Gaelic chieftains measured their wealth in cattle, and cattle-raiding was among the most common forms of Celtic warfare. The trails that preceded Ireland's first roads were likely worn by farmers herding their cattle – and soldiers coming to steal them. *Bó*, the Irish word for cattle, lends itself to *bóthar*, meaning road. Agriculture has affected our genetics as much as our language. The fact that the Irish are the most lactose

"No other development in human history has had a bigger impact on Ireland's landscape than agriculture."

tolerant people on Earth speaks to the influence that farming has had here. It has shaped not only the landscapes of Ireland, but also its inhabitants.

The first farmland in Ireland may just have been natural clearings repurposed for grazing or growing edible plants. But as the population grew, more and more trees were felled to make way for an agrarian lifestyle. From the onset of farming in the fourth millennium BC, it took around 2,000 years to transition from a population of hunters and gatherers to one that depended on farming for its food. By 3,500 years ago, Ireland's people derived most of their sustenance from farming.

This has remained the case right up until the present day. Over millennia, the different groups that settled in Ireland added their own twists to the farming process. Pigs, sheep and goats joined the myriad of Irish farm animals during the Bronze Age. Innovations to the wooden plough around 1,500 years ago allowed for more of the land to be turned over to arable farming. The Normans, who arrived from the twelfth century on, introduced haymaking. The list of grains cultivated by early farmers gradually grew to include barley, wheat, oats and rye (the potato, that signature Irish crop, wouldn't arrive until the late 1500s).

From the 1700s on, hedgerows began to be used to divide fields more often than stone walls. Initially they were made up of thorny species such as hawthorn and blackthorn, designed to keep livestock contained. Soon, though, they would be joined by nettles, docks and a host of scrambling plants such as ivy and bramble, creating a haven for all kinds of wildlife. Hedgerows provided uncultivated refuges on the edges of fields, corridors for creatures to move through and shelter in which they could dig their burrows or build nests.

No other development in human history has had a bigger impact on Ireland's landscape than agriculture. More than 70 per cent of our land area is now used for farming, and scarcely a square kilometre of our countryside has not been grazed or cultivated at one time or another. Undoubtedly, the substitution of forests for farms was to the detriment of some species. It was likely for the protection of their livestock (and themselves) that Ireland's early farmers exterminated the brown bear, our largest native predator. But the new world that emerged also offered unprecedented opportunities for other creatures.

The corncrake was undoubtedly one of these. This is not a species that can readily thrive in dense woodland. Instead, the hay fields and rough pasture that followed in the wake of felled forests made for ideal spaces from which male corncrakes could croak – and female corncrakes could seek out the slugs, spiders and other invertebrates on which to feed their young.

The corncrake was certainly not the only beneficiary of this. It shared the Irish farms of yesteryear with another agricultural specialist, the corn bunting. This streaky songbird was once a common sight on farms across the country, where its thick, notched bill made short work of any grains left behind by the harvest. Perching prominently on a fence or hedge, its distinctive jangling song formed one of the signature sounds of spring about the farm. For years the corn bunting shared Irish farms with its more colourful cousin, the yellowhammer. The male is one of the most resplendent birds about the farm, his rich canary yellow cut through with olive striping. This is another bird that thrives on agricultural land, gobbling up spilt grain after the harvest as well as blackberries and other fruits of the hedgerow.

More retiring species could also be found here. Among them was the grey partridge, crawling silently along like an animate cowpat. Unlike the corncrake, the partridge was resident throughout the year. Where the male corncrake had his call, the male partridge relied on the rich chestnut colouring of his chest – augmenting his orange head and grey uppers – to entice a mate. In another contrast between the species, partridges are social animals, moving about the fields in family groups called coveys. A mated pair is joined by their offspring and other adults who failed to breed that season. Not having the security of a nest mounted high in a tree or hedge, partridge chicks are precocial. They're able to follow their parents around the fields within an hour of being born. Many inevitably succumb to the jaws or talons of predators. Cold and wet weather, and a shortage of insects on which to feed the chicks, can also take their share. To compensate, partridges have lots of offspring; clutches of fifteen eggs or more are common.

Since the 1500s, the native gamebirds of Ireland's countryside have had to share their domain with an altogether larger resident: the pheasant. Pheasants were introduced from Asia as an ideal quarry for hunting. Since then, they have become one of the iconic birds of the Irish countryside. The male is, without doubt, one of the most handsome birds we now have, possessing a shimmering plumage of rich reds, chestnuts and greens. His two-note cry travels far and wide across the countryside, as if compensating for the receding calls of other farmland birds that have since gone into retreat. Among them is the distinctive, three-note 'wet my lips' call of the quail, the pheasant's smaller, native cousin. Once a regular summer visitor to cereal fields, potato plots and rough pasture across the country, like the corncrake, the quail abjured tree cover in favour of more open spaces. Here it could keep itself hidden among the strands of wheat and long grass, feeding on the bounty of seeds and insects the fields had to offer. Were it not for their call, a farmer might not even have known his field was crawling with quail.

Corncrakes, partridges and quail spend the bulk of their time on the ground. But the farms of Ireland have also been the traditional preserve of aerial acrobats. Among them is another long-distant migrant that travels here to make its summertime abode: the swallow.

While the opening up of the countryside made it ideal for the gamebirds, the peppering of that countryside with farms and sheds provided ideal nesting conditions for the swallow. Beams bisecting the barn ceiling, or right angles where the wall meets the roof, offer foundations onto which a nest of mud can be fixed. A furnishing of feathers and dried grass then provides bedding in which the female can lay her eggs.

Swallows are insectivores, using their astonishing speed and agility to poach their prey on the wing. Their forked tail is a huge asset in this, opening and closing to help steer rapid twists and turns. The explosion of insects in the Irish countryside in summer allows swallow pairs to speedily rear two or even three broods in a good season. Once fledged, the young swallows join their parents in darting about the farm, honing their flight skills in preparation for one of the most astonishing migratory feats of any Irish animal: the biannual cross-continental flight of the swallow. It's a gruelling, 10,000-kilometre journey that sees them cross the Mediterranean, the Sahara Desert and the steamy rainforests of the Congo before arriving in their wintering grounds in Southern Africa. The inhospitable sands of the Sahara offer the greatest threat along this mammoth journey. Swallows can lose more than half their weight traversing between hemispheres each year. If wind conditions aren't favourable, mass casualties are not unheard of. But those that do return show remarkable loyalty to the same farms each year. Forty-four per cent of swallows use the exact same nest year after year – phenomenal considering the distance they have covered to do so.

Swallows are only temporary visitors to farms across the country. Other birds make for year-round residents of our rural landscapes, none more evidently than the corvids (crows). Of all the families of Irish birds, few have adapted more readily to human habitation than the crows. A keen intellect – among the sharpest of any bird – and varied diet undoubtedly helped in this endeavour. Today, they are ubiquitous on farms across Ireland, and their cawing forms an ever-present chorus.

Among the most common farmland crows are the jackdaw (the smallest of the lot), the ragged rook – distinct with its bare grey face – and the robust hooded crow, with its plumage of contrasting grey and black. All three manage to find plenty of food about the farm without competing. While the short, conical beak of the jackdaw is adept at harvesting seeds and grubs from the surface of the fields, the longer bill of the rook lets it unearth animal and plant matter from below the soil. Pasture is perfect for rooks, which like short grass and moist soil in which to find their invertebrate prey. Meanwhile, the stronger bill of the hooded crow makes it an accomplished scavenger. It's able to deal with any carrion it finds about the farm, from roadkill to dead livestock.

Ireland's farmland, though, is not the sole preserve of birds. The open, grassy landscape that predominates in rural Ireland has space aplenty for mammals as well. Foremost among these is another introduced species, this one brought here by the Normans in Medieval times. In so doing, they ensured haymaking was not their sole legacy in the Irish countryside. Protein was also needed and rabbits provided it.

Within 200 years of their introduction, rabbits spread out across Ireland. Agriculture – and the abundance of grassland that it provided – had created an ideal habitat for them. Man's animus towards predators (wolves, foxes, birds of prey) certainly helped as well. There are now thought to be up to 13 million of them in the wild, and they are a routine sight on farms across Ireland. Here they live in extensive burrow networks known as warrens. Rabbits are highly social, and so inevitably form pecking orders. Males and females compete separately for status among each other. Dominant males enjoy the most breeding rites, dominant females the most comfortable chambers within the warren.

They have a well-earned reputation for fertility. A female can conceive within twenty-four hours of giving birth to her previous litter. Up to seven litters a year are common. Many of these offspring, however, will not outlive their first year. Rabbits are prey for a host of predators about the farm. To combat this, they use ears that can move independently of each other to give them extensive sonic surveillance for any approaching threat from up to three kilometres away. Eyes on the sides of their head ensure only a direct approach will go unseen.

Rabbits are rivalled in their reproductive prowess by another mammalian inhabitant of Ireland's farms, the wood mouse. It makes its stronghold in the hedgerows that divide the fields. Here it finds the seeds, fungi and insects it likes to feed on, and it can excavate the network of tunnels it needs to cache food and avoid predators. The mouse is a much more ancient inhabitant of our countryside than the rabbit, having arrived here with Stone Age man as far back as the Mesolithic period. Since then, it has adapted well to Ireland's changing landscapes, its ubiquity making it a keystone species in farmland ecosystems. Given Ireland's relative paucity of small rodents, the wood mouse is an important food source for stoats, kestrels and other predators about the farm.

As tiny as they are, mice aren't the smallest mammalian inhabitants of our farmland hedgerows. That distinction belongs to the pygmy shrew, at just five centimetres long and weighing no more than a ten-cent piece. While mice (as with most rodents) will eat almost anything, the shrew is a strict insectivore. Its eyesight might be poor but its long, hypersensitive nose is adept at rooting out spiders, woodlice, beetles and other crawling delicacies in the leaf litter. It has to be. The shrew's tiny heart beats an astonishing 800 times a minute. With such a high metabolism, it has to eat its own

The grey wolf was hunted to extinction in Ireland in the eighteenth century.

Once a common farmland bird, the corncrake has now been largely reduced to enclaves on the Atlantic coast.

Rabbits first arrived in Ireland in the Middle Ages and can now be seen on farmland across the country.

Persecuted to extinction in the 1800s, the red kite was successfully reintroduced into Ireland in 2007.

The golden eagle. This magnificent raptor has been reintroduced into the mountains of Donegal.

Wheatears travel all the way from southern Africa to breed in the uplands of Ireland.

Curlews breed on Ireland's raised bogs. In recent decades, though, their numbers have plummeted.

The red fox is now a common sight in urban areas across Ireland.

The peregrine falcon, the fastest animal on Earth.

The hedgehog is one of the many creatures that now find their food in Irish gardens.

The fin whale, the second largest animal on the planet.

The basking shark, the biggest fish in the North Atlantic and a regular summer visitor to Ireland's Atlantic waters.

Razorbills. Every summer, thousands of these seabirds breed on coastal cliffs around Ireland.

The grey partridge, the subject of major conservation efforts at Lough Boora, County Offaly.

weight in food just to make it through the day – assuming it hasn't been picked off at that point. Fortunately for the shrew, secretions from its scent glands make it hard for most predators to stomach.

With so much game on Ireland's farms, it should come as no surprise that there are predators too. The short, broad wings of the sparrowhawk might predominate in tight, forested spaces, but in open, grassy fields, conditions are ripe for the kestrel. Facing into the wind, the kestrel hangs in the air with relentless patience, hovering above the fields for a mouse to betray itself in the grass below. All birds of prey have impeccable vision. The kestrel needs this to spot prey from up to sixty metres above the grass. It is further aided by eyes that can perceive ultraviolet light. The droplets of urine left by small mammals as they scurry through the pasture reflect this, betraying the location of their maker. Once it's latched onto its target, the kestrel falls to the ground in a staggered descent, readjusting its trajectory for the final pounce.

Although mice might live in fear of the kestrel, larger prey such as rabbits must worry about an altogether larger predator, the buzzard. Broad winged and barrel chested, it's very nearly twice the size of the kestrel. And while the kestrel is at home hovering, the buzzard is at its most iconic soaring, revealing undersides of mottled white and brown as it attracts the ire of rooks and hooded crows. Soaring takes only a twentieth of the energy required for powered flight, allowing the buzzard to survey its vast domain with minimal effort. When not circling the farm, the buzzard often lazes in a tree or on a fence post or telegraph pole, waiting to swoop upon a rabbit that has strayed too far from its burrow. As with the kestrel, exceptionally sharp eyesight helps in this regard. Your eyes have around 200,000 light-sensitive rods each. A buzzard's have a million, allowing their owner to pick out a rabbit in the pasture from more than three kilometres away. Buzzards are famously unfussy though, and will take almost anything they can overpower. Smaller birds about the farm are not spared its lethal attentions. Even worms are taken once they have been exposed by the plough.

Traditionally, the buzzard shared the Irish countryside with another medium-large raptor, the red kite. With its forked tail and rich russet plumage accented with black and silver, it strikes an impressive figure as it weaves over the fields on long pointed wings, shaped like a swallow writ large. Unlike the buzzard, the red kite is too weak-footed to take out large prey. Instead, this bird is a natural scavenger, drawn inexorably to death about the farm, be it a poisoned rat or a sheep downed by illness. The dismembered remains are then ferried back to the kite's nest, usually in a stand of trees fringing more open countryside – the ideal red kite combination.

"The barn owl is not a creature of the forest – and, therefore, not one to have taken to an Ireland before agriculture."

Poisoning (whether deliberate or accidental) was a major reason for the decline – and eventual extinction – of these magnificent birds of prey. Raptors were long regarded as pests, a menace to livestock about the farm. Red kites were (and, by some, still are) considered a threat to lambs. This, as well as active persecution at the point of a gun, saw the red kite extirpated from Ireland during the nineteenth century. The buzzard suffered the same fate, driven to extinction by the late 1890s.

Diurnal raptors like these might have held sway over the fields by day, but at night a different creature emerged to terrorise things that creep and scurry about the farm. The supreme predator of the Irish twilight is another bird of prey, one that has made an indelible impression on Irish folklore. Its haunting shriek once pierced the night sky nationwide, and may have provided a footing from which legends of the banshee could take wing: the barn owl.

Ireland has three owl species. The long-eared owl is the champion of the forest, the dominant habitat in an Ireland undamaged by man. Its close cousin, the short-eared owl, is a winter visitor to coastal heaths and sand dunes across the country. But the barn owl, as its name suggests, is quintessentially a bird of the farm. The pests that proliferate on farms provide it with a ready abundance of prey. And the lofts of barns and other rural outhouses make ideal nesting sites, only a short flight from the fields where the owls do the bulk of their hunting.

Like the gamebirds that populate the fields by day, the barn owl is not a creature of the forest – and, therefore, not one to have taken to an Ireland before agriculture. Its colonisation of Ireland likely came in the wake of farming. Felled trees might have displaced sparrowhawks, pine martens and even wolves, but the new habitat that emerged was ideal for the barn owl to practice its deadly speciality.

Every aspect of the barn owl's anatomy is honed to help it deliver silent death on the wing. Its ghastly white feathers are perfectly structured to minimise noise on approach. Its disk-shaped face forms a well-tuned funnel to shoehorn every rustle in the grass into the owl's ears. The asymmetrical positioning of the ears themselves – one faces out, while the other points to the ground – gives the owl a directional sense of hearing, among the most sensitive of any animal. This steers its talons to their target even in pitch darkness. With such equipment, a pair of barn owls can collect the more than 3,000 rodents they need to rear a brood every year.

Ireland's countryside is not the sole preserve of avian predators. The rabbits that populate our fields have another nemesis – a tiny menace only a tenth of their weight. It's among the most ancient mammals we have. And in the rabbit, it found a ready new source of prey as Ireland's wilderness began to be carved up into farmland: the Irish stoat.

For millennia since the end of the last Ice Age, Ireland's unique stoat had been terrorising the mice and shrews it shared our woodlands with. But from the Middle Ages on, the contest between stoat and rabbit has offered a microcosm of the once great mammalian hunts that played out on Ireland's Pleistocene plains – and one no less dramatic. The rabbit is now the stoat's main prey. Although the rabbit has strength and mass on its side, the wiry stoat is able to exhaust its victim over a long chase across the pasture. Then the stoat's agility comes into play; latching onto the rabbit's back, it's able to twist itself into position to deliver the killer blow, a fatal bite to the back of the neck. Even in their warrens the rabbits are not safe; equipped with the keen sense of smell needed to hunt in near darkness, the stoat is just as eager to take the chase underground.

There are, however, burrowing animals on Ireland's farms that a stoat would be foolish to cross – namely one of its own relatives. With its distinctive black-and-white mask, the badger is among our most iconic native mammals. Where rabbits have their warrens, the badger family has its sett, often entrenched in a hedgerow or at the edge of a field. This is usually shared by three to four adults and their young, who emerge at night to feed about the farm. Badgers can be formidable creatures. Males average around ten kilogrammes, and have the strength to contend with dogs much larger than themselves, as participants in the cruel sport of badger baiting have discovered over the years. Despite their raw power, the mainstay of their diet is the earthworms and other invertebrates to be found wriggling across the farm after dark. They can put away up to 200 earthworms a night. Badgers aren't fussy, though. Fruit will not go to waste, and sometimes even a soft young rabbit caught off guard isn't safe. Badgers in Ireland have adapted well to a landscape dominated by farming; over half of their setts are now to be found in hedgerows.

Agriculture carved out an ideal habitat for all of these creatures, but ironically, changing farming practices have now wrought a terrible toll on biodiversity. For millennia, farming in Ireland was relatively low intensity. This allowed for harmonious co-existence between farmers and the wildlife on their farms. All that would change, however, with the onset of more intensive farming methods in the twentieth century. In Ireland, this process would really kick into overdrive following the Second World War. Arable farming started to disappear. Agricultural grassland began to be managed more intensely. Damp pasture – a treasured breeding site for ground-nesting birds – was increasingly drained. Smaller land holdings would gradually find themselves subsumed into larger, more commercialised farms. Haymaking, a mainstay of Irish agricultural practice since medieval times, would be replaced by silage cutting. This meant earlier harvesting of grass, at enormous cost to the birds and other creatures nesting within it. And the widespread use of herbicides and insecticides deracinated the very roots of farmland ecosystems, destroying the foundation species on which so many others depended.

This process would also take a heavy toll on hedgerows, those vital highways for wildlife between the fields. As hedgerows found themselves replaced by wire, their utility exhausted itself in the eyes of many Irish farmers, and many of them were cut down. The need for larger and larger fields that could accommodate modern farm machinery also played a part in their destruction. As well as hedgerows, this has also spelt doom for grassy margins, those little pockets of wildness on the edges of fields.

The combined effects of all of this have been catastrophic for wildlife on the Irish farm. The corn bunting, once  omnipresent on farms around Ireland, became completely extinct as a breeding bird in the 1990s. Its cousin, the yellowhammer, has seen its numbers fall drastically with the decimation of hedgerows and decline of arable and mixed farming. The corncrake, whose cry once welcomed summer across our countryside, has been driven back to remote outposts on the north and west coasts. Many of these are islands where the soil is too shallow and rocky for modern, mechanised farming. The grey partridge, meanwhile, was devastated to such an extent that by the year 2000 there were as few as twenty wild birds left in the entire country. Our other native gamebird, the quail, has now become a rare summer visitor, restricted to a few holdouts in the Midlands.

Insects have suffered too. Ireland's agricultural grasslands once provided a perfect space for wildflowers – and for the butterflies and bees that fed on them. But the use of herbicides and pesticides, coupled with the ploughing of grasslands and gutting of hedgerows, has taken a heavy toll. Now, their numbers are in freefall; our butterfly population dropped by 12 per cent from 2009–2019. Farmland on poorer western or upland soils is being abandoned and reverting to scrub – a boon for forest butterflies, but a serious blow to grassland species such as the wall brown and dark green fritillary. Meanwhile, our bumblebee numbers fell an alarming 14 per cent over a recent five-year period. Thanks to a dearth of wildflowers on farms and in gardens, the loss of hedgerows and use of pesticides, a third of our bee species are threatened with extinction.

> "Ireland's agricultural grasslands once provided a perfect space for wildflowers – and for the butterflies and bees that fed on them."

Predators have also felt the effects. Barn owls would not be in Ireland were it not for farming. But rodenticide poisoning and the loss of suitable nesting sites in old farm buildings almost halved their numbers from 1970–2010. Badgers, while not nearly as threatened, have increasingly fallen foul of farmers for their ability to spread bovine TB, which many see as a threat to their livestock. In the ten years to 2006, up to one in five badgers in Ireland was culled.

Recent years, though, have brought redoubled efforts to reconcile the needs of farmers and wildlife, in a bid to preserve biodiversity on Irish farms. Whether or not these will be enough to return our countryside to its former wild glory remains to be seen.

The people of Ireland might have gotten their food from the farm, but they got their fuel from the bog. And as we shall see, Ireland's bogs – and the mountains they so often cover – are home to some of our most unique wildlife.

17

The Bogs and Mountains of Ireland

Afine margin divides life from death in the high mountains.

From its hideout in the heather, an Irish hare perks its long ears. That's the giveaway. This hardiest of mammals is a survivor. It once shared the Pleistocene plains with the giant Irish deer, evading wolves and bears. Since then, it has taken to the farms, bogs and mountains of post-Ice Age Ireland. But now it faces a whole new threat.

The hare doesn't know it, but it's already in the scope of its arch nemesis. Eyes eight times sharper than a human's can pick out the flick of a hare's ear up to three kilometres away. Excellent colour vision separates the hare from the mass of purplish heather mantling the mountain slope. Up here, there are no trees for cover, and precious few places to hide.

The golden eagle, therefore, has no canopy to hide its approach. Instead, it hugs the very contours of the landscape itself to shield it from view, hoping to surprise its prey over every crease in the mountainside. This is no bird of the wooded lowlands. Its two-metre wingspan is far too massive

for forest flying. But this allows it to latch on to mountain updrafts with minimal effort, following ridges to scan each slope for prey. After hours of searching, it's finally closing in on its quarry.

The hare doesn't have the benefit of binocular vision. Eyes on the side of its head, though, let it see through nearly 360 degrees. As soon as it spots the eagle closing it, it bolts. With long legs and powerful feet, it can tear down the mountainside at up to seventy kilometres an hour. Fast – but the eagle is faster. Narrowing its wings into a stoop, it can dive at up to 250 kilometres an hour. The hare can turn on a sixpence, sending an eagle careering (sometimes fatally) into the heather. Not this time. Talons longer than a tiger's claws hit their target. They're driven home by a grip eight times stronger than a person's, designed to snap bones, crush skulls and pierce deep into the organs of their victim. With these, a golden eagle can kill prey ten times its weight.

As it struggles into the air with its prize, the clouds break, and the mountainside is washed through with colour, *sfumato* strokes of red, purple and brown. Lumps of quartzite glisten like fallen stars. Caressed by the sun, the eagle's nape lights up, necklaced in the gold from which it takes its name. Then it's off to the nest, a lofty mass of branches high on a remote mountain cliff. Here, a single chick eagerly awaits its next meal, having only dispensed with its weaker sibling that very day. Even bonds of blood are no defence up here.

The mountains of Ireland – and the bogs that cover them – can so often seem a grim and desolate domain. But look and listen, and you will find a space alive with colour, and given voice by its own remarkable collection of creatures. In the heather and pools of the bog, and the skies above it, transpire natural dramas big and small.

Peat – the decomposing remains of long-dead plants – is the bedrock of the bog. Cut out and left to dry, it forms the turf that still fuels many a fire in rural Ireland. Peat is poor in nutrients. Peaty soil, therefore, was never much use for farming. It was also of little interest to the oaks or other indigenous trees that needed a rich substrate in which to spread their roots. But this is not to say the bogs of Ireland where devoid of life. Instead, they were – and still are – home to some of the most unique plants and animals we have, delicate ecosystems that we are now finally going to lengths to preserve.

There are two types of bog in Ireland, blanket and raised. Blanket bogs form in wet conditions, typically where it rains for at least two-thirds of the year. This copious rainfall leaches nutrients from the soil, leaving it unsuitable for all but the hardiest of plants. Blanket bogs are found in upland, mountainous areas across Ireland, as well as along our west coast. They sit atop a foundation of dark peat lying just below the surface. Ancient farmers, clearing what few trees took root in the mountains, might also have had a hand in their formation. Ireland is now home to about 8 per cent of the world's blanket bogs, making it the most important refuge in Europe for this rare habitat.

Most native trees cannot grow in the poor, nutrient-deprived soil of a blanket bog. Other plants can, though. Chief among them is heather. Though it might be able to take root in waterlogged soils, heather cannot thrive in shade. It flourishes, therefore, in the absence of trees. Along with the sun-tanned grasses that pop up between its fronds, it forms a patina atop the bog and sets the mountainside alight with vivid pink flowers in late summer.

Wherever you get heather, red grouse are not far behind. Like the Irish hare, this hardy mountain bird has a long history in Ireland. Genetic evidence suggests our grouse has been here long enough to become distinct from its cousins across the Irish Sea; in the past it was even classed as a subspecies all of its own. Our red grouse are lighter in colour than their counterparts in Scotland, reflecting the lighter colour scheme of our upland areas.

Perhaps more than any other Irish bird, the grouse has formed a symbiotic relationship with one plant – in this case, the heather. One way or another, the grouse depend on the heather from the moment they hatch. As chicks, they are fattened on the insects that thrive in the microclimate created by the heather. As adults they transition to its flowers and soft shoots. And when frightened, it is amid the tumbled branches of the heather that they crouch for cover. The attractive russet-brown plumage of the grouse is designed for maximum camouflage amongst the heather, keeping its owner safe from the prying eyes of a golden eagle contouring the mountains. The only chinks in this perfect disguise are the brilliant red eyebrows of the males, which flush with colour to impress the females in the mating season.

The grouse might content themselves among the heather, but other mountain birds make a spectacle of themselves above it. In spring and summer, the most obvious is often the skylark. While most songbirds recite from a perch, the tenacious skylark does so on the wing. This is an adaptation to a habitat where trees and bushes are few and far between. Wings beating up to twelve times a second to keep itself aloft, it weaves its song out of an endless stream of often discordant themes. Lapping its way around its territory as it sings, it integrates themes borrowed from other upland birds, adding to the complexity of its composition.

Traditionally the skylark was a bird of arable farmland, where the cereal spill-over provided food. But much of Ireland's countryside is under pasture now, and so the skylark has taken to the bogs, uplands and sand dunes in order to weave its song. When it drops to the ground, the skylark's long, straight claws help it clamber about amongst the grass, much as the curved claws of its forest counterparts find purchase on twigs or branches. A dull, streaky plumage, meanwhile, helps it hide when it needs to.

It is in its mountain abode that the skylark resumes its antipathy with the merlin. The merlin is our smallest bird of prey, swapping coastal wetlands in winter for the mountains in spring where it lays its eggs. Like the skylark, the merlin is famed for its aerial prowess. It can reach speeds of over seventy kilometres an hour in full pursuit, exhausting its prey in a high-speed chase. In spring, the skylark is one of its principal sources of prey; only the meadow pipit, the most common bird up here, is taken more often. But in the skylark, the merlin often meets its match. A skylark's fitness is writ large in its song; only the most accomplished singers stand a chance of escaping a merlin on the wing. Poorer vocalists must drop to the ground to avoid being caught, conceding the skies to the merlin. This might spare them the killing embrace of the merlin's talons, but it also leaves them at a disadvantage when it comes to reproducing. By contrast, the stronger males sing proudly mid-air, confident in their ability to outpace a marauding merlin. They are surely a more attractive mating prospect. It's just one more way predator and prey have helped refine each other over millions of years.

The skylark is one of a smattering of passerines – songbirds – that take up residence in Ireland's mountains, at least for part of the year. One of them – the raven – is the largest passerine of all. It's also the largest of the crows, half as big again as a hooded crow. Their deep, guttural croak echoes through the corries and glacial valleys of our uplands as they chase each other in wheeling ecstasy above the heather. Like all crows, ravens will eat almost anything, but have a taste for carrion, including the carcasses of the sheep that graze on the mountains. Wherever there's death in the uplands, you can be sure a raven is never far away.

Smaller songbirds find their home at altitude too. Perhaps the most striking is the male wheatear, with his pinkish-grey back, creamy orange neck and chest and striking black face mask. Each year the wheatears complete one of the longest migrations of any songbird, travelling all the way from southern Africa to make their nests in our upland bogs.

Our rarest mountain bird is another summer visitor, the ring ouzel, a highly retiring relative of the blackbird.

Thrushes in general have taken well to human habitation. This one, though, remains resolute in its devotion to wild upland spaces. Its striking white chest crescent and lilting song can now only be heard in the highest mountains of Kerry and Donegal.

While the other birds of the mountain rely on song to woo a partner, the male hen harrier resorts to dancing. The 'sky-dance' is one of the most celebrated of all the courtship displays that transpire in Ireland each spring. Adorned in stunning silver, the male harrier rises and falls above the heather, spinning elaborate patterns out of the sky with his black-tipped wings. Few birds his size can come close to his aerial grace. It is this that wins the affections of the larger female harrier. The difference between the two is perhaps the most pronounced out of any Irish bird. She's nearly half as big again as her mate. Where he is a striking silver ghost, she is a much more mottled brown from head to yellow legs and feet. The dapper male harrier is built to stand out. The female is coloured to conceal herself (and her eggs) amongst the heather. Side by side, they look almost like two completely different species.

Like merlins, hen harriers haunt our coastal wetlands in winter, but in spring they return to breed in the mountains. Once the eggs are laid, the female uses her camouflage to melt into the mountainside while the male turns his agility to hunting small prey. His disc-shaped face, almost owl-like, hoovers up any rustles in the heather, helping him home in on small creatures scurrying for safety. It is when he returns to the nest that the dimorphism is clearest, as the female rises to complete the 'food pass', almost bullying him to release his catch into her outstretched talons.

While hen harriers, ring ouzels and merlins spend their spring and summer in upland bogs, other birds move in for winter. Ireland's blanket bogs once offered prime winter quarters for the Greenland white-fronted goose, one of the rarest in the world. Around half the world's population makes the 3,000-kilometre trip from the Arctic to overwinter in Ireland, a journey that can cost them a third of their bodyweight. Geese are voracious grazers. In Ireland's blanket bogs they found the ideal forage to last them through the winter and fatten them up for the return flight. Only with the lengthening of days in spring do they depart for the far north once more.

The uplands are not a ubiquitous carpet of heather and grass, however. Every now and then, lumps of bedrock like granite and quartzite punch through, their minerals adding a shimmer to the mountainside. During the mating season they make a fine display post for male red grouse. But as spring wears on and the days grow warmer, they're ideal sunbeds for common lizards. These tiny creatures are the only native land reptile we have. The Ireland of today is largely too cold for reptiles. This species, though dwarfed by its counterparts in the tropics, is among the hardiest of living lizards, able to live further north than any other land-based reptile.

Like all reptiles, though, the common lizard is unable to regulate its own body temperature. On warm mornings, it has to heat up in the sun to infuse itself with the energy needed to chase down insects and spiders in the heather. In winter, the lizards retreat to the nooks and crannies of the mountain to see out the cold, often huddling together for warmth. This camaraderie is quickly jettisoned in spring when the males set up and defend territories for mating. Like their distant mosasaur relatives, these lizards give birth to live young, the eggs incubating within the mother's body before hatching. From the moment they emerge wriggling onto the bog, the lizards are prey for a menagerie of upland predators – both mammal and bird. A secret weapon helps in this regard: a tail that can dislodge in times of need, distracting the predator long enough for the lizard to escape.

If the lizard is one of the smaller creatures to make its home in the mountains, one of the largest is the deer. Sika deer, the smallest of our three deer species, arrived in Ireland in 1860, introduced to Powerscourt, County Wicklow as ornamentation. Many of them subsequently escaped, especially in the chaos that engulfed Ireland during the Civil War. They have since established themselves in the wild, finding the acidic soils of the uplands much to their liking. They are now our commonest non-native deer.

"Mountainsides across the country are now crested with commercial plantations of non-native conifer trees."

These escapees soon intermingled with the native red deer. The hybrids that resulted now predominate in the hills of Wicklow. The roar of the red deer is a distant memory in the mountains. Instead, these halfway-house creatures fill the glacial valleys with their plaintive whistles each autumn. Antlers at the ready, stags file out along the valley floors as they attempt to secure a territory or win access to a harem of hinds.

With no more wolves in the mountains to keep their population in check, these deer have exploded in number. Their sheer mass now adds to the multitude of threats facing upland habitats. As well as deer, our mountains have also been relentlessly overgrazed by livestock. At first it was cattle. These would be grazed in upland areas in summer, a time-honoured practice known as 'booleying'. But from the 1980s onwards, more farmers started to raise flocks of sheep in the uplands. Sheep are much less fussy in their tastes than cattle. They'll eat almost any vegetation, and crop it much closer to the soil than the broad muzzle of a cow can. This has decimated the growth of heather and other upland flora. With all its supportive vegetation either eaten or trampled underfoot, the peat begins to rend. Routine burning of heather and gorse to nourish fresh grazing has further reduced the habitat many of our mountain creatures rely on.

Another blow was afforestation from the mid-twentieth century onwards. Mountainsides across the country are now crested with commercial plantations of non-native conifer trees like Sitka spruce. These resilient trees can grow fast and so yield a healthy return in a relatively short time. Heather, though, cannot thrive in the shade of evergreen leaves. The spread of conifer plantations, although of benefit to the deer that feed and shelter within them, has come at the expense of many of our mountain denizens.

All of these factors have played a part in the sad decline of the wildlife of Ireland's upland blanket bogs. Merlins are now a tragically rare sight. Hen harrier numbers have halved in the last forty years. The red grouse once enjoyed a cherished status, safeguarded by gamekeepers for shooting. But between 1960 and 2000 it saw a 70 per cent contraction in its range. Once renowned as the 'bog goose', the Greenland white-fronted goose has increasingly been forced to spend its winters on marshes and grassland due to habitat loss. Its numbers have fallen by 30 per cent in just twenty years.

Of all the upland creatures in decline, none has been devastated so absolutely as the golden eagle. Together with the extinction of its even larger wetland counterpart, the white-tailed eagle, this amounted to probably the biggest blow to Ireland's birdlife since the coming of man; two apex predators obliterated within a century.

Around the early eighteenth century, falconry, a long-cherished pastime of the well-heeled, began to wane in popularity. Game shooting took its place. When it did, Ireland's raptors went from being a prized asset to a liability. Even before the 1700s, gamekeepers relentlessly hunted Ireland's birds of prey – especially the large ones. The desire to keep grouse moors free from predators led to eagles being shot on sight. Sheep farmers also bore a deep animus towards the birds. From the nineteenth century on, our biggest raptors found themselves being targeted like never before. As well as the bullet, eagles also fell victim to the sinister gin trap, with spring-loaded metal jaws that clamped around the foot or ankle. The latter half of the 1800s saw the arrival of strychnine. This abominable poison probably did more than anything to seal the fate of Ireland's eagles. It would prove particularly devastating for the white-tailed eagle, which last nested in Ireland in 1898 before its untimely demise.

Although not above scavenging, especially in winter, the golden eagle is, by nature, less fond of carrion than the white-tailed. This helped it weather the strychnine storm better in its mountain fastness. Even here, though, its days were numbered. By the end of the 1800s it was facing oblivion across Ireland. As the bird got rarer and rarer, it attained valuable trophy status, and its eggs found themselves in increasing demand from collectors. By 1894, the golden eagle was restricted to patchy outposts on the Atlantic coast. In 1912, it disappeared from the mountains of Donegal, one of its final strongholds. Eagles in Mayo clung on for a few more years before they too vanished. Stragglers would appear on the north and west coasts for some years, but were often shot. When Ireland's fugitive freedom fighters took to the heather in the 1920s, they did so in mountains now shorn of their most magnificent avian predator.

While blanket bogs hold sway in Ireland's mountains, raised bogs predominate in the Midlands. These bogs trace their genesis all the way back to the end of the last Ice Age. As the glaciers went into retreat, the depressions they left in their wake filled in with water and became lakes. Wherever you find lakes, water plants soon follow. The remains of dead plants then built up at the bottom of these lakes. The next ingredients were sphagnum mosses, which thrive on the decay of rotting plant matter. The action of these mosses soon turned both water and soil acidic. Dead plants could no longer decompose, and so started to accumulate. Gradually, what was once a lake filled up with this material until the newly formed bog spilled over its surface and spread itself out across the landscape. In so doing, it gradually edged out the surrounding forests at a rate of around one millimetre a year, eventually adding trees to its collection of pickled plant life.

> "These bogs trace their genesis all the way back to the end of the last Ice Age."

Our raised bogs are some of the oldest living ecosystems in the world. It is in the bronzed peat of Ireland's raised bogs that we find a rich record of life dating back thousands of years, from ancient tree stumps to the antlers of the long dead giant Irish deer. People, and their artefacts, were interred here too. Among the seventeen victims of the bog recovered so far is the oldest 'fleshed' bog body in the world. Unearthed in County Laois, the Cashel Man is over 4,000 years old, his tanned, leathery skin still clinging tight to the bones. Celtic offerings to the gods have also been unearthed, as well as the occasional plank of a *tóchair*, the wooden causeways used to traverse the bog years ago.

Just as with blanket bogs, the nutrient-poor soil of the raised bogs precludes much plant life. Trees are scarce.

Mosses aside, few species can thrive here, but the ones that do number among Ireland's most unique flora. They form a colour palette all of their own, the sickly green and amber hues of the moss augmented by the fluffy whites of the bog cotton, soft pinks of the bell heather and yellow starlets of the bog asphodel.

Of all the plants that make their home here, none are stranger than Ireland's carnivorous plants. These herbaceous booby-traps have developed an ingenious way to supplement the nutrition they can drain from impoverished boggy soils – they have become voracious predators. Each employs its own strategy to ensnare its prey. The leaves of the sundew, for instance, are studded with up to 200 tentacles. Each is tipped with a drop of glistening glue. To a roving insect, it looks like nectar. By the time it realises it's stuck, it's too late. The glue holds fast to its struggling victim as the other tentacles fold in around it.

The bladderwort, on the other hand, prefers to capture its victims underwater. It has the most complex trapping mechanism of any carnivorous plant. This rootless, free floating terror raises its little yellow flowers above the pools of water peppering the bog. Instead of roots, it spreads its green, kidney-shaped bladder traps beneath the surface of the water. When an insect larva or aquatic worm swims too close, it triggers the fastest reaction of any carnivorous plant. Touching a trigger hair causes the hapless victim to be sucked into the trap at speeds of up to one-fifteen thousandth of a second, where it is then broken down by the bladderwort's digestive juices.

The traps of the bladderworts share the pools of the bog with a myriad of smaller creatures – among them monsters. Tadpoles swirl beneath the water, chasing fragments of algae through the murk. They themselves are prey for dragonfly nymphs. As their parents dart about in pursuit of insects above the water, their offspring terrorise things that swim beneath it with a pair of vicious pincers mounted on an extendable, hinged lower lip. This 'mask' can snap forward and back in as little as one hundredth of a second: a chilling weapon, perfected over more than 300 million years.

Tadpoles and nymphs undergo some of the most remarkable metamorphoses in the animal kingdom. Dragonfly nymphs can spend up to three years beneath the water before they emerge and weld themselves to the fronds of a bog plant for their final transformation. Then an adult dragonfly bursts from the eviscerated husk of a nymph, and takes its first tentative wingbeats into the air. After spending so long underwater, this final stage in a dragonfly's life is comparatively brief, lasting weeks or even days.

For the tadpole, the cycle is even faster. It burrows out of a gelatinous, translucent egg, one of up to 4,000 laid by its mother in the same pond where she was spawned years before. At first, the tadpoles – nothing more than black spheres with wriggling tails for propulsion – sustain themselves off yolk affixed to their stomachs. After two days they've grown the mouths with which they can eat tiny, free-floating plants in the pond. Five weeks later, rows of teeth let them add larger water plants to their diet. At seven weeks they have begun to eat the meat that will feed them in adulthood. Even smaller tadpoles are no longer safe.

Other traits of adulthood appear too as a frog slowly emerges. By ten weeks old, this transitional creature has fully formed back legs, and the forelegs erupt from its chest. The tail has all but disappeared by fourteen weeks old, as the young frog now spends more and more of its time out of the water. This is where it will do all of its hunting from now on, although that ancestral amphibian skin will forever bind it to wet habitats. At three years old, the frog is ready to return to its birth pond to breed for the first time. It's thought that frogs can recognise the pool of their birth from the unique scent of its water and flora. Incredible to think that the innumerable pools that once studded Ireland's raised bogs each had an aroma all of their own.

Other animals breed on our raised bogs as well. Mammals are few and far between here. The hardy Irish hare is one of the few that's regularly seen, while otters like to fish in the lakes and rivers that cut through the bog. But ground-nesting birds were once found in large numbers, the treeless landscape allowing them to keep a watchful eye for any approaching threats. Of the ones we have left, one of the biggest is the curlew. This is the largest Irish wader, that great family of birds that throng coastal wetlands across the country, poking both mud and rocky shores with a wide array of mandibular tools. The curlew has the longest instrument of the lot, a fine, delicately down-curved bill, beautifully designed for rooting worms out from their burrows. With its mobile, sensitive tip, little escapes it. More than 70 per cent of our curlews breed on bogs. Streaky brown throughout, they're far from the most resplendent Irish bird, but their haunting song is among the most iconic sounds of the bog, a melancholy thrill rippling across the landscape.

Even curlews were dwarfed by other birds that used to breed here. The raised bogs of Ireland were once home to one of our great lost avian wonders. While the blanket bogs of the mountains still have the solo sky dance of the hen harrier, raised bogs formed a perfect platform for the mass ballet of dancing cranes.

Cranes are gigantic birds; neck outstretched, they are almost as tall as a person. A crimson-and-black face mask and bushy tail plumes added to their visual splendour as they strutted about the bog, beak raised to the sky, suffusing the damp air with their high-pitched honks. As if this weren't enough, the competing cranes might spread their two-metre wingspan to its fullest extent, and rouse a few beats to elevate themselves into the air, hopping about as if on hot coals. Unlike hen harriers, male and female cranes are identical; mutual dancing, therefore is how the best partner is selected – giant birds, dancing over the bones of giant deer.

In the fruits, shoots and seeds of the bog flora, the cranes found the food they needed to sustain themselves and their chicks. Sadly, that same herbivorous diet also made the cranes a prized delicacy on Anglo-Norman dinner plates. The native Irish Celts shied away from eating cranes, probably because of their association with the dark magic of the druids. But from the Middle Ages on, overhunting by these new arrivals (as well as the earlier Vikings) would gradually whittle away Ireland's crane population. Falconry – for sport as much as meat – also took its toll. By the mid-1700s, the bird had ceased breeding here entirely. Before it went, its calligraphic form would imprint itself on the pages of the *Book of Kells*. '*Corr*', the Irish word for crane, found its way into hundreds of place-names, especially in Counties Monaghan and Cavan.

Sadly, the lot of Ireland's raised bogs has only grown worse since the loss of the crane. As Ireland's once vast forests were eviscerated, people increasingly had to turn to the bog for fuel.

"The loss of our bogs has taken a heavy toll on some of our most unique wildlife."

Population growth in the eighteenth and nineteenth centuries – Ireland's population doubled from the 1780s to the 1840s – saw a surge in demand. More and more bogs were cut away for turf. While the Great Famine saw somewhat of a let up in this destructive process, it would continue with renewed vigour into the twentieth century. Coal shortages during World War Two meant turf was needed to power the economy. By 1941, it was being harvested in every county in the Republic. Half of Ireland's raised bogs were destroyed from 1814–1946. Now our active raised bogs cover less than 1 per cent of the nearly 1 million acres they once did. This has been devastating for the plants and animals of the bog – none more so than the curlew. Thanks to habitat loss and fragmentation, it has been almost obliterated as a breeding bird in Ireland, with its numbers falling by 96 per cent since the 1980s. Attempts to preserve the bogs have seen a halt called to all turf-cutting – to the ire of farmers who have relied on turf for generations.

The loss of our bogs has taken a heavy toll on some of our most unique wildlife. But human life in Ireland was not confined to forests, farms or bogs. Freed from the uncertainty of hunting and gathering, people could start to settle down. This allowed them to coalesce together in villages, villages that grew into towns and eventually cities. These are where most Irish people now make their home. And as we shall see, they have a lot to offer wildlife as well.

18

Life Under Lamplight: Ireland's Urban Wildlife

Dusk in the suburbs of South Dublin. The street lamps cast half-moons of yellow light across the pavement. It augments what little glow seeps past the bedroom windows of uniform, detached houses. The incessant din of distant traffic and gentle whisper of the breeze is all that breaks the silence. That is until an incensed dog starts barking furiously from one of the back gardens. The cause of its dissent is nowhere to be seen, leaving its owner bewildered. But it is the dog's nose that has alerted it to the presence of a wild interloper, doing its regular rounds of the neighbourhood in search of food.

As the night wears on, this supreme opportunist grows bolder. Late-night walkers about the estate are treated to tantalisingly brief views; a bushy tail breaking the lamplight, a canid form casting a dark shadow as it scurries across the road. Domestic dogs might be confined to the house or their owner's garden, but at night, the suburbs of Dublin are abandoned to their wild cousin, the red fox.

Few Irish mammals have taken as well to city living as the fox. In fact, there are now thought to be more foxes living in Ireland's urban areas than in the countryside. Hardly surprising; with the abundance of food to be enjoyed in towns and cities, urban foxes can survive in a territory of just twenty hectares, whereas their rural cousins need ten times that or even more. There's plenty of food to be had here, from the rats and mice that also flourish in the orbit of human habitation to the crisps, offal and fruit that people leave behind. The introduction of wheelie bins in an attempt to fortify refuse doesn't seem to have harmed our foxes. Crafty to a fault, they know where and how to get food – and how to avoid danger while doing it.

Traditionally, foxes dug their dens under hedgerows or trees. Now, a garden shed will suffice. Here the cubs are fed and tended before the males are evicted by their parents in late autumn (females often hang around to help in the rearing of the next litter). At this time of year, the adventurous young males are more likely to be seen wandering the streets by day. Sadly, this is also when their naivety and inexperience

ensures mortality is at its highest. City life may be good, but it is not without its perils.

Regardless, the success of the red fox in Ireland's towns and cities is testament to how life can thrive even in this most human of landscapes. It gives us hope that, in an increasingly urbanised Ireland, wildlife can still find a home.

Towns and cities are relatively new phenomena in Ireland. For most of our early history, the vast majority of people lived in small settlements of often no more than a few dwellings, scattered across the countryside. It took the arrival of the Vikings in the eighth and ninth centuries for the first towns to be set up, often in natural harbours around our coasts. Later in the Middle Ages, the Anglo-Normans established yet more towns, some of them further inland. From the sixteenth century on, English and Scottish planters augmented Ireland's urban landscape with settlements of their own. Then, during the nineteenth century, estate towns such as Westport, County Mayo and Skerries, County Dublin were added to the mix.

The trend of urbanisation has continued to the present day. Now, the majority of Ireland's people live in towns or cities. Centuries ago, Ireland's urban spaces consisted of narrow streets with buildings packed together in a tight squeeze. These unsanitary conditions were often poor for wildlife – and, for that matter, for people. That began to change in the eighteenth and nineteenth centuries. This is when houses became topped and tailed by gardens and more open areas were introduced for recreation. The trend for low-density housing with gardens and green spaces continued into the twentieth century. This has allowed more and more wildlife to flourish in our urban areas.

Some Irish wildlife has adapted well to urban living. Feral pigeons, for instance, are a ubiquitous site on city streets across the country. These descend from domesticated rock doves that have reverted to a wild state. In towns and cities nationwide, they have found pigeon paradise, vacuuming up bread and seeds discarded by humans and making their nests on the arches of bridges. They can rear up to four broods a year, such is the surplus of food to be found here. The courtship display of the male, as he puffs out his iridescent neck and fans the pavement with his tail in amorous pursuit of a partner, is an accessible natural drama playing out right in front of our eyes.

It is these pigeons that have helped open up Ireland's urban landscapes to the fastest animal on Earth. Stooping from a great height, the peregrine falcon can reach speeds of up to 320 kilometres an hour as it folds its wings back and plunges towards its victim. A supremely aerodynamic, teardrop shape enables it to reach these incredible speeds. Bony cones in each nostril, called tubercles, help regulate its intake of air while diving, preventing its lungs from filling up and bursting. A third eyelid helps to lubricate its black eyes, keeping the peregrine's sight razor sharp during high-speed pursuit, as well as shielding them from wind and dust. And a heart that can beat up to 900 times a minute gives it all the momentum it needs for this high-octane chase.

Traditionally, the peregrine bred on mountains and coastal cliffs. Like many other raptors, it was devastated by DDT poisoning. Now it's making a recovery – and in more recent decades, has found a new home amidst the concrete cliffs of Ireland's urban sprawl. Here, church towers, office blocks and old quarries fill in for cliff-top crannies as ideal nesting sites, while an abundance of pigeons and other urban birds provides all the food it needs.

The peregrine is rivalled in its aerial prowess by the swift, another bird that has taken well to Ireland's urban spaces. Swifts are among the last of our summer migrants to arrive (mid-May) and also the earliest to leave (mid-August). During the brief spell in between, their cigar-shaped bodies and sickle wings weave their shadows across urban streets nationwide as they fill the air with their shrill screaming.

Of all Ireland's birds, none has adapted better to life in the air than the swift. The peregrine has its dive, but when it comes to powered flight, no bird on Earth can move faster than a swift (over 111 kilometres an hour). This helps them catch all the food they need in the air. While swallows chase down large insects one at a time, swifts simply hang their gaping bills wide open and allow midges and other airborne minutia to stumble in.

Swifts can even sleep and mate in the air, the occasional flick of a wing keeping them aloft in the breeze. They can go more than two years without touching terra firma. Indeed, once a swift touches solid ground it can find it hard to become airborne again.

The swift has become so used to life on the wing that its feet have largely atrophied. Unusual among birds, its four toes point forward; they cannot gain purchase on a tree branch, being instead evolved for clinging on to the sheer cliff faces where they once laid their eggs. Now, it's more often on the soffit boards of old Georgian houses that they choose to raise their young (new or renovated buildings often lack the nooks and crannies swifts need to nest in). When a swift departs from its Dublin nest in August to overwinter in Africa, it may not touch ground until it returns to that same nest nine months later. A swift can live up to eighteen years in the wild. During that time, the milage it has clocked up on its biannual sojourns between Ireland and Africa could take it to the moon and back eight times over.

Below the aerial acrobatics of the swifts, more terrestrial birds have also found the city to their liking. Pied wagtails, which poach insects in open areas, now bob up and down after prey in car parks. Equally familiar are the house sparrows, omnipresent with human habitation in Ireland. They travel about towns and cities in flocks – all the better for exploiting every food resource available, while providing more eyes to look out for danger. There are few foods they won't turn their beaks to, from garden plants to all manner of human leftovers – whether they're spilling from a bin or left out for the birds to enjoy. The sparrows nest and roost communally. The nooks and crannies of buildings provide perfect places to do so.

Another urban bird that nests in buildings is the starling. Its numbers ballooned across Europe in tandem with the rising human population. The clearance of forests undoubtedly played a part in this; short-cropped grass suits the starling, and now they can be found probing for insects in gardens and football pitches nationwide. They feed together, sharing knowledge of where to find the best foraging while benefitting from the warmth and safety that comes with a flock – and the balmier conditions that pervade in urban areas. These flocks can grow to include hundreds or even thousands of individuals. Every once in a while, the skies above Ireland's towns and cities bear witness to one of our most breathtaking natural wonders: a murmuration, a writhing mass of starlings wheeling and folding in and out of itself in synchronised undulation. By matching the speed and movements of the birds around them, the starlings harmonise into a great, swirling ball. This mesmerising display is the ultimate communal defence mechanism. By moving as one, the starlings can confuse the efforts of a peregrine or sparrowhawk, making it harder to zero in on a single target.

Sparrows and starling share suburbia with birds that traditionally dwelt in Ireland's forests, but have found a new abode in the parks and gardens of the city. Perhaps the most familiar is the robin, a stalwart of Irish folklore for generations. Robins are highly territorial. Their characteristic red breast is used by the males to establish dominance – in a face off, each tries to gain a higher vantage point from which to display his chest in the hope that the other will back down. This determination to hold on to territory is also why robins sing right through the winter. They're among the most vocal songbirds we have – and the most belligerent, with up to 10 per cent of fatalities resulting from territorial clashes. In urban areas, the presence of street lights even encourages robins to sing long after the sun has gone down.

Like the robin, the blackbird traditionally got its food on the forest floor, but has found towns and cities much to its liking. There's clearly good living to be had here; urban blackbirds not only migrate less than their forest-dwelling kin, but also breed earlier and are able to live at higher population densities. They fledge more chicks than blackbirds in the countryside, despite laying fewer eggs per clutch. Incredibly, blackbirds in urban areas sing at a higher pitch than those in the forests. They have refined their sound to complement this new concrete-and-glass jungle they find themselves living in. Urban blackbirds have also been shown to be less curious and more cautious than those living in woodlands; clearly it pays to be street smart in the city. They even have a lower stress response than woodland blackbirds, so as not to find themselves exhausted by the constant clamour (humans, cats, cars) of city living. What's more, these behavioural quirks aren't merely learned, but appear to be hardwired in blackbirds inhabiting different habitats. The selection pressures of the city could even be shaping the very genetics of life itself.

The vocal prowess of the blackbird is matched by its close cousin, the song thrush, another bird that has taken well to urban Ireland. Here, television aerials and other man-made structures take on the role of trees as song posts from which to project their melodies far and wide across their domain. Along with the raucous calling of the robin and bomb-drop whistles of the starling, this helps create an urban bird chorus all of its own. In more recent decades, another theme in this avian symphony has arrived in the form of the soft, burring coo of the collared dove. Traditionally a bird of Southern Europe, the collared dove has undergone a rapid expansion in its range. It first arrived in Ireland in 1959. Now, its call is one of the signature sounds of small towns and suburbs across the country.

All of these suburban songbirds need to be careful, however, that their eggs and chicks don't fall foul of another bird – one that has probably taken to suburbia better than any other. The corvids (crows) are among the most intelligent and adaptable of birds, and the magpie is no exception. It is thought to have first arrived in Ireland in the late seventeenth century. Since then, it has gone from tormenting gamekeepers in the countryside to being the great menace of nesting garden birds. Opinions vary as to the impact this has on songbird numbers. In any case, the sinister cackle of the magpie is now one of the most familiar bird calls to be heard in housing estates across Ireland.

Magpies possess the keen intellect of a crow; they're among the only birds in the world capable of self-recognition, an ability once thought unique to primates, elephants and dolphins. This, combined with a highly variable diet, has seen them exploit urban Ireland to the fullest extent, from peeling open milk bottles to get at their contents to soaking dry bread in water to make it easier to eat. Their boundless curiosity ensures few food sources escape them. Like their forest-dwelling cousin the jay, magpies will hoard surplus food for leaner times ahead, and can learn from each other in order to survive. All of this has made the magpie a suburban success story. Across Ireland and Britain, its population has quadrupled in recent decades, with suburban areas seeing the greatest increase.

What the cackle of the magpie is to the suburbs, the raucous cry of the herring gull is to the city centre. Like the magpie, this large gull is an opportunistic scavenger, and has gravitated away from its traditional coastal domain to the high street. Here, copious amounts of food left in overflowing bins provide a feast for the highly adaptable herring gull. Swollen refuse tips and sewage systems have also contributed to the explosion in herring gull numbers across Europe. In response to this urban bonanza, herring gulls have taken to nesting on rooftops or even chimneys. The birds have grown increasingly bold as more and more exposure to humans erodes their natural fear of man. Many urbanites now feel beset by aggressive gulls in pursuit of a meal. Temperature has probably played a part in the transition too; with all that concrete, steel and biomass, cities are four to six degrees warmer than the

"The corvids (crows) are among the most intelligent and adaptable of birds, and the magpie is no exception. It is thought to have first arrived in Ireland in the late seventeenth century."

surrounding countryside, extending the bird's breeding season. Moreover, street lights allow urban herring gulls to forage long after their coastal kin have settled down for the night.

Those same streetlights that guide the crepuscular feeding of herring gulls also waylay moths on their nightly foraging forays around the city. For millions of years, moths are thought to have used the moon and stars to navigate at night. That worked well in a world before the streetlamp. Now it's a major handicap, keeping them swirling around man-made lights in towns and cities nationwide. And when they do, they become easy targets for bats.

Bats are the only mammals to have achieved true powered flight, following a path first blazed by the insects, then by pterosaurs and birds. We have nine species of bat in Ireland, ranging from the tiny common pipistrelle – the weight of a twenty-cent piece – to the more robust Leisler's bat, which has found a stronghold in Ireland. This is the species often seen poaching the insects that swarm around urban street lamps.

All of our bats use sound (echolocation) to find their prey. They emit up to 200 short, sharp pulses a second, collating the echoes from these to pinpoint their target. Each bat produces a different frequency, tailored to a different type of prey. This allows multiple bat species to coexist in the same environment, avoiding competition with each other. Their prey, however, is not completely defenceless. Some moths even emit sounds of their own, false feedback that confuses the bat's sophisticated navigation.

Most of Ireland's bats were originally woodland creatures to one degree or another. They made their roosts in tree-holes, caves or other natural crannies. Now though, some have taken to spending their day hanging upside down from the roofs of old buildings such as churches. The brown long-eared bat, in particular, has adapted well to urban living, and now frequently seeks shelter in attics or other cosy cavities offered by man-made structures. On top of its echolocation, this bat uses the largest ears for its body size of any animal (three-quarters the length of the bat itself) to amplify the miniscule beat of insect wings.

Other insectivores have taken up residence in Ireland's towns and cities as well. Foxes aren't the only creatures that make dogs go apoplectic at night. Quite possibly, their insolence is directed at a hedgehog, venturing into the garden in search of prey.

Hedgehogs became part of Ireland's fauna in the thirteenth century. They were introduced either by accident or possibly even for food. Since then, they have taken to the forests, farms and now to the parks and gardens of suburban Ireland in their nightly pursuit of slugs, worms and millipedes. A bowl of tasty dog food isn't overlooked either. They can roam over four kilometres through the suburbs each night in search of food.

Alone among Irish mammals, the hedgehog brandishes its own suit of armour. It is protected by up to 5,000 spines, each lasting up to eighteen months before being replaced. Each one is affixed to a muscle. This allows the hedgehog to erect them for defence or roll itself into a ball to confound predators. Sadly, some foxes may have learned to overcome this by rolling hedgehogs downhill into water, forcing them to unseal their defence and swim for safety.

Like foxes, it appears that suburban hedgehogs have much smaller home ranges than their counterparts in the countryside, and cities tend to harbour higher numbers than rural areas. From one of multiple nests, they set off on their nightly rounds about the gardens in search of food. This routine comes to a dramatic halt in October, when they are ready to hibernate. To do this, they acquire two types of fat throughout the year: white for fuel, brown for insulation.

Then they stow themselves away in hibernation nests made of leaves or grass, many of them built in gardens. Here, the hedgehog allows its bodily temperature to mirror that of its surroundings. Its heartrate plummets from over 150 beats per minute to just twenty. It may wake from this stasis several times before normal business resumes in March or April.

Hedgehogs aren't the only creatures that see out the winter asleep in the undergrowth. As well as mammals and birds, gardens across Ireland offer refuge for another creature – of far more ancient stock.

The onset of spring is the cue for a remarkable transformation to take place. This is when smooth newts emerge from hibernation on land and make their way to water to start breeding. Ten centimetres long, these tiny, lizard-like creatures are living echoes of the once spectacular amphibian diversity to be seen in Ireland's Carboniferous swamps. The newt spends much of its time on land. But like its ancestors 300 million years ago, this amphibian can't reproduce on terra firma. For this, it prefers still or slow-moving bodies of water. Garden ponds are ideal. They have become important breeding sites for newts nationwide.

For his size, the metamorphosis of a male newt in spring is as spectacular as that of a red deer stag ready to rut. The black spots that pepper his body swell. His belly lights up a vivid orange. A fleshy ridge sprouts from his back, running to the end of his paddle-like tail. He then wriggles about in the water to display these assets to a prospective mate. If he succeeds, he fertilises the jelly-like eggs she festoons around plants in the pond. Two to three weeks later, the larval newts emerge to begin this amazing lifecycle all over again. There are ripples here from a bygone age.

Of all Ireland's urban creatures, however, there is one that has truly mastered the art of living alongside humans – so much so, in fact, it now outnumbers them in many cities right around the world. It's perhaps the most hated creature we have in Ireland. This makes its sheer success all the more remarkable.

Though not native, rats have a long history here. The black rat even found itself ensconced on the pages of the *Book of Kells* as far back as the eighth century. It would return to Ireland with a vengeance later in the Middle Ages, a stowaway on one of the many vessels making their way through our bustling ports. Its second coming would coincide with one of the deadliest plagues the world has ever seen, killing tens of millions of people across Europe. The bubonic plague broke out in Ireland in the summer of 1348. The disease spread fast in the cramped, insanitary conditions of cities and large towns like Dublin, Drogheda and Dundalk. By Christmas that year, it had already claimed up to 14,000 lives in Dublin alone. Recent studies might absolve the black rat of some of the blame for this, citing human parasites such as lice, and not the fleas of rats, as the main vectors of the disease. The taint of this deadly illness, however, still hangs heavy over the black rat.

The black rat is now actually one of the rarest mammals we have. In 1722, the larger brown rat arrived in Ireland from Eastern Europe. This is the rat you're likely to see scurrying furtively along roadside verges at night. Rat reproduction is simply incredible. Females are ready to breed at just three months old, and can produce up to five litters every year. Because of this, a female rat can have up to a thousand descendants within a year. Within ten years of its arrival, the brown rat had already become a serious pest on the streets of Dublin, a status it retains to this day. In the process, it largely outmuscled and usurped the smaller black rat.

"Today Ireland's rat population numbers in the millions, despite all the efforts of people to exterminate them."

Today Ireland's rat population numbers in the millions, despite all the efforts of people to exterminate them. They can make their home in almost any man-made structure – even sewers. Sewers, in fact, are a rat paradise: warm in winter, cool in summer, and with an endless bounty of food floating by. Brown rats can tolerate much damper conditions than most other rodents. They are excellent swimmers, able to hold their breath for up to three minutes at a time. This – combined with hinged ribs that can fold in like an umbrella – allows the rat to squeeze through holes the size of a fifty-cent piece, and colonise urban waterways across Ireland. Walls are no deterrent either; long claws allow them to scale brickwork with ease.

An omnivorous diet is key to the success of much urban wildlife, and the brown rat is no different. The sugary, fatty foods to be found in urban refuse help city rats grow faster and live longer than their rural counterparts. They can get significantly bigger too; perhaps the urban legend of giant rats has some basis in fact. Incisors that grow nearly thirteen centimetres every year are forever sharpened against each other. With these, rats can gnaw through almost anything, even metal, and handle just about any food source they come across, from cardboard and hair to soap and even toenails. Poisoned bait won't stop them – its use has led to the rise of resistant rats, and does more harm to the raptors and other predators that eat them.

Rats, like all of the creatures that now inhabit Ireland's towns and cities, once made their abode elsewhere, just like the herring gulls that now beg for bread and chips in Dublin's St Stephen's Green. These once made their living following trawlers and poaching fish from smaller seabirds. In other words, they got their food, at least indirectly, from the sea. And it is in the sea that life in Ireland is at its most spectacular.

19

Life Beneath the Waves

The signs that giants have returned to the waters off West Cork are often subtle. Far out to sea, you notice a sequence of bubbles slowly and silently forming a patina on the pulsating surface of the ocean. One by one, the bubbles link together to fill out a loose circle. The trap is now complete. Kittiwakes and fulmars hang in the air or alight on the water's surface. They know what's about to happen.

Above the water, things look calm. But just below the surface, chaos is ensuing. A shoal of sprat is now trapped. Penned in by the ring of bubbles, there's no escape as they pack tighter and tighter together. This behaviour has evolved to help them confuse their enemies. Most predators are after only one fish, and swirling together makes it harder for them to single out a target. Not this one. This is exactly the response it's counting on. It's not after one sprat. It wants the whole shoal.

Having completed its bubble net, their tormentor also relies on another weapon in its arsenal: noise. Weaving the ring of bubbles from its blowhole emits an intense sound.

Sound is more potent underwater. It's unbearable to the fish, resonating within their very swim bladders, a death note that won't relent. With no hope of breaking the bubbles, and descent downwards blocked by the gargantuan predator below, the sprat are forced to the surface.

This is when the space between the bubbles is broken by one or more enormous maws. The cavernous mouth of a humpback whale can take in up to 19,000 litres of water in one great gulp – and thousands of small fish. It can put away up to 2,500 kilogrammes of prey a day. Weighing in at thirty-six tonnes, it has to.

One whale is a scary enough prospect for a school of sprat, but humpbacks can hunt in groups. While one whale blows the bubble net, others circle the shoal, corralling them further into the trap. Yet more whales prevent escape from below, and by synchronising their lunge, the whales ensure that any fish that evade one giant maw inevitably find themselves in another. What's left gets picked off by the raucous seabirds. Sometimes, humpbacks take a different approach entirely.

Lounging at the surface with their lower jaw hanging open, they stir up a soft current with their enormous white flippers, channelling everything into their mouths. Unlike bubble netting, this approach is best employed when prey are not tightly packed together. Sadly, falling fish stocks in Irish waters might be forcing them to do this.

This ability to work together and tailor their approach to suit the situation speaks to the immense intelligence of these giants. It's one more reason to preserve the incredible wildlife harboured in our seas.

As an island nation, the sea exerts an inescapable influence on life in Ireland. Much of the food for Ireland's Mesolithic people came from the sea. Many of the remains they left behind have been found close to the coast. Their campsites are replete with the shells of cockles, oysters and scallops, as well as the bones of cod, wrasse, haddock and ray. Fishing would provide sustenance for coastal communities for millennia to follow. Even creatures as large as seals were not spared. The need to exploit the ocean's bounty would lead fishermen up and down the west coast to develop an extraordinary range of *currachs*, rowing boats crafted for the specific conditions of the local coastline and islands. They shared the fruits of our oceans with a spectacular array of marine creatures, among them some of the largest animals ever to live on the planet.

Life in Ireland's seas is shaped by events originating thousands of kilometres away. Rising in the Gulf of Mexico, the aptly named Gulf Stream marches up the coast of North America before steamrolling across the Atlantic (in the form of the North Atlantic Drift) to encircle Ireland, bringing warm, sub-tropical waters with it. Thousands of years ago, the disruption of the stream by melting ice sheets spelt doom for the last giant Irish deer. But now, the warming influence of the stream ensures Ireland enjoys a pleasantly temperate climate year round – and warmer waters than might be expected given our latitude. These, in turn, are a haven for marine life.

Fish are the mainstay of our marine ecosystems, just as they have been for hundreds of millions of years. Some, like the sand eel, make their living off the smallest creatures that hang in the current, including plankton and the hatchlings of other, larger fish. This dynamic is reversed when those larvae survive against all the odds to reach maturity. Now, the sand eels find themselves on the menu for larger fish such as the sea bass and Atlantic cod. Others, such as flounder, have evolved to conceal themselves on the sea floor. At birth, flounders are symmetrical like most other fish. Gradually, though, one eye migrates to what will become the top side of the fish, and the other side loses its colour. Now it's ready for a lifetime of lying in ambush on the seabed. Yet more fish make a living closer to the surface. Among them are the mackerel, herring and sprat that poach plankton in open water.

These fish rely on speed and coordinated schooling to evade larger predators – among them, sharks. Sharks have a legacy in Irish waters dating back over 300 million years. The super-predatory sharks of the Cretaceous might be long gone, but their more modest living counterparts are hardly less fearsome.

Ireland's seas are home to more than seventy shark species. Catsharks – in Ireland, ironically, known more often as dogfish – are among the most familiar. These sandy brown sharks are the ones you find stinking out fish crates in harbours, or whose egg cases entwine seaweed on shorelines nationwide. At around sixty to seventy centimetres long, they're about the same size as the Carboniferous sharks that swam over what is now The Burren more than 300 million years ago. Catsharks cling to the seafloor, searching for crabs and molluscs to sink their teeth into. The rough skin, like sandpaper, for which they are famed helps keep them safe from their own predators.

Of all Ireland's extant sharks, the blue shark is the most formidable. At over three metres long, and armed with the razor-sharp teeth sharks are infamous for, these are ferocious predators of small schooling fish – and anything else in the water they can overpower. This shark can travel thousands of kilometres across the oceans of the world in search of food. Its royal blue colouring encapsulates both the beauty and the danger of the open sea. Sadly, they are also among the most heavily fished of all sharks, calling the future of this once plentiful predator into question.

In summer, Ireland's seas are home to another, even bigger shark. Being fish, they don't need to surface to breathe. Often, the first sign of their presence is the rounded tips of the dorsal and tail fins, gently breaking the surface. These are the calling cards of a basking shark. It's the largest fish in the North Atlantic, with adults averaging seven to nearly nine metres long. Worldwide, only the whale shark overshadows it.

With its enormous white mouth opening up to more than a metre wide, the basking shark can strike a terrifying figure as it slowly ploughs the waters of Kerry, Mayo or Donegal, sometimes just a few metres from the shore. But this benign giant is a far cry from the flesh-eating sharks that plied Ireland's prehistoric seas. It's harmless to humans. The serrated teeth of predatory sharks are altogether absent from this leviathan. For all its impressive bulk, the teeth of the basking shark are modest. At seven millimetres long, they can be hard to even see as the shark exposes its vacuous white gullet. Instead, this giant relies on its gill-rakers – bristle-like structures festooned from its gill slits – to filter out the plankton as it swims along, mouth open. It gets all the food it needs to sustain its massive size this way, straining up to 1,800 tonnes of seawater an hour.

Impressive though it may be, the basking shark is still dwarfed by the largest creatures to make their home in Ireland's waters. The demise of the dinosaurs sixty-six million years ago also saw the end of the great marine reptiles – the ichthyosaurs, plesiosaurs and mosasaurs – that once swam the seas of the world. Their disappearance left a vacancy at the top of the ocean food chain. And nature seldom leaves a niche unoccupied.

About fifty million years ago, on the coast of what is now Pakistan, a small, wolf-like creature waded into the shallows, probably in search of fish. Gradually, its descendants became more adept at underwater living. Their tails would elongate into a fluke. Their feet became webbed, transforming into flippers. Eventually the hind limbs would atrophy entirely as their owners found themselves so at home in the sea they could no longer return to land.

The apogee of this remarkable process can now be seen in the phenomenal diversity of cetaceans – whales, dolphins and porpoises – to be spotted around Ireland's coasts. Ireland is one of the best places in Europe to see these magnificent creatures in the wild. To date, twenty-four species have passed through our waters or washed up on our shores, more than a quarter of the world's total. Our most commonly sighted species range in size from the one-and-a-half-metre harbour porpoise to the gargantuan fin whale. At up to twenty-four metres long and seventy tonnes in weight, it's the second largest animal ever to live on Earth. Living in water has freed the great whales from the constraint of having to support their own weight, allowing them to surpass even the largest dinosaurs in mass. Size, though, has not come at the expense of speed. With its superbly streamlined body, the fin whale can motor through the water at up to forty-five kilometres an hour. It's one of the fastest creatures in the sea.

The great whales have another secret behind their size: their food. On land, almost all of the largest animals are herbivores. The opposite is true of the oceans, where animal biomass exceeds that of plants. Here, all the biggest animals are carnivores. Meat, of course, is more energy dense and nutritious than vegetation. Large whales, therefore, not only have access to more energy-rich food, but conveniently, it tends to swarm together, making it easier to catch. An elephant has to guzzle through poor quality grass for up to eighteen hours out of every twenty-four to get the calories it needs. A fin whale – ten times bigger than an elephant – can get far more nutrition with just one enormous gulp. By ingesting hundreds if not thousands of prey items in one go, a creature this size is also far more efficient than its smaller dolphin relatives, which have to pick off one fish at a time.

Like the humpback, the fin is a baleen whale. Over millions of years, these creatures have substituted teeth for a series of hairy bristles – baleen – that hang from the upper jaw. Grooves in the throat help it to expand, allowing them to take in huge mouthfuls of water. This is then forced through the baleen, sieving out fish and other small prey.

The humpback and fin whales share Ireland's marine bounty with the smaller minke whale. It's the most modest

"Living in water has freed the great whales from the constraint of having to support their own weight, allowing them to surpass even the largest dinosaurs in mass."

[227]

of the baleen whales but still a huge animal, at around eight metres long and weighing up to ten tonnes. It is also our commonest whale. Smaller species still – the dolphins and porpoises – have retained their teeth, and have used them to become voracious predators of small fish in our coastal waters.

Our larger whales are seasonal visitors, with sightings peaking around late autumn and winter as they move inshore in pursuit of spawning fish. Other cetaceans, though, can be seen year round. The Shannon estuary that divides Counties Clare and Limerick is home to our only resident population of bottlenose dolphins. Here they pursue their prey through the water with the same streamlined shape evolved by the ichthyosaurs before them. A remarkable example of evolution arriving at the same solution in unrelated animals, 200 million years apart.

In their conquest of the oceans, cetaceans developed another weapon the marine reptiles never had: sound. Sound travels four-and-a-half times faster underwater than it does through air, a fact that whales and dolphins have exploited to the fullest extent. With other senses compromised by their underwater existence, sound is essential to their survival.

Baleen whales, like the fin and humpback, produce complex 'whale songs' using clicks and pulses. These are among the most powerful noises in the animal kingdom. They can travel hundreds of kilometres underwater as the whales vie to attract mates and orientate themselves in the often-featureless expanse of the open ocean. The humpback whale in particular is a renowned virtuoso singer. The male weaves complex themes into his song, from deep bass notes to high, thrilling whistles that throb through the water. The song varies widely across the humpback's global range. Males in different regions incorporate different themes. Like any cultural trope, the song is not fixed but changes subtly year on year.

While the mysticetes (baleen whales) are the ultimate long-distance singers, the odontocetes (toothed whales, including dolphins and porpoises) have become the true masters of echolocation. The bottlenose dolphin navigates its world using clicks, focused through the fat-filled melon on its forehead. The clicks bounce back off anything they caress in the form of an echo. The dolphin's more than eighty cone-shaped teeth funnel these echoes into the cavities of the lower jaw. Like the outer ear in humans, these act as conduits to steer the sound into the middle ear, inner ear and ultimately the brain. With such a sophisticated sonar system, the dolphin can navigate its underwater world with phenomenal dexterity. It can even tell the difference between a ping pong and a golf ball, based purely on the types of echo they return.

Sound plays a vital part in dolphin family life as well. In their repertoire of clicks, groans and whistles, Ireland's bottlenose dolphins communicate in a different way – a different 'dialect' – to their counterparts off the coast of Wales. This is not instinctual but has to be learned and passed on, just like any human language. Each dolphin even has its own signature whistle, a name all of its own, used by itself and others to identify it. And in the disparate hunting techniques

favoured by dolphin cultures spread across the world, sound is the means by which the pod coordinates and synchronises its efforts to devastating effect.

Sound therefore facilitates a degree of behavioural complexity in cetaceans that we've only begun to fully comprehend in recent years. Whales and dolphins are now ranked among the smartest animals on Earth. Their brains have more surface area and cortical convolutions than ours. Such equipment is thought to help them navigate the intricate social and cultural lives we now know they lead. They also possess spindle cells, those conduits of complex emotional response once thought exclusive to great apes (including us) as well as elephants. But there's more. Cetacean brains have a whole other cortical lobe – called the paralimbic lobe – that humans lack altogether. This additional segment lets them perceive and process the information they receive from their environment to a degree surpassing what is possible in humans. With such formidable brainpower, some scientists speculate that whales and dolphins could possess a level of emotional sophistication that is beyond what we can experience.

For all their splendour, cetaceans can be difficult to observe from the land. Other marine mammals, though, make for easier viewing. The pinnipeds (seals and sea lions) took to the water much later than whales did, around 23 million years ago. They can still leave the water when they need to, spending much time resting on beaches or rocks. While dolphins use hearing to find their prey, seals can call upon another sense: touch. Their whiskers each have up to 1,500 nerve endings, compared to just 200 apiece in cats. This, combined with their unique elliptical shape, helps them pick up even the slightest vibrations made by fish in the water. With such precision instruments, the common seal – which can be found on sandy coastlines and sheltered bays around Ireland – can zero in on prey it can't even see.

The grey seal is the larger of our two seal species. At up to 300 kilogrammes, the bulls are formidable creatures. From August, the seals gather on beaches, give birth and begin the breeding cycle once again. To survive the chilly waters of the North Atlantic, grey seal pups need to fill out fast – up to two kilogrammes a day when suckling on the rich, fatty milk provided by their mothers. During this time, they have to avoid the ire of rampaging bulls, vying for mastery of the beach. Just as with red deer in the forest, the contest to breed takes a heavy toll. The need to hold on to a territory can see males foregoing food for up to eight weeks. During this time, they're left exhausted as the bodyweight they put on over the preceding months plummets. Casualties are inevitable.

The spectacle of fighting grey seals might be a staple of autumnal Ireland, but the most breathtaking manifestation of the bounty of Ireland's seas can be observed around our coasts each summer. This is when some of Europe's largest seabird colonies come ashore at sites such as Great Saltee (County Wexford), Rathlin Island (County Antrim) and Skellig Michael (County Kerry). Bit by bit, steep sea cliffs fill with thousands upon thousands of seabirds, a great squawking mass of flesh and feather, calling and reeking as one. No space goes to waste, from the sheer cliff edges lined with guillemots to the abandoned rabbit burrows repurposed by puffins.

"Whales and dolphins could possess a level of emotional sophistication that is beyond what we can experience."

Of all the birds that make up these mass congregations, among the noisiest are the kittiwakes. Their eponymous, high-pitched cry, echoing through the cliffs, is one of the first sounds that greets you upon approaching a seabird colony in summer. These are the only gull we have truly worthy of the name 'seagull'. While the likes of the herring gull hug the coast year round, the kittiwake spends the bulk of its year at sea, catching whatever prey comes within reach of the surface or scooping up the waste from commercial fishing vessels. Sometimes it even dives to catch food – the only gull that can do so. This ability to divorce itself from the coastal domain of most other gulls is what made the kittiwake such a success. It is now far more numerous than the larger herring and black-backed gulls it shares the colony with.

Other seagoing birds, however, are more adept at pursuing prey underwater. Water is 850 times denser than air, and so balancing the need to hunt underwater with the necessity of flight is quite a challenge. Some birds have risen to this. Cormorants and shags are among them. In these birds, all four toes on each foot are bound together by webbing, forming two enormous propellers to sweep their owner through the water. With such propulsion, these large seabirds have the speed to catch fish with their vicious hooked beaks.

Cormorants can't waterproof their feathers to the extent that other aquatic birds (such as ducks) can. This helps them lose buoyancy and sink to the sea bed after fish. But it also means they have to hang themselves out to dry after they come ashore; wings spread in the classic cormorant pose, crowning rocks and buoys around our coasts. They are among the most ancient of all birds, with a design that hasn't changed much since the time of the dinosaurs. Cormorant-like birds kept a wary eye out for marauding theropods as they dried their wings under the Cretaceous sun – and risked the teeth of mosasaurs beneath the waves.

When it comes to the underwater pursuit though, even the cormorants are left behind by the auks. Of all our birds,

these are the most adapted for life in the water. The
auks – guillemots, razorbills and puffins – are the
North Atlantic's answer to the penguins. Stand
a guillemot side by side with a penguin and
the resemblance is obvious. Even the colour
scheme is uniform between the families.
A dark back helps the bird disguise itself
to prey looking down, while a white belly
helps it blend in with the sky above and go
unnoticed by any predator circling beneath.

Auks can still fly. There are simply too many foxes, stoats
and other mammal predators here for them to abandon flight
entirely. Their wings, though, are much reduced. These make
for great paddles but poor flying. Together with cormorants,
the poor aerodynamic design of auks gives them the highest
flight cost of any birds. Their breathless wingbeats over the
waves look even more pathetic when contrasted with the aerial
ease of the fulmars and gulls soaring above them. Puffins, for
example, have to beat their dumpy wings up to 600 times a
minute just to stay airborne. A razorbill needs 64 per cent more
energy to fly a given distance than a petrel of the same size.

Underwater, however, is where they come into their
own. Unlike cormorants, the auks use their wings to propel
themselves beneath the waves. Their streamlined shape,
powered by those stubby wings, helps them pursue fish with
singular efficiency and grace. Guillemots, for instance, can
reach depths of 180 metres, and stay submerged for three
minutes at a time. This is a remarkable feat of endurance for
so small an animal; the pressure at these depths compresses
their lungs to one-twentieth of their volume at the surface. This
is where the auks can deploy their weaponry to devastating
effect. The stunning red and blue bill of the puffin is not only
used to attract a mate. It can hold over sixty sand eels in its

gape. A rough tongue and spiny palette work in concert to prevent the fish from slipping out.

If cormorants and auks pursue fish underwater, the gannet rains chaos on them from above. This is the largest seabird we have, unmistakable with its long white wings tipped in black, and buttery flush around the head and neck. The spear-like bill of the gannet – a vastly different weapon from the colourful cleaver of the puffin or fish-hook of the cormorant – is perfect for this. When the gannet folds its wings back, it morphs into a living javelin. Razor sharp eyes steer the gannet to its target from a height of up to forty-five metres above the surface. At full pelt, this huge bird can hit speeds of up to 100 kilometres an hour – and may have to dive up to 100 times per foraging trip. The gannet is beautifully designed to mitigate this. Its long, narrow beak ensures it enters the water with minimal impact. The beak has no nostrils on it, preventing water from rushing in. And the bird's skull is cushioned with air sacs to soften the blow. Their catch is ferried back to the nest at sites such as Little Skellig, off the coast of County Kerry, where the gannet chicks – scrawny, sepulchral bags of leathery black skin – await their next meal. In summer, this towering pyramid of rock punching out of the Atlantic is home to around 70,000 gannets – the second largest colony in the world.

Of all our seabirds, though, the most adept on the wing are the tube-noses. This magnificent family of birds counts the albatrosses, petrels, fulmars and shearwaters among its members. The fulmar is a relatively recent arrival in Ireland. It first bred here in 1911, enticed by the delectable waste discharged from trawlers. Now it can be found nesting all around our coasts. Its stiff-winged flight is diagnostic of its family, and easily lets you pick out a fulmar amid the mass of kittiwakes with which it shares its white and grey colouring.

Those long, stiff wings let the fulmar exploit ocean winds to the fullest extent, covering vast distances with minimal effort. Tube-noses have a phenomenal sense of smell. With a favourable wind, fulmars can zero in on the scent of fish oil up to twenty-five kilometres away. Tagged birds have covered over 6,000 kilometres in a fishing trip of just over two weeks. Fulmars are among the longest lived of all birds, able to survive for over forty years in the wild. During this time, they accrue an unparalleled knowledge of the seas above which they forage, able to remember and navigate to rich patches in the featureless ocean with a precision we're still struggling to understand.

Mass gatherings of seabirds and their chicks inevitably attract both predators and pirates, thieves that steal the catches of more skilled fishermen. Among the most fearsome is the great black-backed gull, the largest in the world. It weighs at least twice as much as a herring gull – a very big bird in itself. This gull strikes an imposing figure as it circles seabird colonies around our coasts, its white body bisected by long black wings, topped by a heavy yellow bill. It dwarfs most of our regularly occurring seabirds apart from the gannet and cormorants. This, combined with its sheer aggression, helps it force smaller birds such as auks to cough up their catch when returning to the nest. The gull is so voracious, though, that sometimes it will kill its victim outright. The dead puffin or shearwater is then turned inside out, allowing the gull to dine on the tender flesh without ingesting the feathers.

In their sheer mass of feathers and noise, Ireland's seabirds create one of the country's great summer spectacles. However, there is one Irish seabird that remains conspicuous in its absence. It was perhaps the most unique creature found around our coasts. This is why, of all the species we've lost, its demise is, without doubt, the most tragic.

20

The Tragedy of
the Great Auk

In May 1834, one of the rarest birds in the world was caught off Ballymacaw, County Waterford. Exhausted, half-starved and unable to fly to safety, this large, emaciated seabird was tempted near a fisherman's boat by the promise of sprats and caught with a landing net.

The locals who saw the bird must scarcely have been able to believe their eyes. The *garefowl*, as it was widely known then, was so scarce that by the early 1800s it had largely passed into legend along the coastal parts of Europe it once called home.

This incredibly valuable bird – a young female – would go on a remarkable journey over the ensuing months and years. The fisherman who caught her (named in sources only as Kirby) sold her to Francis Davis of Waterford ten days later. Eventually she wound up in the home of Jacob Goff in Horetown, County Wexford, where she remained for four months. At times, she had to be force fed potatoes and milk – but when she did eat, it was with ravenous hunger. She was fond of fish, which she swallowed whole, and was said to prefer trout over marine fish.

When she died, the bird traded hands once more, finding her way into the ownership of Dr Robert J. Burkitt on 7 September 1834. Ten years later, Burkitt presented her stuffed and mounted body to Trinity College, Dublin, where it has remained ever since. Such was the value of the specimen that the college gave Burkitt a pension of £50 a year (over €7,000 in today's terms) for the rest of his life.

It was the rarity of this bird, now known as the great auk, that saw its value skyrocket in the years preceding its extinction. This led to its ultimate demise.

Today, the Ballymacaw bird is one of just seventy-eight stuffed great auks in the world, and the only one in immature plumage. Together with twenty-four skeletons and seventy-five eggs, these are the meagre remains of a species that once numbered in the millions. Not long after its arrival at Trinity College, the last great auks on Earth perished.

While the creature caught by Kirby was a dishevelled wreck, in full health the great auk was a magnificent bird. Its striking black and white plumage was capped by a heavy, hatchet-like bill, opening into a bright yellow maw. (Like its closest living cousin, the razorbill, it's thought this was used to help attract a mate.) Around seventy-five centimetres tall and weighing up to five kilogrammes, it was the largest Irish seabird, the only flightless Irish bird and the only flightless seabird in the northern hemisphere. It also holds the grim distinction of being the only Irish bird to become completely extinct within historical times.

To the unknowing eye, the auk looks like a penguin. It was this resemblance that may have led penguins to be given

"It was arguably the greatest avian aquanaut that ever lived."

their name. The word 'penguin' comes from the Welsh *pen gwyn* ('white head'), a name initially applied to the great auk due to the white patch on its face. When European sailors began exploring the southern hemisphere (the domain of the penguins) they discovered flightless seabirds similar to those back home. This is how the birds now called penguins came to be known as such. The great auk went by many other names throughout history, including *garefowl* and *geirfugl* (in Icelandic). To centuries of Irish sailors, it was *an falcóg mhór* ('the big auk').

Although similar to penguins in form and lifestyle, the great auk was not related to them. Its closest living relatives – razorbills, guillemots, black guillemots and puffins – still throng Irish coastal cliffs each summer.

All of these birds are excellent swimmers. But the great auk took this even further. It was arguably the greatest avian aquanaut that ever lived, as perfectly evolved for the sea as the swift is for the sky. Like the penguins south of the equator, it had sacrificed the ability to fly in order to become the consummate living torpedo. Unimpeded by the bulky wings needed to get into the air, the great auk could develop a superbly hydrodynamic shape, able to power through the water with devastating speed and agility. Equipped with its laterally compressed, razor-sharp bill, this bird would have been a formidable underwater predator. Each feather was anchored in its own muscle, allowing them all to be flattened, trapping less air and reducing buoyancy. Flat eyes were perfect for taking in light underwater, allowing the auk to spot its prey in the murky depths.

A larger body size also entails a slower metabolic rate, which consumes oxygen more slowly. This would have made the great auk an even more efficient diver than its living relatives, able to remain underwater for up to fifteen minutes at a time. Within the auk family, diving depth correlates nicely with size. Puffins can go down around 60 metres, razorbills 140 and guillemots 180. But the great auk was up to five times larger than its surviving relatives. How far could its feeding forays take it into the abyss? Tragically, we might never know for sure.

Like all of its clan, the great auk was a piscivore, a fish eater. Most of its life was spent at sea feeding on schooling fish such as capelin. The bird thrived for millions of years throughout the North Atlantic, from Newfoundland in the west to Norway in the east. It could be found as far south as the Channel Islands and Florida on either side of the Atlantic. Fossil finds link the bird to Gibraltar and Italy, suggesting it once swam the Mediterranean. Cave paintings of the great auk dating from 20,000 years ago have been found in southern France. These (and the fossil evidence) imply that advancing ice sheets during the Pleistocene forced the auk south to warmer climes. Unlike the penguins, it seems that this was a bird unsuited to polar conditions.

That aside, the similarities between the two were manifold. The great auk filled the same ecological niche in the northern hemisphere as penguins did to the south. The resemblance between the two stemmed from convergent evolution – when two unrelated species grow to look alike on account of similar lifestyles.

Being flightless, the auk was incredibly vulnerable on dry land. Webbed feet placed very far back on the body made great propellers. But on land, their owner could only waddle awkwardly. This put the bird at great risk of predation once it came ashore to lay its eggs on bare rock.

Because of this, the auk could only breed on isolated islands with no land-based predators, and flat, gently ascending shores so it could access the sea by foot. In short, it needed the opposite of what most other Irish seabirds look for: towering cliffs and promontories accessible only on the wing. These criteria left very few sites in the North Atlantic where the auks could congregate safely.

One possible former breeding ground is the Keeragh Islands off County Wexford. Flat, low-lying and devoid of rats and foxes, these were just the sort of nest site a flightless seabird needed. However, it is likely that these colonies (if they ever existed) were exterminated by human predation.

"Every breeding season, sailors arrived in growing numbers to reap a gruesome harvest."

Man had hunted the great auk in Ireland since antiquity. Kitchen middens found in Tramore Bay, County Waterford (less than thirty kilometres from the Keeragh Islands) have yielded great auk bones, as have similar sites in Antrim, Clare and Donegal. This hunting could have decimated what nesting great auks there were in Ireland.

Nesting on isolated islands may have saved the auk from most terrestrial threats, but as human populations around the world expanded, auk colonies came under attack like never before. Such a large, flightless bird was perfect for the pot. Natives of both Europe and North America hunted the auk for food.

However, it wasn't until European colonisation of the New World that this slaughter racked up a gear. Auks provided protein for settlers as well as fishermen and whalers bound for the far north. The auk's eggs attracted the interest of wealthy collectors. They were prized for their exquisite black and white patterning. No two were alike, and this drove up their collectability (and value) even more. Meanwhile, its feathers – ever a shield against the North Atlantic chill – came into demand for duvets, pillows and even ladies' hats.

As a result, killing which until then had been merely at subsistence level kicked into overdrive. Every breeding season, sailors arrived in growing numbers to reap a gruesome harvest. Auks were herded into pens, clubbed, stripped of their feathers and boiled down for their fat, often while they were still alive. The fat from dead auks would then feed the fires over which more birds were boiled.

At the time, extinction and sustainable slaughter were nascent concepts. The idea that such an abundant bird could ever be wiped out entirely held little currency. One by one, the vast great auk colonies of the North Atlantic were destroyed. By 1794, this wholesale killing was prohibited by law, but irreversible damage had already been done.

Only in Iceland did the great auk find a safe haven, until that country's cruel geology dealt it yet another blow. The Geirfuglaskr ('Great Auk Rock'), the island that housed one of the world's last colonies, was obliterated by a volcanic eruption in 1830, sinking into the Atlantic and taking most of the remaining auks with it. The survivors sought refuge on another island, Eldey, closer to the Icelandic mainland – and therefore within easier reach of sailors.

In the final years of its existence, a new threat arose that would ultimately seal the auk's fate: science. Today, science and conservation go hand in hand. But in the nineteenth-century, scientists were more concerned with collecting and stuffing than they were with the long-term survival of species. Dead specimens were often more valuable than live ones. As the great auk became rarer and rarer, the price of a body skyrocketed. Competing museums, universities and private collectors paid handsomely to augment their exhibits. Dr Burkitt would find this out when Trinity College agreed to pay him that hefty pension for the Ballymacaw bird.

Cash-starved sailors eagerly took commissions to hunt down the remaining auks. The price of an auk (alive or dead) would have been a godsend to men like the ones who rowed ashore on Eldey. It was here that the last recorded pair of great auks was caught and killed on 3 June 1844. Once spotted, both birds had their necks rung. The female was sitting on an egg at the time of her death.

It is likely that some birds lingered on throughout the North Atlantic. Reported sightings persisted for a few more years. A great auk was rumoured to have washed ashore in West Cork in 1844. Two more were supposedly spotted on Belfast Lough a year later. But these sightings have never been confirmed and after 1852, it can only be assumed that the auk was finally extinct – lost not just to Ireland, but to the world.

It was arrogantly assumed at the time that more colonies survived in as-yet unexplored Arctic waters. These never materialised, and years of fruitless searching finally forced scientists to come to terms with the auk's demise. It lingered on only in folk memory, museum collections and in literature, weaving its way into the dreams of Leopold Bloom in James Joyce's *Ulysses*. Since then, the great auk has become an icon of extinction on par with the dodo, a lesson to all about the avarice of man and the fragility of the natural world.

Epilogue

Back from the Brink: The Rewilding of Ireland

In 2007, the red kite took to the skies of County Wicklow for the first time in well over a hundred years.

This magnificent raptor had been absent from the Irish countryside since the 1800s. That changed with the release of 120 red kites in Wicklow from 2007–2011. This was supplemented by the release of another eighty birds in County Down and forty in South Dublin.

It didn't take long for the kites to pick up where they left off all those years ago. By 2010, the Wicklow population had already produced at least eighty-one native-born red kites. Sadly, poisoned bait – the old bane of birds of prey in Ireland – has not disappeared entirely, and has claimed its share of kites. But for the most part, the project has been a stunning success. I'm reminded of this every time I drive through the Wicklow countryside. I'm regularly treated to the sight of a long-winged, fork-tailed raptor, hanging in the air, resplendent in all its russet and silver. A lost piece of our natural heritage, finally back where it belongs.

Arguably no group of animals in Ireland has suffered more at the hands of man than birds of prey. Owls aside, Ireland once had twelve breeding raptors. Seven of these – the golden eagle, the white-tailed eagle, the goshawk, the marsh harrier, the red kite, the buzzard and the osprey – were obliterated by human persecution. Others, such as the peregrine, nearly joined them. Now, amazing efforts to reverse this damage are starting to pay dividends.

The return of the red kite to Wicklow followed the successful reintroduction of our eagles to their former haunts. It all began in 2001 with the release of sixty-one golden eagles from Scotland back into the wilds of Donegal's Glenveagh National Park. In 2018, this project enjoyed a major boost when an Irish-born golden eagle hatched a chick for the first time in over a century. Meanwhile, the white-tailed eagle made its grand return to Killarney National Park in Kerry in 2007. A pair of these new arrivals bred in 2013, and others soon followed.

The return of this enormous predator was greeted with scepticism at first. Farmers feared that livestock would be taken. But in over a decade, this fear has not been realised. Eagle and farmer now coexist in Kerry. The scaremongering has largely subsided. So too has the poisoning.

The story of life in Ireland can so often seem a story of death. Looking back, it's hard to not feel disheartened by all the damage that has been done, and grieve

"Now more than ever, people are waking up to the importance of nature."

a little for what has been lost. No other country in Europe has had its native forests ravaged to the extent that Ireland has. The primal wilderness we once had is almost completely gone. Much of our wildlife has gone with it. We've lost more of our wildlife in the last fifty years than we did in thousands of years before it. Many of our most charismatic creatures are now extinct, among the 120 or so plants and animals known to have met their doom since man set foot here.

Those we have left are under pressure like never before. All told, around 300 species are in danger of extinction in Ireland. Our butterfly populations have fallen 12 per cent in just a decade. Ireland's once bountiful seas are now heavily overfished. This, and other factors such as pollution, has led to a decline in seabirds like the kittiwake and puffin. Two-thirds of our regularly occurring birds are now under some degree of conservation concern. Even species that have taken well to human habitation – like herring gulls, starlings and swifts – are not as plentiful as they once were, victims of an ever-changing world. Our rivers and lakes have also been hit hard; the number of pristine rivers in Ireland has fallen from over 500 in the 1980s to just twenty now. Years of pollution, as well as overexploitation, have taken their toll. Waterways that once heaved with fish are now almost completely barren. The number of salmon now spawning in Irish rivers is less than a fifth of what it was in the 1970s.

And yet, all of this has come at a time when appreciation of the natural world – and its plight – has never been higher. Now more than ever, people are waking up to the importance of nature, and the pressing need to preserve it. This is manifesting in amazing efforts all across the country to save the wildlife we can still see all around us.

Sometimes, if left unhindered, nature has a remarkable ability to right itself. When I was a boy, a buzzard circling above the fields of rural Wicklow would have been a rare sight. Now it's almost a given every time I return home. Rampant poisoning and shooting had seen this predator wiped out by the end of the 1800s. The cessation of these brutal practices has allowed the buzzard to reconquer the Irish countryside once more. It's been a phenomenal natural success story. (Arguably, though, this has come at the expense of another farmland raptor, the kestrel.) Like the buzzard, the peregrine was decimated by poison – particularly DDT. However, since the 1970s, the ban on this insidious substance has allowed their numbers to rebound slowly.

The buzzard is not the only bird to have recolonised Ireland from scratch. The great spotted woodpecker was also completely extinct here, likely a casualty of the forest clearances that swept the country in centuries past. In recent times it has made a tentative return. The bird was first confirmed breeding in County Down in 2007, and its population continues to grow. Meanwhile, woodland birds in more northern counties are, once again, finding themselves living in fear of the mighty goshawk. In one of the most exciting ornithological developments of recent years, this apex forest predator has started to nest here in small numbers after an absence of centuries. It's not the only raptor to return of its own accord. And in December 2020, just as this book was preparing to go to print, the Irish Raptor Study Group released the thrilling news that the marsh harrier had bred successfully in the Republic for the first time since *c.* 1917, with two pairs rearing chicks in Counties Galway and Westmeath.

Another, far bigger bird could also be on the cusp of making a return. In May 2021, Bord na Móna confirmed that a pair of cranes were nesting on a rewetted bog in the Midlands. Hopes are now high that these could become the first cranes to breed in Ireland for 300 years. Could these magnificent giants go on to re-establish themselves on our rehabilitated blanket bogs? Only time will tell.

At the same time, our lingering forests are home to another conservation success. The red squirrel and the pine marten are primordial enemies. Now, in a fortuitous twist of fate, the pine marten could be helping the red squirrel regain ground from its newer nemesis, the invasive grey squirrel. Larger and more aggressive than its native cousin, the grey squirrel had largely usurped the red in woodlands across Ireland. But the rebounding pine marten population is helping to reverse this. The bulkier grey squirrel is easier prey for the pine marten, being less nimble and more likely to descend to the ground. Having evolved with the pine marten in the primeval forests of Europe, red squirrels are wiser to the threat of this furtive

forest predator than their grey cousins, being more vigilant when they catch scent of a pine marten in the area. Thus, the pine marten's taste for grey squirrels is helping our red squirrel reclaim its former strongholds across the country.

Larger forest denizens have benefitted from conservation efforts too. Centuries of deforestation and hunting had taken a heavy toll on our native red deer. Large stags with trophy antlers were particularly prized, and their elimination from the gene pool weakened the native stock even more. This left our red deer more vulnerable to yet another threat: hybridisation with the closely related sika deer introduced from Asia, with which they also competed for space and food. By the mid-nineteenth century, Killarney and its surrounding areas had become the last redoubt of Ireland's native red deer, beasts with a blood line stretching back before the first Celts set foot here. By 1960, there were as few as sixty of these magnificent creatures left. The protection afforded to them has allowed their numbers to increase more than tenfold since then – so much so that the abundance of deer is now, in itself, a conservation concern. This is also the case elsewhere in Ireland, where the profusion of sika, fallow and hybrid deer poses a major threat to farmland and forestry. With no predators to control them, human hunters have had to fill the void.

Culling, though, remains a sensitive subject – particularly when it comes to so iconic a creature as Killarney's red deer. More recently, conversations have turned towards culling foxes and crows in a bid to preserve ground-nesting birds like the curlew. Foxes have taken well to modern, urban Ireland. Now, however, preserving some wild creatures may come at the expense of the lives of others.

The success of recent reintroductions has raised the controversial sceptre of returning Ireland's apex predator –

the grey wolf – to its former haunt. Since its demise more than 200 years ago, the Irish countryside has been shorn of its top mammalian carnivore. Proponents of the wolf's return cite the ecological benefits that would result. As top predators, wolves exert an enormous influence on the environment. Advocates argue that they would bring Ireland's rampant deer population back to a sustainable level. As a result, foliage could flourish more easily. This in turn would benefit all the smaller creatures that inhabit our mountains and forests, helping whole ecosystems return to their former splendour. Some argue it could even benefit farmers. Wolves are masters at eliminating sick and unhealthy deer, animals that might otherwise impart their pestilence to livestock. Opponents insist that Ireland simply does not have the wild space for wolves anymore, and that reintroduced animals would inevitably attack sheep or even people. The debate continues.

Reintroductions of charismatic predators like wolves and eagles might illicit strong emotions – for good or for bad. But many of Ireland's conservation successes involve humbler creatures. The tiny lesser horseshoe bat, one of our smallest mammals, needs old, unused buildings in which to make its summer roost. Fears for its survival led conservationists to acquire thirteen of these as reserves. Its population increased by more than 60 per cent in just over twenty years. The roseate tern has been another notable Irish success story. Over the past thirty years, its breeding population on Dublin's Rockabill Island has increased tenfold. This is now the largest colony of this endangered seabird in Europe.

Perhaps even more amazing has been the recovery of the grey partridge. By the 1990s there were as few as twenty partridges left in the wild in the whole of Ireland. Drastic action was needed. All of our remaining partridges were caught and moved to a new reserve created on 600 acres of exhausted industrial peatland at Lough Boora, County Offaly. This was restored in a manner perfect for partridges,  with plenty of wildflowers and cover crops in which they can find the food and shelter they need. Polish birds were brought in to supplement our dwindling numbers. Now there are around 900 grey partridges living in and around Lough Boora. At the opposite end of the scale, Ireland's wildlife can also benefit from conservation efforts beyond our shores. Once decimated by hunting, the humpback whales that bubble-net feed off the coast of West Cork are no longer an endangered species.

As well as efforts to save individual species, attempts to preserve and restore entire habitats are also underway. In cultivating an ideal space for grey partridges at Lough Boora, conservationists also created a safe haven for other bog and farmland species such as the lapwing, skylark and Irish hare. Similar projects at sites like Abbeyleix Bog and the Bog of Allen are helping preserve Ireland's remaining bogs and all of the unique plants and animals that live in them. All told, Ireland now has over 250,000 hectares of peatland under conservation.

What of Ireland's native trees? In recent years, renewed efforts have been made by citizens and governments alike to regrow Ireland's lost woodlands. Over a million native trees have been planted nationwide since 2013. In 2019, the government committed to planting another 600,000 native trees, such as birch and alder, over a three-year period. Perhaps in time, these will create new hedgerows and corridors along which wildlife can flourish.

Conservation is something everyone can play a part in. Farmers on Mayo's Mullet Peninsula are now taking advantage of a scheme that pays them to work the land in a more wildlife-friendly manner. They have begun mowing later in the year to protect ground-nesting birds, and leaving aside patches of nettles and irises to provide cover. The result? Fields that once fell silent in summer are now ringing with the unmistakable cry of the corncrake. Further south, in County Kerry, farmers have become the custodians of dozens of ponds built as nurseries for the natterjack toad, found nowhere else in the country. More proof that agriculture and nature can coexist.

You don't need a farm to get in on the act either. Ireland's more than two million gardens cover nearly 360,000 acres between them. That's more than twice the area of all our national parks combined – a huge resource for wildlife. Recent years have seen a phenomenal rise in gardens adorned with native shrubs and wildflowers. These in turn create food and shelter for bees, butterflies and birds, oases of nature at the heart of suburbia. Ponds are another major boost for biodiversity in gardens, providing drinking water for birds and hedgehogs as well as breeding sites for insects and amphibians; up to a third of Ireland's frogs now reproduce in garden ponds. With rivers polluted and bogs depleted, these are now more valuable than ever.

All of this gives me hope that people and nature can coexist in modern Ireland. I cast my mind forward to a country a few decades from now, coalescing from the combined fruits of conservation efforts big and small. Back garden after back garden buzzes to the hum of bees harvesting from the golden flowers of the birds-foot trefoil. A profusion of butterflies adds silent colour to the scene; the shimmering glory of the common blue, the striking crimson and black of the peacock. In the branches of the holly and hazel above them, a host

"Recent years have seen a phenomenal rise in gardens adorned with native shrubs and wildflowers." of tits and finches feasts as robins and starlings fill the air with their cries, and a sparrowhawk waits in ambush. Dragonflies cast their shadows on garden ponds, fleeting shade for newts wriggling about in the weedy water.

The space between the houses and farms is filled out with oaks, elms and the healthy understorey that flourishes in their shadows. Along their branches, pine martens and red squirrels resume their ancient rivalry; grey squirrels are now long gone. The trees are awash with birdsong: the effervescent babble of the goldfinch and machine-gun trill of the wren set to the percussion of the great spotted woodpecker. As night sets in, badgers and foxes head off on their nightly rounds while hedgehogs and pygmy shrews rustle through the leaf-litter. Red kites and buzzards surrender the countryside to barn owls, their nightly raids emanating from special nest boxes strung up about the farm. All three now thrive without fear of poison, swooping over fields crawling by day with partridge and quail and resonating to the song of the yellowhammer.

From deep within a bed of nettles left aside just for him, a male corncrake braces himself for a night of calling.

A New Frontier:
Bringing Extinct
Species Back to Life

Siberian reindeer herder Yuri Khudi and his sons were leading their stock down to the Yuribey River for their fill of water. The river cuts through the permafrost that sits like a mantle over this wild expanse of eastern Russia. Ice Age secrets are locked in it, and every once in a while, the action of the river throws them up for the world to see: the occasional bison horn, the odd mammoth tusk or tooth. But on this fateful day in 2007, something on a whole new scale was to emerge.

Looking around, one of Yuri's sons spotted a leathery bag of skin, laid bare by the thawing frost. Neither Yuri nor his sons were scientists – but they didn't need to be to see the value in this shrivelled body peeling out of the riverbank.

They returned to the scene as soon as they could, reinforced by experts better suited to examine the carcass. It was gone. Panic and dismay set in. But a find like this could not be kept hidden for long.

While the scent was fresh, the group tracked the body to one of the villages strewn across Siberia's frozen wastes. Its new owner made little effort to hide his prize, propping it against the front entrance of his shop. As it turned out, one of Yuri's own cousins had parted with the specimen for two snow mobiles and a year's supply of food. Vital stocks in the harsh Siberian winter – but small wages, some might say, for the most complete woolly mammoth specimen ever discovered.

Lyuba – as this mammoth is now known – was only a month old when she died, a mere infant. She is not the most imposing of her kind. But she is the most precious. It is thought that she got stuck in a riverbank and drowned in the mud before her mother could save her. Now, more than 40,000 years later, her almost perfectly preserved body could be the salvation of her species.

Bar some cosmetic damage to her ears and tail, Lyuba is more or less intact. All of her organs are still encased in her mummified form. Contained within them are vital fragments of DNA – the recipe for resurrecting a mammoth.

Tragically, the conditions at Castlepook, Shandon Cave and Drumurcher were less than ideal for preserving the soft tissues of Ireland's dead mammoths. As the Irish climate warmed, there was no chance for them to find themselves locked in a permafrost prison. Not so Siberia. Here, on the fringes of the Arctic, frigid conditions endured long after the last Ice Age ended. These would help entomb not just baby mammoths but full-grown adults, who have since been pried out (tusks and all) in enormous ice blocks to be ferried off by helicopter for examination.

The discovery of remarkable mammoth specimens like Lyuba has coincided with the birth of the amazing (if controversial) new science of cloning. It first really made headlines on 3 February 1997, when Dolly the sheep was revealed to the world. Dolly, a Finnish Dorset, was the first mammal in history to be cloned from the cell of another individual. Her birth opened up (literally) a Brave New World of possibilities.

These possibilities could soon be realised with the resurrection of the mammoth. The technology that made Dolly possible has improved exponentially in the two decades since she first shocked the world. And our understanding of genetics and how organisms all fit into the intricate web of life past and present has also grown with the passage of time.

Given all this, we have the means to bring Ireland's extinct animals back to life.

The first step in the process involves harvesting what intact mammoth DNA still exists, in order to map the species' genome (i.e. what makes a mammoth a mammoth). Thanks to specimens of the calibre of Lyuba and the frozen mammoths of Siberia, scientists already have some material to work from. However, given that DNA degrades over time, the genetic material that can be extracted from even the most perfectly preserved mammoth will be incomplete. You can't clone a mammoth from this alone. That's where modern elephants come in. Living elephants in Asia (the mammoth's closest living relatives) not only help us reconstruct mammoth behaviour. By comparing their genomes side by side, scientists can see how the two species differ – and edit the elephant genome to resemble that of its dead cousin.

Once this stage is complete, you're almost ready to build a mammoth. You have the ingredients with which to recreate mammoth cells, seeds to be implanted within eggs to take route in a womb.* Initially, it was thought an Asian elephant

---

* Incredibly, this has already been achieved with an extinct animal, when the fertilised egg of a Pyrenean ibex – an extinct wild goat – was implanted into a domestic goat and brought to term back in 2007. The resulting offspring only lasted seven minutes outside the womb, but its short life was still a milestone in the resurrection of lost life on Earth.

would have to stand in as a surrogate for a mammoth. Now, scientists are increasingly confident that an artificial womb will suffice to help birth the first mammoth in over 4,000 years.

In 2019, another small milestone towards this remarkable end was achieved when muscle cell nuclei from a woolly mammoth were inserted into the ova of a mouse. Previous attempts at reviving mammoth cells in this way had come to naught – but not this one. Sure enough, when placed within a living substrate, the mammoth nuclei started to show the first tentative signs of life. This was a significant step forward in understanding how long dormant cells react when roused from their slumber beneath the ice. With this knowledge, the sceptre of recreating an extinct mammoth raised its head once more.

Given the elephant admixture, the resulting creature will not be 100 per cent mammoth. Instead, it will be a weird halfway house between species living and dead. However, with further genetic editing, and maybe a bit of selective breeding over successive generations, the mammoth traits could slowly be teased out. Eventually, we would arrive at a creature virtually indistinguishable from the woolly mammoths that grazed the plains of Cork 35,000 years ago.

Even if this succeeds, it will all be in vain if nothing is to be done with the resurrected mammoths. That's where Siberia once again plays a part. The mammoth steppe of Ireland may be long gone, but there are still enclaves of habitat that look much as they did when mammoths ranged far and wide across the northern hemisphere. And much of this can be found in Siberia.

One piece of this – sixteen square kilometres in total – has already been earmarked as a potential haven for these neo-mammoths. Called Pleistocene Park in a nod to its fictional

Jurassic counterpart, this reserve will provide a refuge for mammoths to roam much as they did during the last Ice Age. Eventually, an entire Ice Age ecosystem could be reproduced.

Revive & Restore, the organisation spearheading efforts to resurrect extinct species, argues that there are environmental as well as aesthetic reasons for bringing the mammoth back. The mammoth steppe – the largest terrestrial habitat that has ever existed – was as dependent upon the mammoths as the mammoths were dependent upon it. Using their huge, curved tusks as snowploughs, mammoths exposed swathes of grass beneath the snow for smaller grazers (muskox, reindeer, bison) to feed on. The grazing of mammoths (and other herbivores) pruned back the grass enough for the sun to warm the soil. This promoted the growth of fresh grass at the expense of boggy vegetation, which could freeze into permafrost, locking away nutrients and consuming less carbon dioxide. Because of this, some scientists even think that rewilding Siberia with mammoths will help in the fight against climate change.

Sadly, Irish punters will likely have to travel a long way if they ever want to see a mammoth in the wild again. But other creatures – whose demise traces back not thousands, but mere hundreds of years – might wind up closer to home. The great auk is the only Irish bird to become extinct within historical times. It left a genetic legacy in the numerous skins, skeletons and eggs that stand guard in museum cases across Europe, as well as a suite of organs interred in jars in the Natural History Museum of Denmark. Scraped together, they could yield usable DNA. Supplemented with that of the razorbill (the great auk's closest cousin), this could be enough to resurrect the auk from its watery grave. Once implanted within the egg of a bird large enough to accommodate the bulky great auk chick (a goose, perhaps) you have everything you need to bring another lost species back to life.

Unlike the mammoth, the great auk would not need a relict habitat far removed from civilisation in which to survive. Having only succumbed to extinction within the last 200 years, its North Atlantic domicile remains much as it was when the bird still swam Irish waters. Nor has it been gone long enough for its niche within the ocean ecosystem to be usurped. This offers the exciting possibility that – in the distant future – great auks might once again swim or even breed around the coasts of Ireland.

Currently, the Farne Islands off the east coast of England have been touted as a potential reintroduction site for the auk. Once a population has been established there, it is hoped that the bird's natural inclination to wander during the winter months will see it eventually re-colonise former haunts across the Atlantic. Perhaps these neo-great auks will find the Keeragh Islands off Wexford or Rathlin Island off Antrim to their liking.

De-extinction has a long and chequered history. Among its first targets was another extinct Irish animal, the wild horse, or tarpan. The mammoth or great auk have no living descendants. But the genes of the tarpan are thought to still flow in the domestic horse breeds of Europe and Russia. Intrepid scientists have sought to use these to revive the long-dead tarpan. The Heck brothers were the first to attempt this audacious experiment at the Munich Zoo nearly 100 years ago. They began an extensive cross-breeding programme, incorporating Swedish, Polish and Icelandic horses as well as the wild Przewalski's horse. By 1933 they finally produced a specimen with the dull dun pelage we now know the tarpan possessed.

"This knowledge and technology might one day be used to bring mammoths back from the grave."

Heck horses still adorn zoological and private collections today. In the end, though, the resemblance is merely cosmetic. They are a poor imitation of the beasts that once cantered across the Ice Age plains of Waterford. This has not stopped conservationists today from trying to resurrect Europe's lost wild horse. Scientists are now selectively breeding horses sourced from primitive breeds across Europe with the hope of recreating the wild horse from the genes of its descendants. The plan is to reintroduce these horses into selected rewilding areas from the Iberian Peninsula to the Balkans. The wild horse was a keystone species in a European wilderness now lost. Its grazing once helped open up space for a host of other creatures to thrive in, and its dung fertilised plants that helped sustain a whole ecosystem. If this project succeeds, perhaps it will again.

Meanwhile, in September 2020, Revive & Restore announced that the Przewalski's horse – a species that was once extinct in the wild – had been successfully cloned for the first time. A Przewalski's foal was cloned from DNA that had been kept frozen for forty years, and brought to term after being implanted in a domestic horse. As this book was going to print in December 2020, the foal was still alive and well. This is the largest species of wild animal that has been cloned to date. The knowledge and technology that made it possible might one day be used to bring mammoths – or other extinct animals – back from the grave.

Resurrecting lost species is not without its critics. It naturally lends itself to accusations of 'playing God' and attempting to master nature. But the main critiques arise over resources. As charismatic as they may be, mammoths and great auks are gone. Meanwhile, thousands of species still with us are in urgent need of help. We're starting to learn this here in Ireland. Birds that were common decades ago have plummeted in numbers, their ranges contracted by changing use of the land they depend on. Other animals are in even more dire straits, threatened not just with regional extinction but total elimination from the wild. Human compassion for the natural world is finite – as is the funding allocated to save it. Surely, the argument goes, we should focus on saving the creatures still with us instead of pursuing a vanity project to resurrect beasts long dead, a project whose success is still uncertain.

There's also the issue of which species should even be brought back. Mammoths and other megafauna are easy candidates. But does size make any species worthier of resuscitation? Should we not love all creatures great and small? It's not just the mammoths of this world that can have a huge impact on the environment. We're now discovering this in Ireland at great cost. The miniscule insects we depend upon to pollinate our flowers are going into unprecedented decline. Their loss could lead to the collapse of fragile ecosystems that larger creatures (ourselves included) rely on. Only when the bees stop buzzing will we remember that we needed them to help fields bloom and crops flourish.

Our planet is undergoing yet another mass extinction right now. It's not known for certain how many species of plant and animal die out every day. Most of them ebb away without anyone to remember them; they don't make a lasting impression the way a mammoth would. The extinction of the orangutan, were it to happen, would be mourned by millions. But if the Cuban solenodon – a poisonous, shrew-like oddity – were to meet the same fate, would anyone even shed a tear? And does this make it any less worthy of salvation?

If, in the end, we can just bring them all back, will this lead us to discard conservation in the here and now? Why worry over something that can be regrown and replaced with ease?

I'd like to hope that this won't become the case. The need to preserve what is already here, the authentic wild lineages that still endure in a fragile, degraded state, will not give way to apathy in this new genetic age. We should not try to resurrect the past for its own sake, but focus our efforts on species that are only absent now thanks to the past misdeeds of man. And, where possible, the wonders of cloning could also be employed to help supplement fragile populations of existing species, injecting genetic vigour to ensure they don't succumb to inbreeding and disease. If a species is on the brink, and not reproducing fast enough to replenish its own numbers, then cloning could again be called on to help (together with captive breeding programmes).

For us here in Ireland, we should watch the flowering of de-extinction with interest – and not lose sight of the phenomenal conservation efforts that have already taken place on our shores. It is through these that we have helped protect the wild things we have, and restocked our wild spaces with denizens once lost.

Meanwhile, on a grassy steppe far from here, the wonders of the present and future could help resurrect scenes from an Ireland long gone – a land given voice by the neighing of horses, the howls of wolves and the rumblings of mammoths.

Select Sources

Anderson, Glynn, *Birds of Ireland: Facts, Folklore & History* (Cork: The Collins Press, 2008).

Attenborough, David, *The Life of Birds* (London: BBC Books, 1998).

Attenborough, David, *The Life of Mammals* (London: BBC Books, 2002).

Byrne, R., Collins, P.C., Martill, D.M., Simms, M.J. and Smyth, R.H.S., 'First dinosaur remains from Ireland' (*Proceedings of the Geologists' Association*, 2020).

Castlecomer Discovery Park, Castlecomer, County Kilkenny.

Chritz, K., Dyke, G.J., Lister, A., Monaghan, N. and Zazzo, A., 'New Insights on Giant Deer (Megaloceros Giganteus) Paleobiology Inferred from Stable Isotope and Cementum Analysis', *Journal of Vertebrate Paleontology*, 282, pp. 133–44, (2009).

Clack, Jennifer A., *Gaining Ground: The Origin and Evolution of Tetrapods* (Bloomington: Indiana University Press, 2012).

Conserve Ireland, viewable online at *Conserveireland.com* (last accessed 22 December 2020).

Coxon, Peter, 'Landscapes and environments of the last glacial–interglacial transition: a time of amazingly rapid change in Ireland', *Irish Naturalists Journal*, Vol. 29, pp. 45–61 (2008).

D'Arcy, Gordon, *Ireland's Lost Birds* (Dublin: Four Courts Press, 2000).

de Buitléar, Éamon, *Wild Ireland* (Dublin: Amach Faoin Aer Publishing, 1984).

Discover Wildlife, viewable online at *Discoverwildlife.com* (accessed 22 December 2020).

Doughty, Phillip, 'A Big Mystery: Did Elephant and Hippopotamus roam the Belfast region just before the last Ice Age?' *Earth Science*, Issue 2, pp. 12–15 (2007).

Doyle, E., Hennessy, R., Hoctor, Z. and McNamara, M., *Stone, Water and Ice: A geology trip through the Burren* (Ennistymon: The Burren and Cliffs of Moher UNESCO Global Geopark, 2017).

Ellis, Richard, *Sea Dragons: Predators of the Prehistoric Oceans* (Lawrence, KS: University Press of Kansas, 2003).

Flannery, Tim, *Europe: A Natural History* (London: Allen Lane, 2018).

Flegg, Jim, *Birds of the British Isles* (London: Black Cat, 1998).

Fogarty, Pádraic, *Whittled Away: Ireland's Vanishing Nature* (Cork: The Collins Press, 2017).

Fuller, Errol, *Extinct Birds* (Oxford: Oxford University Press, 2000).

Gaskell, Jeremy, *Who Killed the Great Auk?* (Oxford: Oxford University Press, 2000).

Geist, Valerius, *Deer of the World: Their Evolution, Behaviour, and Ecology* (Mechanicsburg, PA: Stackpole Books, 1998).

Hall, Valerie, *The Making of Ireland's Landscapes Since the Last Ice Age* (Cork: The Collins Press, 2011).

Harrington, Rory and Hayden, Tom, *Exploring Irish Mammals* (Dublin: Town House and Country House Ltd, 2001).

Hickey, Kieran, *Wolves in Ireland: A Natural and Cultural History* (Dublin: Four Courts Press, 2013).

Irish Bog Restoration Project website, viewable online at *Irishbogrestorationproject.ie* (last accessed 23 December 2020).

Irish Deer Commission website, viewable online at *Irishdeercommission.ie* (last accessed 23 December 2020).

Irish Deer Society website, viewable online at *Irishdeersociety.com* (last accessed 23 December 2020).

Irish Peatland Conservation Council website, viewable online at *Ipcc.ie* (last accessed 23 December 2020).

Irish Wildlife Trust website, viewable online at *Iwt.ie* (last accessed 23 December 2020).

Jackson, Patrick N. Wyse, *Introducing Paleontology: A Guide to Ancient Life* (Edinburgh: Dunedin Academic Press, 2003).

Jeffery, Jonathan, 'The Carboniferous fish genera Strepsodus and Archichtys (Sarcopterygii: Rhizodontida): Clarifying 150 years of confusion', *Paleontology*, Vol. 49, Part I, pp. 113–32 (2006).

Jones, Calvin, *Ireland's Wildlife*, viewable online at *Irelandswildlife.com* (last accessed 23 December 2020).

Lambert, D., Naish, D. and Wyse, E., *Encyclopaedia of Dinosaurs & Prehistoric Life* (London: DK, 2001).

Larramendi, A. and Molina-Pérez, R., *Encyclopaedia of Dinosaurs: The Theropods* (London: The Natural History Museum, 2019).

Lister, Adrian M., 'The extinction of the giant deer Megaloceros giganteus (Blumenbach): New radiocarbon evidence', *Quaternary International*, 500, pp. 185–203 (2019).

Lloyd Praeger, Robert, *The Way That I Went* (Dublin: Hodges, Figgis & Co. 1937).

Lysaght, L. and Marnell, F., *Atlas of Mammals in Ireland: 2010–2015* (Waterford: National Biodiversity Data Centre, 2016).

Monaghan, Nigel T., 'Fossil Insect from Carboniferous Rocks of Co Clare', *The Irish Naturalists' Journal*, Vol. 25, No. 4, p. 155 (Oct., 1995).

Monaghan, Nigel T., 'Irish Quaternary Vertebrates', *Advances in Irish Quaternary Studies*, pp. 255–92 (2017).

Moth Light Media (YouTube channel), viewable online at *Youtube.com/channel/UCOh5Ht3eB4914hMUfJkKa9g* (last accessed 23 December 2020).

National Museum of Ireland – Natural History, Dublin.

Nicolson, Adam, *The Seabird's Cry: The Lives and Loves of Puffins, Gannets and Other Ocean Voyagers* (London: William Collins, 2017).

Ní Lamhna, Eanna, *Wild Dublin: Exploring Nature in the City* (Dublin: O'Brien Press, 2008).

Norman, D.B., 'Scelidosaurus harrisonii (Dinosauria: Ornithischia) from the Early Jurassic of Dorset, England: Biology and phylogenetic relationships', *Zoological Journal of the Linnean Society*, Volume 191, Issue 1, pp. 1–86 (January 2021).

Ó Liatháin, Concubhar, 'Hyenas and woolly mammoths in Doneraile', *The Corkman*, 12 October 2019.

PBS Eons (YouTube channel), viewable online at *Youtube.com/channel/UCzRrom72PHN9Zg7RML9EbA* (last accessed 23 December 2020).

Parkes, Matthew, *The Valentia Island Tetrapod Trackway* (Naas: The Geological Survey of Ireland, 2004).

Paul, Gregory S., *Predatory Dinosaurs of the World: A Complete Illustrated Guide* (New York: Simon & Schuster, 1990).

Prehistoric Life: The Definitive Visual History of Life on Earth (London: DK, 2012).

Revive & Restore website, viewable online at *Reviverestore.org* (last accessed 23 December 2020).

Rewilding Europe website, viewable online at *Rewildingeurope.com* (last accessed 23 December 2020).

Shapiro, Beth, 'Pathways to de-extinction: How close can we get to resurrection of an extinct species?', *Functional Ecology*, 2017, 31, pp. 996–1002 (2016).

Smith, Adam S., 'Rare Ichthyosaur and Plesiosaur Material from the Lower Jurassic of Ireland', *Irish Journal of Earth Sciences*, 28, pp. 47–52 (2010).

Thomas, Ben G. (YouTube channel), viewable online at *Youtube.com/channel/UCDSzwZqgtJEnUzacq3ddoOQ* (last accessed 23 December 2020).

Tipling, David and Unwin, Mike, *Empire of the Eagle: An Illustrated Natural History* (London: Yale University Press, 2018).

Ulster Museum, Belfast.

Vincent Wildlife website, viewable online at *Vincentwildlife.ie* (last accessed 23 December 2020).

Wicklow Mountains National Park website, viewable online at *Wicklowmountainsnationalpark.ie* (last accessed 23 December 2020).

Wild Ireland website, viewable online at *Wildireland.org* (last accessed 23 December 2020).